Happily Never After: A 20-Something's Guide to Breaking Up, Looking for Love, and Surviving Singledom in the Modern Age of Dating

Britany Ederveen

ISBN: 0692549803
ISBN 13: 9780692549803

"Keep love in your heart. A life without it is like a sunless garden when the flowers are dead. The consciousness of loving and being loved brings a warmth and a richness to life that nothing else can bring" –Oscar Wilde

Thank you to all the sung and unsung voices who made this project possible.

To my editors, who helped craft the final product: Brittny, Jill, Julie, Michelle, Stephanie

To my family who let me talk their ears off: my mom, my dad and Tami, my grandma, my siblings Cameron and Kayla, my aunts Kellie and Susan, Dan and Cathy

To my friends who were my biggest cheerleaders: Aimee, Anika, Angela, Anna, Briana, Brittany, Brenda, and Brooke, Dani, Deb, Jenna, Kate, Lauren, Lisa, Nicole, Peggy, Sarabeth, Sarah

To my roommates, who cooked, cleaned, and did my laundry so I could write: Christiane and Logan (and, of course, thank you to the dogs as well)

To God, who abruptly woke me up one morning in July with a book title and an urgency to write.

To Simon, who showed me what a real relationship should be like.

And, to Kent: getting dumped was the best thing that ever happened to me.

Table of Contents

Introduction

Once upon a time, there lived this girl named Britany. One day, as Britany walked down senior hall of her high school, wearing a red, flannel shirt, denim jeans, and a cowboy hat (it was homecoming week at her school), she collided into a boy named Kent. At 6'3", 145 pounds, Kent was awkward and gangly. He liked Britany since freshmen year of high school and would sit in English class and throw used staples at her, poke her in math, and whip her with his keychain during passing periods to get her attention. Britany always rejected him because she was always interested in some other stud. However, on this bright sunny day, as Kent and Britany passed each other in the hallway, Kent decided to stop, scoop Britany up in one of his famous bear hugs, spin her around, and as they gazed into each other's eyes, something inside Britany changed; something fluttered, caught her attention, and she decided that maybe Kent wasn't so awkward and so gangly after all. The two ended up ditching their dates to dance the night away at homecoming and decided to become an 'item' the very next day.

The couple dated all through senior year, went to prom together, and graduation. When fall came, Kent went off to play lacrosse and study business; Britany went to dance on her college dance team and study English and secondary education. Every weekend, Britany would drive down to watch her boyfriend play college lacrosse. She would sit in the stands, proudly wearing her boyfriend's number, cheering him on, and when he came out of the locker room, she would run and jump to give him a big hug, tell him how proud she was of him demolishing that other player. After the lacrosse games, the two would parade around the small town together, holding hands, and make appearances at the celebratory parties as a couple. They were so much in love that hearts literally pervaded their eyes whenever they looked at each other, like amorous cartoon characters. Britany's favorite thing to do was show up at Kent's apartment unannounced, bringing a love note, accompanied by his favorite food items (and because he was a lacrosse player, he sure did love to eat). One summer, Britany went on a European excursion for three weeks and they missed each other so much that Kent almost got on a flight to pick Britany up and bring her back home. They always had a playful relationship; Kent picked on Britany and Britany pretended to be mad. And, they took care of each other. When Kent suffered from mold poisoning and almost stopped breathing, Britany dragged Kent up the stairs, pulled him in the car, and drove him to the ER. When Britany got sick with the flu, Kent let her sleep in his bed, fed her soup and Gatorade, and rented a marathon of Netflix movies. They would spend Sunday afternoons at the library together, helping each other with homework; Britany would write Kent's papers and Kent would do Britany's math problems.

Soon, Britany graduated college and got a job teaching, Kent stayed to play lacrosse an extra year. And still, Britany would drive up each weekend to watch Kent play. By Thursday of each week, the anticipation would almost kill her, thinking about how excited she was to see her boyfriend play in the game that weekend. When Kent graduated and moved home, the two started thinking about their future together: what kind of dog they would get, what kind of living situation they desired, when would be the ideal time to get married. Kent began applying for jobs in New York; Britany began looking for opportunities to follow him. One weekend, Kent flew out for a job interview, came back, and . . .

Well, that is the end of this love story.

What actually ended up happening was Kent went to New York for that job interview, came home, realized Britany was not going to be the girl he would marry, called her, and dumped her.

(And, in case you were wondering, I am Britany).

Of course, there was much, much more to the break up than just Kent deciding we were not meant for each other. However, if you survived that sappy love story above, you will be happy to know that this book is not a love story; this is a break up story.

As I begin to write this, it has been about a year since I received that 'dreaded break up phone call.' I have officially been through one year's cycle without Kent: I went through a Christmas without him, our birthdays, Valentine's Day, our what-would-have-been six year anniversary. So many things in my life have changed; obviously, the major one is my relationship status. But also included: my outlook on life, my goals for myself, my interactions with people, and the resurrection of my faith. I call it my *existential crisis* and while it has certainly been no easy journey, and I certainly have suffered a great deal in between, the break up is the best thing that has ever happened to me because, through the pain and suffering, I emerged a more authentic version of myself.

What you will find in the proceeding pages will not be about how I wish I had Kent back or what a jerk I think he is. What you will find, however, is how I vowed to pull myself out of the wreckage, how I managed to heal, how I made a commitment to learn from every post-break up experience, and how I continue to navigate as a dumped, newly found "single-ite."

I write from pure honesty and sincerity of how I see this modern dating world shaping me. I am just your everyday 20-Something. The good news is, since it is not anything atypical or unusual, if I could overcome it, you can too.

Part I:

Pre Break Up

Before we get into the nitty-gritty details, let's back up to the year before the break up, when the relationship actually started unraveling.

The summer before I started my first teaching job, my mom and I got into an argument, she told me it was time to move out of the house, and I went to live with Kent's parents (while he was still in college). At the time, Kent and I had been dating for five years; we were waiting for him to graduate college the next spring, and then we would plan our future from there.

But, as we all know, two women living together inevitably ends in disaster. It was clear that Kent's mom and I had conflicting views on what a relationship should look like: I only wanted to see Kent once a week, and she thought I should see him three. I stayed home one weekend from his lacrosse game to get caught up on work, and she thought I should go no matter what. Tensions started rising between us, no one brought it up to the other, and Kent got the brunt of the issues. One day, I walked into the kitchen to hear Kent's mom on the phone, talking to Kent about me. I was crushed. But, I still hoped to marry Kent someday, so I kept pretending like I knew nothing, that nothing was wrong, that our lives and our relationship were "perfect."

When I returned home one day, Kent's mom pulled me into the office to tell me she thought *I needed to get on hormone medicine to regulate my emotions,* that she felt *I was the most ungrateful person ever because I never offered to buy dinner,* and that she was afraid *I was turning into my family.* Deeply offended and flabbergasted, I recruited my siblings the next morning, packed up my stuff, and moved out.

Of course, I still hoped to maintain a relationship with Kent, and to try to resolve things with his mom. The next weekend, despite my newly bruised ego, I called Kent's mom to invite myself to ride with them to Kent's game. I took an 18 hour car ride with his parents to see him play lacrosse. I went over to his house after Thanksgiving dinner. I asked his mom repeatedly if she wanted to get pedicures, go to coffee or lunch so that we could try to resolve some of the conflicts. But, those conflicts never got confronted, she never accepted my invitation, and I had to resign myself to the fact that I may never get to apologize like I so desperately hoped for.

And then the local town fair happened.

The local town fair is the town festival that occurs every June. As usual, Kent and I met up with a couple of our friends at the local town fair. As we were walking around, we ran into his parents. Kent's mom pulled him over to the side to meet an older lady, and avoided acknowledging my presence. When she finally did make eye contact with me, I blurted out, "It's nice to see you are back from your trip." Kent, finally seeing the tension that arose between his mom and I, stormed off. I ran after him, trying to get him to talk to me, but he turned abruptly around, told me to leave him alone and kept walking off. He sat in his car in the parking lot for about an hour until he finally called me, apologized, and said he wanted to fix things between us, that he wanted to make things work.

We spent the rest of that summer pretending that everything was going to work out: we made our usual date night Friday nights, hung out with our mutual friends, took a trip to Cheyenne Frontier Days at the end of July, talked about our future, planned his resume, and worked on finding him a job. Eventually, summer ran out. I started my second year of teaching, and about a week later, he was on his way to New York to interview for jobs.

That Dreaded Phone Call

I remember distinctly the phone call. It was a Monday, the second week we were back to school. I had just arrived home from yoga, my roommates were grocery shopping, and I worked on preparing my lesson plans for the next day. At 8:17, Kent called me. I had not heard from him since he left for New York three days prior (which, really was not unusual for us), so I was really eager to hear how his job interviews went. Of course, I already had started researching school districts, calculating sick days and blocking out three-day weekends in my calendar that I could visit him, and began thinking about how I needed to diet for professional cheerleader auditions. When I answered the phone call, there was an eerie silence for what seemed like eternity and he just stuttered, "I think it's time to start seeing other people." Shocked and speechless, all I could muster out was, "I think you need to come to my house and do this in person."

6

So, Kent hopped in this car, drove the ten minutes to my house. He called me; I walked out of my house, and jumped in his car. We spent about an hour, sitting in the parking lot, discussing the terms of this break up. That conversation is now a complete blur; I remember sitting in his front seat, my knees curled up to my chest, staring out the windshield, shaking my head and sobbing uncontrollably. I remember him staring blankly out the windshield, unable to make eye contact with me, in his once-too-big-old white t-shirt. I remember bits and pieces of, *I don't see myself marrying you, my morals and values just don't allow me to continue this, I want my grandchildren to have a relationship with their grandparents and I just don't see that happening with you, I am so exhausted trying to make this work.*

I remember trying to refute his statements, to try to talk him back into loving me; "But we have been through so much together," "But what about the sacrifices I have made for you?", "But I was planning on moving to New York when you got a job." I remember him begging me not to cry, that it "made him uncomfortable."

When it appeared that my efforts would make no difference, he was really breaking up with me, this wasn't just another fight we were getting in, and that this really was the end, I excused myself, unbuckled from the front seat, and sauntered back into my house, alone, single, and completely shaken. I remember passing my neighbors, who continued their Monday night rituals, unaware of the life-changing conversation I just witnessed and the crumbling of my soul that was beginning.

And, that was the end of it.

I remember lying in my bed and thinking, "Well, this really sucks, but I am 23 years old and need to figure out how to get through this." A break up, in many ways, serves as a form of loss. While Kent may physically still be present on this earth, that fateful Monday evening, he departed from my life, and from that moment on, I began on a journey that would completely alter my interactions with the world. I had just lost what was one of the most important pieces of my identity--Kent.

Step One: Survive the Shock

I remember Kent driving away, and instead of feeling hurt, sad, or angry, all I could feel was shocked and confused. Two weeks ago, we were at Cheyenne Frontier Days, and he was telling the old couple who offered us a ride home we would get married once he got a job. How did things change so drastically? I remember I spent that entire next night tossing and turning in my bed, trying to make sense of what just happened. Bits and pieces of the conversation kept replaying in my head: "You just aren't it," "I still care about you," "I don't want you to come to New York with me." Visions of his white t-shirt, his sunken eyes, the awkward red patch in his beard floated in my brain.

One of my favorite disorders to study is Post-Traumatic Stress Disorder, or PTSD. One theory suggests that we have two parts of our brain: the right side, which handles emotions, and the left side, which handles language and logic. When we go through a traumatic situation, the memories first get stored in the right hemisphere, which is why we experience flashbacks, arousal, and hyperviligence (you know, when every little sound tips you off). In our society, we often think of these long-term relationship break ups as insignificant because the term *boyfriend* seems frivolous and childish, compared to calling someone a *husband* (because, when *husband* is attached, we KNOW it's going to be bad). Because Kent was just my *boyfriend,* it should seem that the break up shouldn't waver me too much; I might be sad for a few days, but since we were never officially *married,* it should seem that it wouldn't be a big deal. However, as it turns out, these long-term relationship break ups *are* significant and do take a toll on our emotional states. Just because we never called someone *husband* does not mean we did not have our identity wrapped up in our relationship. Even though we never officially lived together, Kent and I spent six years of our lives adapting to one another and learning about each other, and to lose that could potentially mimic similar processes to divorce.

I know that I experienced some trauma symptoms because so many aspects of the break up are forever engrained in my brain. I remember exactly what I was wearing when he called: sweaty yoga pants and a black tank top. I remember exactly what I did when I walked back into my house: sat on the blue, floral patterned couch, stared vacantly at the wall. I even remember the remnants of the bacon-grease scent that infiltrated our kitchen, post-dinner. At first, I could not talk about it. I told my roommates, I told my best friend, and I told my department chair (in the event that I accidentally threw a chair at a student or dropped the "F" bomb in class out of sleep deprivation). But, I could not tell my friends, I could not tell my co-workers, I could not even tell my dad because I did not quite know what to even say. When my best friend heard the news, she packed her bags and was on her way to my house, but I didn't even want her over because I was so shocked. I didn't yet have the language to understand what had just happened.

While my brain was still comprehending that there was no more Kent, I knew that I needed to keep myself busy in order to survive the shock. Sometimes we need to take some time away, to distract ourselves before we can come to terms with situations. The first step was to go to work the next day and pretend like nothing had changed. I knew had I not gone back to work, I would sit and wallow in my room by myself; just like my neighbors completing their Monday evening rituals, everyone else's lives must still go on; mine must too. Even though everything was not all right, I needed to pretend that it was. Unfortunately, my teaching suffered; my students did a slew of busy work at that time because I just needed to get through my day. I made my sophomores copy down vocabulary words for an entire class period because I could not mentally process anything more complex; all that I could do was mutter written words off the projector screen. I remember mispronouncing "heinous" and profusely apologizing for my inadequacy (as a young teacher, admitting my shortcomings could be detrimental). Word got around somehow to the faculty, so that first day at school people sent me milkshakes, wrote me cards, gave me endless amounts of hugs, constantly sent me Google-chat messages or funny pictures via e-mail. Throughout the first few weeks, my friends sent me thoughts of love in the mail and secretly planned social events that I was forced to attend. I woke up each morning, thought about what I was about to tackle, planned how I was going to keep myself busy, and surrendered myself to sleep at the end of each night; I was always so exhausted. And, the next day, I woke up and did it all again: I woke up, took a shower, made my breakfast. I drove to school, taught my classes, went to dance practice. I came home, ate dinner, took the dogs on a walk, and went to bed.

Throughout the next few weeks, I made sure to overbook my calendar. I made sure that I went to the gym or yoga every single day. On the weekends, I worked extra hours, signed up for extra duties, went to the pool with a friend, made dinner plans. The weekend I was supposed to visit Kent in New York, my roommates and I planned a mountain getaway and we went rafting and hiking. I spent the first three Friday nights, (which would have been our 'date' nights) at my grandma's house, crying on her shoulder and listening to her expert counseling advice. The times that I knew I would be completely alone, I would try to call a friend or relative for small talk, just to keep my mind occupied. When I drove to school in the morning, and no one was awake enough for me to call, I would blast my music and sing along. Even though thoughts of Kent constantly ran through the back of my head, I tried to keep myself and my immediate consciousness busy because dealing with the feelings of loss were still too painful to tackle, and I wasn't ready to talk about them yet.

One really important survival technique I learned during this stage was how to self-motivate. In my head, I kept replaying, "I am fine. This is no big deal. I am going to survive. Life goes on. This doesn't even phase me. I can live without him." When I look back on it, I was *not* fine and it *was* a big deal, but I needed to believe at the time that my life was going on just as pleasantly as it was during-Kent. Like the self-fulfilling prophecy suggests, the act of self-motivating allowed me *to* survive, *to* continue on, *to* live without him. We have this motto in dance: "Fake it until you make it." Just like going to school the morning after that "dreaded phone call," I needed to pretend like everything was okay; pretending was fake, but it was necessary. Especially when experiencing loss, sometimes these self-talk defense mechanisms become the only way to survive at the time. It is important to recognize that there will come a time to process, but perhaps not right away.

Like Post-Traumatic Stress Disorder also produces anxiety, I would be overcome by it anytime I went somewhere by myself—walking into the bar to meet my friends, the grocery store, the gas station— in the event that I might run into Kent, or his mom. My hands would clam up, my forehead perspire, my heartbeat increase. I would freeze. As he left it, I knew nothing about Kent's whereabouts. I knew he got a job in New York, but I had no idea when he was leaving, where he was going, what company he was working for. When we were dating, I could track him, but this new scenario we were in was strange, and now I could not. I was constantly afraid that I would run into him, turn into an emotional wreck, and all the hard work I had been doing would be reversed. However, I also knew that anxiety comes from fear, especially of not being in control, and that the best way to conquer that fear was to expose myself to it. I related it to flying on an airplane: I am anxious anytime I get on an airplane, and as soon as I step on, I started making up scenarios in my head of what could go wrong. However, first I have to tell myself that if something *does* go wrong, I can't do anything about it, and second of all, not flying will extremely limit my experience of the world. I used the same techniques with Kent. I could not control if we showed up at the same places, and if I didn't go somewhere because I was afraid of running into him, then I was severely limiting my opportunities (and, risking my car running out of gas and really not being able to travel anywhere). So, anytime I arrived somewhere, I got out of my car, took a deep breath, rolled back my shoulders, tipped my chin, and told myself I was going to conquer this break up, no matter what. If I did run into him, I would figure that out when it happened, but there was no use ruminating over "what could happen" (to this day, I still have never run into Kent).

I probably spent about a month, waltzing around the world like a zombie, bags under my eyes, my already-frizzy-hair resembling Albert Einstein's, crinkled cardigan sweaters. I was a robot, passing through the motions, doing what I needed to survive, taking it day by day, and then surrendering myself to sleep at the end of each night. I did some really irrational things during this time. I contacted some of his college friends, whom I had not spoken to in years. My message said something along the lines of, "Hey I am not sure if you heard, but Kent and I broke up. I am concerned that his mom put him up to this and I was wondering if you could talk to him." For some illogical reason, I thought his friends might be able to talk him into taking me back. But, if they got back to me even at all, their responses were always, "It sounds like his mind is made up".

Although completely irrational, I felt a sense of anxiety that I could potentially be carrying his child, and spent some time worrying over that: how would I break the news to him? How would we divvy out the child support? How would the child bounce back and forth between Denver and New York? Of course, when that turned out to not be a possibility at all, I felt relieved. But, this is what trauma does to you. You think and do irrational things.

And then one day I woke up. The vivid images running through my brain began taking on different forms, and I finally felt strong enough to think about it. Once I pulled myself out of the shock and I began finding language to start processing the emotions I was feeling, I turned to writing to help. I would be teaching my class and suddenly an idea would pop into my head; I would pause class, run over to my desk, and jot down a note for me to come back to later; I used my blog as a response to Kent's break up because I needed to dump whatever my brain was trying to figure out. I kept a journal for all of the things that could not be posted online. Because I was so shocked and caught off guard by his sudden heartlessness, I felt that I never had an opportunity to defend myself, to tell him: that, yes, I would be an excellent mother. That, yes, I did try to mend things with his mom and she would never respond to me. That, yes, I did clean and go grocery shopping inconspicuously when I lived with his parents. There were so many things I wish I could say to him. So, I tactfully wrote about it on my blog. For some reason, writing and knowing that he could potentially be reading what I was writing was just as good as actually saying it to him.

August 22nd, 2013: Emotionally Bankrupt

I recently have been reflecting on the term 'emotionally bankrupt'. To me, it is a term that is used to describe someone who does not express any emotions.

During Greek times, the idea was that, if you wanted to ask someone for forgiveness, all you had to do was give them a gift. Perhaps this is where materialism stemmed from—we can erase anything and everything with something tangible, never mind the unconscious desires we carry with us. Perhaps this reasoning is why the Greeks were known to be so aggressive—they had so much rage built up in them because they were emotionally bankrupt—they covered up their emotions which then lead to a physical expression. I think there is definitely something to this idea. My grandmother, for example, grew during World War II in The Netherlands. She immigrated over to the Unites States in the 1950's and forever lived her life under those same traits—suppress your emotions. She was a wonderful lady and ended up dying from breast cancer about ten years ago. I think you find a similar trend, even at a smaller scale of getting colds: when emotions are not expressed and are so pent up, the human body has to find a way to break the stress and therefore refers to a physical experience, whether that be through aggression, symptoms, or sickness.

My aunt recently told me, "Our family is not any crazier than any other family. The only difference is that we let our skeletons out to dance in the street and other families just leave their skeletons in the closet". I come from a long line of educators, nurses, and counselors. I am not sure if those collective professions together have caused us to know the consequences of inhibiting emotions. In my opinion, I would rather go through a short period of catharsis and relieve my emotions rather than bottle them up, let them ruminate in my head, and ultimately prohibit my success.

I think as a society, we are making moves towards a more forgiving society. We can see this through many popular trends and cultural icons: we are more concerned with what we eat and stores are packed with 'organic' and 'gluten free' items; everyone is flocking to yoga/pilates/zumba/jazzercise classes; some places have passed gay marriage vows. As a society, I believe we are learning the consequences of sweeping things under the rug, and we are flourishing. I, for fact, am not ashamed to share the crazy, quirky stories from my family because in the end, the experiences I share with them have made me who I am today.

August 25th, 2013: Family Thoughts

I have been contemplating this idea of family. What is their function? How should we handle them? What are they responsible for?

You see, we often have a misconstrued view of family—that we need to remain loyal to our family, no matter what because they raised us, give us money, and provide for us. Is it OUR duty to acknowledge and dote on their efforts, or is it their ethical duty to take care of us the best they can because they made the decision to bring us into the world? Is it our gratitude we must express, or is it merely their responsibility?

I believe that family does not have to include just those we share bloodlines with, but also those we hold close to us. If I were to get married, a small fraction of my guest list would include my grandparents, aunts, uncles, cousins, etc. And, the remainder of the guest list would contain my dance friends, my coaches, my co-workers, my mentors, and people I have met along the way who influenced me to become who I am today.

I think, too often, we judge people based on their families. We often find ourselves saying, "That girl's family is just white trash", or "Those kids come from dysfunctional parents", or "That family can barely afford to buy new clothes" but I think we need to shift our thinking from what kind of family does someone come from towards what are those people doing with the family they are given. Someone coming from a poor upbringing that does something significant with their lives I think means way more than someone who comes from an average household and does something semi-significant.

I do believe that much of our schemas, understandings of the world, perceptions, attitudes, judgements, and behaviors do stem from our upbringing. However, I also believe that those things can be changed. The brain is a wonderful muscle that, especially in your early 20's, is pliable and adaptable. So, if you are willing to put in the cognitive efforts, I believe you can overcome any kind of programming that occurred throughout your early years.

This is something I constantly strive to do myself, all by constantly reflecting on my own life, attending yoga classes, going to life coaching classes, carefully observing the world around me, and exposing myself to a diverse array of ideas before making a decision. At my job, we recently took a personality/behavior profile. As I thought about my own results, I thought to myself that this was NOT the profile I would have received four years ago, when I started college. When I first started (and please remember that I went to CU Boulder), I would define myself as very liberal. In fact, I even registered as a liberal the first time I voted. Now that I am older (and wiser), I find myself swaying a little more to the right on some of these issues. It is strange how just a few years and experiences can impact your perceptions so drastically.

I think the people you keep close to you that are not your family are almost more telling of who you are as a person. In our culture, we put so much emphasis on 'family values'. For example, we force ourselves to spend Thanksgiving, Christmas, Easter, Mother's Day, Father's Day, birthdays, Fourth of July, Memorial Day, Labor Day, etc. with our families. How many of us truly LOVE spending that time with our families, and how many of us does that time end up so stressful that you stop eating/ lose weight/get in fights with other people, everyone ends up in a big fight, you see someone you don't want to and get irritated that you have to be nice to them, or you end up drinking way more than you ever wanted just to deal with them? How many people actually like and have the best relationship ever with their in laws? From what I have observed, this is very slim to none because your parents, since they raised you themselves, will never find anyone 100% acceptable for you, unless of course you end up marrying an exact replica of your mother.

I think when we grow up, go to college, start our first jobs, and find our first (and second, and third) loves, we are exposed to more diverse ideas and we start looking critically at our upbringing and our relationships with our family. We learn that, perhaps our parents are not always right, perhaps our parents are judgmental, perhaps we do not agree with the views of our parents. For some, it is a very difficult concept to grasp because we have been so close for so long and feel like we owe allegiance to our family. But perhaps sometimes, we need to stand up for ourselves, our own values, and our own destinies.

In my opinion, those friends you keep close to you say more about who you are as a person than your family ever will because your friends are the ones you choose to have around you; they are a direct reflection of you. Are your friends loyal to you? Are they ready to come pick you up at the drop of a hat when you get stranded at a concert? Do your friends offer your support and advice? Are they able to let loose with you and dance the night away, and then not leave you when they find a cute guy? Do your friends weigh you down? Are they always ditching you, never following through, never inviting you to things? It is the phrase "birds like a feather flock together", so we keep those close to us that reflect our own personalities, desires, and hopes.

We cannot help who we are born into; we can only help how we handle it and how we choose to move forward in our lives.

August 26th, 2013: The Importance of Diversity

I went to the University of Colorado—Boulder, hippie central. And, not only that, but I entered one of the most liberal professions of them all—teaching. Throughout my teaching school, we were constantly discussing the term of 'diversity'. Diversity does not necessarily just mean differences in ethnicity. It also means differences in backgrounds, perceptions, histories, and an overall experience in the world. Throughout my teaching school and short teaching career, I do preach diversity, but I never quite understood the value of diversity until this week.

On a daily basis, I check in with over 200 different people: 172 students, 12 faculty members, 6 family members, 10 dance team girls, and whoever else I might encounter during my day. This is a privilege because I can hear over 200 diverse opinions and perceptions of the world in just one day. This allows me the ability to listen, synthesize, and analyze over 200 opinions before I make my own interpretations. For example, our bell schedule changed this year. As I am deciding whether or not I like this new schedule, I listen to the students' opinions, the old teachers' opinions, the new teachers' opinions, the admin opinion, and so on, so forth. Then, I make my own opinion based on what other people have said and what I have thought. I think this is also very beneficial in relationships. A few months ago, I had a conflict with someone very close to me about a family issue. Before I made my own rash decision, I checked in with many older adults that I know who have had successful marriages; a successful marriage, to me, means that you have done something right throughout the years and you have some kind of wisdom. By doing this, it allowed me to make the most informed decision possible.

This week, I have been exposed to the danger of not experiencing diversity. We become closed minded, ignorant, judgmental, and risk making informed decisions. We do not allow ourselves to see other perspectives and allow ourselves to be manipulated, controlled, and taken advantage of. This is especially true when we vote: without seeking other opinions, I might make an emotional decision to vote for a candidate just because they are charismatic, but at the end of the day, their values and work ethic may not be up to par. I believe this same thing occurs in relationships. For example, people my age are in a difficult position because they are stuck between what was and what they want to become. In what was, we trust our parent's opinions because they raised us, so their opinions and advice must be accurate, correct? But, in the situation of what we want to become, we struggle because we might be finding inaccuracies in our parent's advice; we are NOT our parents, so what worked for them may not necessarily work for us. Without seeking a diversity of opinions, we might make a decision solely on our parents opinions that may not necessarily be as accurate as we think. This might also happen when we go to buy a car: without researching around about safety features, price, gas mileage, etc. we might get sucked into purchasing an uneconomic car, or one that will might break down two years down the road. Or, when we are accepting jobs: it is important to look at a diverse amount of aspects of the job, the benefits, the hours, the location, the employee moral, instead of just looking at how much money we might make. We make decisions on a daily basis that are more beneficial when we use diversity.

The situation I witnessed this week was a prime example of this and as I reflect back on it, I realize just how sheltered and closed minded some people can be for the simple fact that they do not open themselves up to a diversity of opinions. It makes feel sympathetic for them because they are missing the wonderful, grandiose visions of the world; they are stuck in whatever closed off world they entered when they shut off the diversity. The consequence is undoubtedly less progress, growing, and learning. If we do not expose ourselves to diversity, we will continue to do the same thing over and over again, not realizing the perhaps times have changed (think about your grandparents who are computer illiterate) or that perhaps something is broken about the cycle we are taking.

I took a trip to Europe last summer, which was perhaps one of the most eye opening experiences of my life and forever changed my view of the world (well, going to Europe and reading "The Poisonwood Bible" by Barbara Kingsolver). I learned that, although someone may use a different path to get somewhere—they might choose to use public transportation instead of their own car, or they might think allowing citizens to have guns is a bad idea—we all do what we think is right; so, just because someone has a different perspective than we do does not necessarily mean they are in the wrong; it just means they have different reasons and experiences for doing what they do.

As I go into another week of teaching, this revelation of the importance of diversity will continue to ring vivid and authentic as I remind my students the importance of critical thoughts; I always say that I do not care what you believe, as long as you have enough evidence to support your ideas. When I was in teaching school, I knew that we should preach diversity, but I never really understood the benefit of it until now.

August 27th, 2013: Choices

Today, I am thinking about the idea of choices.

There are two different philosophies that choices can fall under. Calvinism, and many religions, believe that we have a set destiny, so no matter which choices we make, we will always come up with the same outcome. So, we are meant to have one soul mate, and no matter how many people that come before them, how many times we break up, how many issues there are, we will end up with that person because 'it is meant to be'. Or, no matter how much we slack in college, no matter how hard we work, we will end up with the same job and the same career path no matter what.

Existentialism and modernism offers us the viewpoint that our choices will lead us down different paths. So, there is no prescribed destiny for us, but each choice leads us towards a different outcome. So, perhaps we do not have a set soul mate, but when we meet someone at the right place and right time in our lives, it fits and we end up together. We could meet the same person five years earlier and it would not have worked out due to the choices and place we were in our lives at the time. Or, the job we accept could be a conglomeration of choices we made—we decided to write this on our resume, shop for this outfit, research this amount of information, etc.

This happens with athletes and their rituals. On my dance team, before competition, we had an entire set of things we would go through. On my list of things to do was brush my teeth. I felt like, if I made the decision not to brush my teeth, it could hinder our chance at winning. The Calvinist might say that it does not matter if I brush my teeth or not because we would win the state championship no matter what. Or, if a girl fell out of her turns, we weren't meant to win anyways so it didn't matter what happened.

I have been considering this perplexity and am not sure which one I believe. On one hand, I can think of aspects of my life that definitely were led up to destiny, such as my job. On the other hand, I can think of many other aspects that the outcome was due to a choice that I made, such as friendships and places I decided to go.

Teaching high school, I have the interesting experience to go back and reflect on myself and my own behaviors. For one, I thought I was the most put together person ever. When I look back at my old diary entries, I know for sure I was probably a mess, all the time. High school is such a unique time—kids are testing their boundaries, discovering themselves, trying out different activities, tempting relationships. At just the ripe age of 14-18, do these kids have official destinies, or do the choices they make now influence their paths? If a freshmen fails my English class, was it meant to happen for some reason, or did the student make the choice to fail that will then result in consequences and an altered path?

I think in some ways, it is comforting to use destiny as the guiding force in life; we give up our anxiety of the unknown by prescribing the thought that someone or something else is controlling the outcome anyways. So, when we break up with a significant other, we do not feel as bad about it because, "If it is meant to happen in the end, it will work out" (think about The Notebook). It is discomforting to think that "all of my choices have lead me to this point" because you have to take personal accountability for it. My choice to purchase a cheap car ended up with an blown engine and in the end, I had to send more money on a new car anyways; the fact that destiny has nothing to do with my choice but that I myself am responsible can be disheartening.

I think the important thing to note is that we all have choices to make. We can choose a job with a lot of money, or we can choose a job that makes us happy. We can choose to dwell on an obstacle in our life, or we can choose to pick up and move on. We can choose to push our boundaries, or we can choose to stay safe. We can choose to get ourselves sucked into a whirlpool of negativity and closed minded-ness, or we can choose to look at the big picture and expose ourselves to diversity. We can choose to get involved in the drama, or we can choose to keep our mouths shut.

Choices are something I am constantly contemplating. How will changing my hairstyle alter my life? How will expressing my emotions make someone think differently of me? Because my ultimate goal is to keep myself as happy and as productive as possible, I often make the choice that is going to help me remain in control and out of conflict/emotional distress. This was something I had to learn as to give up as I student taught: that sometimes I cannot always be in control of everything that happens. I cannot control what a student will blurt out during my evaluation, I cannot control how a discussion will go, I cannot control whether my students study for a test or not. I think the same thing is true in relationships and friendships. I cannot control whether a person accepts an apology or not; I cannot control whether a person cares enough to call me or not; I cannot control whether someone buys me a birthday present or not. All that I can do is control myself.

Sometimes the most disappointing concept is that we cannot control other people's decisions. I cannot change how someone might decide to act, no matter how detrimental, idiotic, or ignorant it may seem, but ultimately, their choices are in their hands. We all have the potential to make all kinds of choices for ourselves and sometimes, it just depends on what path you take.

August 29th, 2013: This is Living.

Shit has hit the fan in the last couple of weeks. Literally. The last couple weeks, I have been afraid to check my phone or my email because so many issues have surfaced. It has felt like a snowball, one thing after another, I am finding myself to be stronger than I ever imagined.

This week, I asked myself, "When is this ever going to stop?" I have felt like, especially in the last year, one thing has happened after another. It has been family issues, relationship issues, integrity issues, school issues, car issues, gym issues, management issues, technology issues, food issues, etc. I thought that, at 23, I had already overcome so many hurdles that what else could possibly go wrong? I am beginning to learn that this is just life and things happen all the time and I can't imagine how coarse I will become at the end of all of this.

I spend a lot of time protecting myself so I can be the happiest and most productive possible. I analyze situations, make careful choices, and keep strict standards so that I do not find myself in this place. It is uncomfortable. It feels unsafe. It is unknown, frightening, anxiety producing. However, I have been amazed at my resiliency throughout the last couple of weeks. I did not think I was this strong and I see now that all of the obstacles, situations, and challenges I was faced with in these last few months have helped me to focus on reality. I think about myself at 18, immature, emotional, impulsive. When my boyfriend broke up with me, I was devastated. I laid in my bed, moped around my house, and stopped eating for about a week. I think I desperately texted or called him everyday because I was so sad; I let myself wallow in pity. I even remember going to work (which, at the time was a maternity store) and welling up with tears in the middle of a check out. It was embarrassing, especially with the pregnant ladies around who were asking me what color their breast milk should be. I thought I was strong then and now when I look back on it; I never knew what more life had planned.

I started noticing all of these things happen when I began to student teach. Perhaps it is just my profession. I think applying for jobs is one of the worst experiences ever, especially when you have something to lose: your dignity. Applying and interviewing for jobs sucks because you take it personally. You have to rely on someone else to approve your resume, someone else to get you into an interview, someone else to like your responses, all the while worrying about the other candidates. You yourself know that you are the best candidate for the job, but do they? There was a period of two weeks that I was a disaster. I would get super excited when one school called for an interview and in the same hour, get a call from another that rejected me. It sucked, I felt like a failure, and at the end of the day, I am where I was supposed to be.

A good friend of mine called to check in with me last night. She said, "I am just so amazed at how well you are handling it, with everything you have going on". And I told her, "I am amazed at myself as well. I am not exactly sure how I am getting through my days, but I think I am beginning to realize that life throws curve balls that we sometimes cannot control and all I can do is pick up myself and keep living". It has been one thing after another in these last couple of years, so many things that I could have never anticipated. I keep asking myself if this happens to everyone, and through my research: Yes, yes it does. This is life.

I thought I would graduate, get a job, and that would be it. I never even questioned that it might not work out that way. Being a grown up sucks. But, as I find these curve balls being thrown at me, I find myself spending less time ruminating, less time grieving, and less time feeling personally attacked. I am maturing and becoming a stronger, more educated person through each situation.

Today, I am feeling sad. Perhaps it is hormones, perhaps it is exhaustion, or perhaps it is nostalgia. I am an English teacher and throughout my year, I am teaching my students what the human condition means. I think it means exactly this. It means feeling raw, passionate, strong emotions. It means losing the best thing that ever happened to you, only to realize in the end why it happened. It means surrendering your destiny to time because time can only answer these uncertain questions. It means building patience and acceptance towards the unknown. It means fighting for what you think is right, figuring out who you are, and experiencing all of those emotions in between. I woke up sad today, but I know being sad is an all too human emotion. We have sadness, we have happiness, and we have to experience it all. This is life and this is what it means to live.

Step Two: Rid The Kent

*A*fter I got over the shock of being dumped, the next thing I knew I had to do for myself was to take his presence out of my life. This does not mean to "delete" him completely, but I knew in order to heal and move forward, I had to get rid of all the daily reminders so that I would stop weeping in the corner and start moving forward.

We live in a society of instantaneous gratification and easily accessible information. If I wanted to be reminded of my relationship with Kent, all I had to do was check my Facebook, and sit in my room with the curtains drawn, and cry. If I wanted to see which company had hired him, all I had to do was Google his name (or, hope that he hadn't yet changed his password to his e-mail yet). If I wanted to see what he was doing on the weekends, all I had to do was Twitterstalk his friends. However, I also knew that searching for this information was not going to make the break up any easier. So, I boxed up every picture, every card, every gift that he ever gave me and put it in my mom's basement (except the really nice yoga mat and pair of jeans he bought me—I could still use those). I had a slight moment of weakness where I wanted to mail that box to his parents' house, but then got talked out of that one.

I "unfollowed" him on social media and his friends (this sounds like such a juvenile thing to do, but is unfortunately such an established part of our modern day society). I knew that I was about to embark upon a journey of healing from a six plus year relationship, and that if I continued to keep up with his where-abouts, I was going to add more onto the processing the stuff I already needed to re-think. At 23, I did not necessarily have time for added-bonuses (new girlfriends, weddings I was supposed to attend, work trips). I threw away the pictures of us at his lacrosse game that I kept in my plan book, and replaced them with a goofy picture of my sisters. I deleted his phone number from my phone so that I was not tempted to call him and locked up all of his text messages; it would not be healthy if I re-read them over and over again. I left my phone in my car during school hours, so I was not tempted to check it every two minutes to see if he had called me; if people needed to contact me, they could go through the office. Going through my Facebook and deleting all of our sta-tuses, pictures, and chats together was a little too painful (that comes later) but I felt like these immediate reminders that I had just been dumped served as an adequate start. Like sobering up from kind of "addiction," the first two days are the hardest, but as each day passed, it got better, and I actually enjoyed not hav-ing my phone connected to my hip all day. I am a do-er and I was relieved to begin do-ing something about the break up, and starting a new journey Kent-Free.

It would be dishonest of me to say I hoped Kent would never contact me because I secretly hoped that he would. But, every time I went back to my car, picked up my phone, my heart sank when there was no missed call, no unread text message. I was crushed every single day. How could someone I spent six years with just wipe me out of his life so nonchalantly? There were so many questions I still had and so many things I wanted to tell him. I wanted to tell him I was concerned about his relationship with his mom, I wanted to ask him when he knew things were not going to work out, and I wanted to know why he continued to string me along if he knew it wasn't going to work anyway.

Unfortunately, I would never get the answer to those questions. I felt very hurt that I had devoted six years to taking care of this guy, and one day, he never wanted to talk to me again. But, what I had to remember was that he was going through the same break up that I was going through. Whether he checked out of the relationship two months before or not, he was still going to have to adjust to life without me, which meant no nightly phone calls, no text during the middle of the day, no Friday night plans, no back massages. And, in fact, perhaps he was not contacting me because he did in fact care about me, and knew how hard the break up would be for me, and wanted to respect my needs. Regardless of whether Kent not contacting me was out of care and concern was the true reason, or he was just a selfish jerk, is irrelevant. Rationalizing and making myself believe this narrative in that way made me feel better, and allowed me to begin moving on.

Step Three: Go Through Catharsis

And, once I was able to accept that we were broken up, the storm drains flew open, and I began grieving. Allowing ourselves to grieve, as painful as it can be, is a really, really important process to partake in. As a culture, we do not allow ourselves to utilize this cathartic process enough. We are too busy trying to maintain an external appearance of perfection, too busy trying to beat our competitors, too busy caught up in the daily chores. In the end, we forget to take care of ourselves and we forget that our emotional stability is one of the most necessary aspects of our physical well-being.

But really, we need to deal with it. There are times when we can't deal with it, and there are times we must. A couple weeks into the post-Kent stage, I was in yoga class and as we were laying in final savasana, "Find Yourself" by Brad Paisley came on. This song always makes me tear up (mostly because I think about *Cars*, the movie itself—Disney always has a way to make me emotional) and at this point in my life, it had special meaning, especially the lyrics that sing, "When you find yourself/In some far off place/ And it causes you/To rethink some things." I could not control myself; my eyes just started welling up. Luckily, I had one of those fabulous lemon-lavender washcloths on my face so no one could tell that I was bawling uncontrollably. I laid on that yoga floor for at least an extra ten minutes, tears flowing like a hiccuping stream underneath my washcloth until everyone else left the room, and I could exit inconspicuously.

I have learned to never hold back tears. I want to be productive, successful, and I don't want anything to get in the way of my happiness. So, when I feel like crying, I let myself cry. I spend a few minutes going through this cathartic process and magically, when my tears dry up, I am over it and ready to go on with my day. I cry for all kind of reasons: because I am proud of my dancers, because I am excited for my students to enter college, because I have the best people in my life. Tears do not necessarily mean sadness, but sometimes overcoming of some kind of emotion—happiness, compassion, anxiety, gratitude, affection.

I have also learned in my life that, when I need to cry, I need to cry. Sometimes, I will go months without crying and, without any real reason, decide I just need to have a good cry. Nothing in my life alludes to this; I just need to go through this cathartic process every once in a while. Growing up as a dancer, music holds a special power over me. Music has this magical quality to sing the exact words from my heart that my mind cannot craft. I put on my iTunes, sit in the bathtub (depending on how clean I feel it is), and give myself 15-20 minutes to let it all out.

So, I turned on my playlist, and I cried. I cried by myself, I cried with my grandma, I cried with my co-workers during my plan period. And, soon, the need to cry stopped. I marked my progress by "days of not crying." Eventually, I went an entire week, and the need to grieve turned into the need to understand the events leading up to the break up, and I could start talking about Kent.

September 10th, 2013: Just Shut Up and Cry

Here is my playlist of songs that I put on whenever I need a good cry:

Landslide–Dixie Chicks *(try playing this song with a group of rowdy teenage girls—there is something soothing, calming about this song—everyone just stops, sings softly, and is admitted into some kind of deep reflection)*

Free Falling–Tom Petty

Help Me Believe–Nicole Nordeman *(this song is from my glory days as a pom—when I hear it, I get flooded back with the feelings of being in high school, on that team, growing, maturing, and looking towards something bigger than myself)*

Find Yourself–Brad Paisely *(I don't really know why, but this song just gets me every time. I think I relate it back to myself and my students—there is something so magical about this journey we call life—I connect it to the feelings of growing up, of finding yourself, of having to let people go, of having to let yourself go, etc. It really is a feeling I cannot describe)*

Better Together–Jack Johnson *(Just a simple, easy song. I remember, after breaking up with a boyfriend in high school, this song came on the radio and a wave of sereneness came over me and I knew that everything was going to be ok).*

Make You Feel My Love–Adele/Garth Brooks *(There is something very lyrical, something stuck and emotional about this song—it is very beautiful, you can feel the desperation and heartbreak in between the lyrics).*

Didn't You Know How Much I Love You–Kellie Pickler *(Nothing like a good belting song)*

I'm Still Here–Vertical Horizon *(I put this song on a CD for a dear friend going through a difficult time. I went back a few years later and realized that the lyrics were not what I thought they were at all, but I still like the song and it still takes me back to a place).*

Long Black Train–Josh Gracin (*This song reminds me of a wonderful family I encountered a few years ago and have been an inspiration to me. It reminds me that people are always tackling more obstacles than we are*).

He Ain't Worth Missing–Toby Keith (*Toby Keith just speaks right to my heart*)

Daddy Let Me Drive–Alan Jackson (*This song reminds me of my brother and also reminds me of going to Cheyenne Frontier Days with my sister. I always end my 'Trauig' playlist with something a little simpler, a little more light hearted so I can end my grieving session with a smile*).

September 13th, 2013: What's Love Got to Do?

I tried an experiment the other day. I turned on my iPod shuffle and made a list of the all topics the songs were about. Here is what came up:

Love Story by Taylor Swift–*how timely. No explanation needed here.*

Evacuate the Dancefloor by Rhianna–*A song about two people who are hot for each other and want to hook up on the dance floor*

I Want You Back by Jackson 5–*A song about someone who broke up with someone else and now realizes they made a mistake*

Whatever It Is by Zac Brown Band–*A guy singing a song about a girl that he likes and can't decide what he likes about her but just knows she has something special.*

You get the picture. Above all aspects in our world, why are we so captivated, so focused on finding companionship? I see this theme beginning at a very young age—a majority of our high school experience revolves around who likes who, who is dating whom, who got ditched at prom, etc. And, the older I get, the more I realize that my peers and I are discussing the exact same topics, only using better words that, "He is so hot" and "I think he made eye contact with me today". Instead, we say things like, "I really like his strong jawline" and "I enjoy his intellect".

There is something inherent in our genetic makeup to find 'the perfect mate'. We spend our entire lives hoping, searching, dreaming about who our significant other is going to be. We can see this everywhere: how many movies can you think of that don't include some kind of love story? How many songs can you list are not about love/re-lationships/break ups? How many books have you read that don't focus on two people searching for companionship?

So, I have been asking myself: Why is finding a mate so important to us?

For one, we can look at it evolutionarily: we want our gene pool to reproduce. We want our legacy, physically, to last on. When our traits continue on, it is a re-minder that we were an influence on humanity. My family always jokes because we are known to be tall, skinny, long limbs, bony, big noses, big ears, blonde (with like twenty pieces of very thin hair). I remember getting off the plane in Europe and feeling like I was amongst my people. My cousins share a story about when they were in Australia and saw a guy walking with an Ederveen stance. Sure enough, as they drove by, it turned out he was an Ederveen—my Opa's cousin, in fact.

Having a companion allows us to experience emotions that are outside our realm. Mostly, we focus on the butterflies, the smitten-ness, the excitement. But, it also allows us to feel sorrow, disappointment, and sympathy. In my class this week, we read the story of Prometheus and discussed whether the concept of ig-norance is bliss or knowledge is power is better. In this aspect, not being in a relationship saves you from heartache, but at the same time, you are not exposed to the expansive spectrum of emotions: being ignorant and withheld from those feelings, you maintain a safe, but small range of emotions. Companionship, while we do suffer from those hurtful emotions, we also get to experience the love, the jubilation, the spark.

We often define ourselves by being in a relationship with someone else. For some reason, 'single' sometimes has negative connotation in our society. We use terms like "she is way out of your league" and "she is quite a catch" to make ourselves feel better. We create standards for ourselves. As one of my favorite young adult novels, The Perks of Being a Wallflower (which revolutionized the way I look at the world), quotes, "We accept the love we think we think we deserve". So, having a significant other means something about ourselves. For one, it obviously means that we are stable enough people to have someone stick around us. It means that we are good enough to be loved. It means that, whatever attractive traits our partner has, we must be just as quality.

I think another reason is because we want to validate our own existence. It really is a selfish reason when you inspect it. One of the best parts about being in a relationship with someone is to be able to share life experiences with someone else. We want someone to hear the funny story about the smelly kid we encountered; we want someone to praise us for blowing up balloons in our sister's car for her birthday; we want someone to protect us when a fugitive is on the loose; we want someone to check in with us if there is severe weather in the area. There is something validating about having someone laugh at the same stories, show concern, point out things you didn't see yourself. We want someone to care about us because that means we are living and doing something meaningful.

We have all heard the dream about "sitting in a rocking chair next to your loved one at 85 years old, reminiscing about the old days". Companionship allows us to expand our boundaries, our emotions, our world, and share it with someone special. I don't know why we are so focused on finding "the perfect one" but perhaps someday, when I find mine, I will understand.

Step Four: Learn Mindfulness

$\mathcal{I}$f I was going to deal with the issues Kent left me with, I first had to figure out what those issues were. I learned mindfulness in two settings: yoga and counseling. Mindfulness basically means that you are consciously paying attention to your state of mind; in your head, you are figuring out, "I think I am feeling really agitated right now because the room smells really funny and that funny smell reminds me of this time in college when…". It is actually very difficult and requires introspection and a whole lot of patience. I knew that, in order to figure out what I needed to heal from the break up, I needed to be in tune to my consciousness' needs. If my mind wanted to go back to that scene at the local town fair two months prior to our break up, then I needed to allow myself to wander there. If my mind wanted me to be angry, then I needed to allow myself to be angry. If my mind wanted to focus on all the things I loved about Kent, then that is what I needed to do.

Mindfulness kind of goes like this:

At the end of yoga, we sometimes take an extended savasana. If you are not familiar with yoga, it is the best and last pose in class where you lay on the ground. So an "extended savasana" means, in this class, we lay on the ground for a longer period of time than usual, and you are supposed to "relax your tongue from the roof of your mouth" and neither think or move.

This is how my extended savasana usually goes: "———————" (that means my brain is blank for, oh I would say about 15 seconds). Then my line of thinking usually proceeds like this: *"Ok, so after class, I need to invite my sister to my game night tonight and see if she can preview some dance stuff for me. When I get home, I probably need to clean my bathroom and see if Christiane wants to go on a hike. Later, I need to make sure I have my lesson plans done for Monday and I really want to start reading my new book. Oh wow, I am really hungry. I wonder if I should use my Starbucks gift card on my way home so I don't pass out from hypertension or whatever that disease is called. Oh, that reminds me of a story from last weekend that I forgot to tell Christiane about . . . ."*

Wow! What a really "relaxing" savasana that is!

My high school dance team teacher forced us to go to yoga, and when I stopped dancing, I just continued because it was part of my routine. I go to yoga for many reasons, but one particular reason is because it helps me to clear my mind. I might suffer from an adult version of ADHD; I often have at least ten thoughts ping ponging around my head at any given moment. So, when I am in the midst of a yoga class, I try really hard to focus only on my breath and what my body is doing (and, of course, since I am super competitive, I try focusing on how I can push myself to my edge and be the best).

Having a dance background, I feel like I have an advantage in my yoga classes. I can hold my leg above my head during Birds of Paradise. Throw any inversion at me—Crow, Headstand, Hurdler—and I will stay up for at least three breaths. I can do a kick ass flow and I can balance in Tree like no one's business. Yet the most challenging pose for me is the simplest pose in yoga—literally, all you have to do is lie on the ground, with your arms and legs splayed open, and not think about anything; some people even fall asleep.

So, of course, as I am lying in extended savansa and realizing my inadequacies, I begin thinking about how this uncomfortable position translates to how I live my life (ah because of course, yoga IS life).

As I write this, I am 24, which is a really awkward age because there are so many unknowns. My friends and I are always discussing how difficult this time in our lives is because we are suddenly faced with potentially damaging or potentially opportunistic decisions. Up until this point in our lives, we have had strict deadlines: in four years, I am going to graduate high school and need to pick a college. In four years from then, I am going to graduate college and need to get a job. And, now that I have a job, the future is limitless; I could be at my job for three years or be at my job for twenty. I could meet a guy next weekend and be married by Christmas or I could never meet one and become a single cat lady. I could have one kid, four kids, no kids, and that could happen before I turn thirty.

We are used to everyone being on the same track, with the same deadlines, hitting the same developmental milestones. And, suddenly, now everyone is in completely different spots. Some of us are married with children. Some of us are very single and career oriented. Some of us are in between marriage and singleness and not sure if we should move with our potential spouse or not.

When I talk to my co-workers or other seasoned, older adults, they often have these marvelous stories about spontaneously quitting their job to enter a new industry on a whim, moving across the country with only a Corolla and a box of belongings, taking the unguarded chance to go on a blind date or join an adult softball league. And, you know what? All of them have turned out just fine and they all gloat about how taking those chances opened their eyes to opportunity.

As I typically lie in my final savasna, I decided that I needed to stop worrying so much about the future, be present in the moment, have faith that things will work out the way they are supposed to, and enjoy the excitement of the unknown. This is a challenge, especially for someone so conscientious as me because I want answers and a plan for everything. I always tell myself that *if* I knew whom I was going to marry and when, and how long I would stay in teaching, and if I would ever coach a state championship team, my life would be so much less stressful. But, life is surprising. Things happen that we can't foresee. I can't predict if that boy will ever call me again. I can't predict when I will graduate my Master's program or if a position will open up at that school again.

So, like lying in extended savasna, I need to just be present in the current moment and have faith the future will pan out the way it is supposed to.

As I continued practicing these mindfulness techniques, a strange phenomenon started occurring: I began having vivid dreams about Kent and his mom. I remember dreaming that I literally beat Kent's mom up. Another time, I dreamt that Kent was chasing me at some party and I kept rejecting him. After all of these dreams, I woke up the next day, feeling incredibly refreshed, relieved, and much happier.

In psychology, there are a few theories regarding dreams. Freud and the psycho-analytics believe that dreams are symbolic and a representation of something else, usually a repressed or sexual desire. In his famous lecture, Freud says, "Dreams are disguised fulfillment of repressed wishes." So, I want something in my life that I can't have, and since that is harbored in the psyche, I dream about it instead. I am getting what I want to an extent and my consciousness can have some sort of fulfillment or closure.

The Activation-Synthesis Model of dreaming suggests that when our brains are shut down, we experience extra sensory processes. As Freud says, this is when our brains experience, "our most creative, conscious state, one in which the chaotic, spontaneous recombination of cognitive elements produces novel configurations of information: new ideas. While many or even most have these ideas may be nonsensical, if even a few have its fanciful products are truly useful, our dream time will not have been wasted." So, basically, our brains are so stimulated all the time that when we are asleep, our brains still think and still generate ideas. My roommate, who is a diesel mechanic, reports fixing engines in his dreams, and then waking up to be able to solve a complicated problem at work the next day.

Of course, there are many other dream theories: we dream from random neuron impulses, so dreams don't really mean anything; we dream to send important information from our short to long term memories; we dream to get rid of unnecessary material in our brains.

The more in touch I become with my "emotional intelligence," the more vivid my dreams become. It has actually become a very interesting experience. When I was in college, I started having these dreams about my teeth falling out. I think this was my brain's way of expressing just how anxious and distressed my emotional state was. When I dreamt about Kent's mom, it was a full-on, girl fight brawl. We met up at a social gathering somewhere, I walked over, tapped her on the shoulder, and just started screaming at her angrily but incoherently. It was actually quite therapeutic. I remember waking up the next morning and feeling completely over the situation.

I think we dream for a variety of reasons: to attain wish fulfillment, to solve problems, to expend frustration, anger, and anxiety. Dreams become another avenue for processing this thing we call "life." It is a really satisfying experience and the better I know my conscious and unconscious processes, the more helpful and revealing my dreams are.

Of course, some of my dreams are random, like the dream I had about the black and white dinosaurs who wore neon sunglasses or the annual dream every teacher has about walking in on the first day, not being prepared and not remembering anyone's name, or my sister stealing my conditioner (oh wait, that one actually came true).

Interestingly enough, many of my friends who also have extensive yoga training and attend counseling also report having these vivid, therapeutic dreams; I think it is a testament to the mind-body-spirit connection. And, the stronger the mind-body-spirit connection, the more intuitive the individual. I needed these dreams to figure out what parts of the relationship and the break up I needed to process and rationalize--which ones were bothering me the most.

At the beginning stages of a break up, perhaps the most tumultuous and confusing question you must ask yourself is whether you will get back together or not. Kent broke up with me once before we went to college because he "wasn't sure if he really wanted to be with me," spent a week not communicating, tracked me down at a movie-in-the-park while I was with my friends, pulled me out, and we decided to get back together. I broke up with him one summer when we were in college, drove up to his apartment the next day, and profusely apologized for my irrational behavior. I toyed with the possibility that we would get back together this time, but then again, he was going to New York...

So, I started researching. I asked everyone I knew who had successful relationships when they knew they were going to marry their significant others. My aunt and uncle dated in college, he went on an internship, they broke up, he came back, missed her so much, and they got married. One of Kent's lacrosse friends met his future wife in high school, got married in college, and just knew they would be together. In synthesizing these stories, I realized that the only commonality was, "when you know, you just know." There is no magic moment that everyone experiences, no paper that falls purposefully from the sky to tell you are "in love", no choir of angels that sing when you find that person, or a symphony that immediately starts parading around you.

As I began researching and practicing mindfulness and dreaming, a really interesting phenomenon occurred. A few weeks after That Dreaded Phone Call, my sister and I were riding bikes at LifeTime Fitness (one of the many tasks I did to keep myself busy), making fun of all the kids jumping off the diving board. Practicing my clairvoyance that I gained from practicing my mindfulness techniques, I was trying to determine if I thought Kent and I would ever get back together. Suddenly, as one overweight girl in a pink and lime green bikini belly flopped into the pool below, I acquired this pit in my stomach. No, Kent was *not* the one I was supposed to marry. No, we would never get back together. No, I hoped to never to see him again. He was not it.

What all of this mindfulness training revealed to me was that this was not about losing Kent, but rather about finding myself. This realization was incredibly freeing, and I decided to put myself on a turbo speed mission to heal from Kent so that I could focus on myself instead; eventually, I went from writing all about Kent and relationships, to writing more about teaching, about going to church, about the books I recently read and the movies I recently watched.

October 1st, 2013: How I (So Far) Survived My break up:

Yes. It happened. I am ready to publicly announce for the first time in six years that—I am a single lady. He called me on the phone, did the little, "I think we should see other people, it's not you, it's me" blah blah blah. (I have some other opinions about the matter that are not appropriate to share via public blog, but this is about post-break up Britany, so those are not the important details). The first thought that came to my head was, "Shit. How long is this going to take to get over?" I like to be successful and productive; I have a lot going on in my life and when something is blocking my emotional capacity to be so, I get kind of irritated. So, of course, the fact of having to 'get over someone' irritated me because I thought it would inhibit my busy lifestyle and prevent me from being myself. What I have discovered is this could not have been further from the truth.

*1. **The first thing that I vowed to do was to take care of myself, however that might look**. If it meant I needed to light some spearmint candles, sit in my room with my playlist of trauig songs grab a whole roll of toilet paper, then that I what I was going to do. If it meant I was going to call every single person I could think of to tell my story to, then I certainly was going to do that too. If it meant I needed to sit with a carton of rocky road ice cream and watch Breakfast at Tiffany's, I was going to do that as well. I was going to do whatever it would take to purge myself of the emotions and move on with my life. What actually ended up happening was I walked into my class the day after, looked at my students, and was completely overcome with gratefulness. Just looking at the innocence, the playfulness,* the desire to please and learn and grow and mature cheered me up. Some of my kids also turned in personal narrative essays at the same time. After reading some of their experiences, I decided that life is so much greater than 'a break up'. People have tragic life experiences that would not even amount to what I was 'going through'.

2. So, the next thing I did was I decided to start focusing on the positive things I have in my life. For one, I have amazing family, co-workers and friends. Throughout the first week, I was being showered with cards from afar, flowers, Starbursts and Starbucks, milkshakes, notes, check-ins. Honestly, if I were to die tomorrow, I would say I have already lived a pretty fulfilling life. I think one of the most difficult parts of losing someone is not having someone to check in with—someone to ensure you are still alive and ticking, to share your accomplishments with, or to bounce ideas off. But, what I have found is that I have many people in my life who can fit that same exact role.

Everyone started offering me their own personal break up and marriage stories. The common thread was, "I thought I was going to marry so-and-so and now I look back on it and know exactly why it didn't work out". I realized that **4. I was not any different than anyone else**; in fact, we all share the same exact experiences and **5. I needed to take some time to observe other people's relationships**. We are taught our entire lives that we 'are special' and 'one in a million' and 'a needle in a haystack', blah blah blah. Basically, we are taught that we are the most special person in the world and everything that happens to us is a uniquely individual experience. While I do agree we are all noteworthy in our own special ways (some of us more than others....), most of the experiences we go through are the same experiences that everyone else goes through. Everyone experiences a crappy roommate. Everyone has conflict with a co-worker. Everyone has liked someone that doesn't like them back. Everyone has blown up two cars (ok, so that one might be unique to me, but you get my point). By hearing everyone else's stories, I realized that break ups are just part of life and everyone goes through at least one, whether it be in a relationship, a divorce, a friendship, a familial circumstance. And, everyone moves on. No one died of heartbreak (except the couple on The Notebook, but that is obviously a scripted case). I began asking those I knew who were in respectable relationships (and those who had gotten out of rotten relationships) questions, such as "How did you know it was going to be forever?", or for the other ones, "At what point did you know it was over?" Since then, I have been observing relationships and watching how couples treat each other, what makes them 'tick', and deciding what traits and behaviors I like, and which ones I do not like. I think so many of us do not take the adequate time to sit back and observe from a clinical perspective. We do not allow ourselves to see the truth, the obstacles, and the determination to mend. I think we would be a much less divorced society if we allowed ourselves some time to just observe (shout out here to everyone who has answered my pesky questions—you are awesome!)

When I looked back at other people who went through/are going through rough break ups, I realized one common thread that prevented them from moving on. It was the attitude of, "I wasted time on you". I decided to change my perspective and **6. Focus on the things that I learned from the relationship**. It was never a waste of time because I was able to grow as a person. I learned the importance of communication, I was able to feel some emotions that not many people are privy to, and I realized that, if I were to go back, I would not change one thing I did in the relationship because each of those things made me who I am today.

7. I decided I was not going to dwell. It is what it was. I wasn't going to change any decisions that were made so I was going to live my life accordingly. When I turn on 'country shuffle' on my iPod, there are so many songs about "we broke up five years ago and now you are with someone else and I am still not over it yet" (especially Rascal Flatts!). I did not want to be that pathetic. I found that my life did not change that much and in fact, almost got better. I made a list for myself of what I wanted to do: travel the world (or, just the places in the United States that I have friends in…), go to graduate school, take a vacation with my siblings, attend more social events, bond with my girlfriends that I have neglected, read more books, write more on my blog, etc. I had no idea what I was missing out on and as I trudge forward, I am excited for all the opportunities that are awaiting me. I can't wait.

I can't say that I have definitely survived this break up just yet because, let's face it, I am still 23 and so many things can still happen. But, the experiences I have been through thus far have been incredibly positive and inspirational. This break up *allowed me to re-discover myself. And, what I have learned in this 're-discovery' is that I am exactly who I thought I was.*

October 24th, 2013: Defining "Happiness"

About a year or so ago, I was having a conversation with someone, discussing my (very meager) teacher's salary. I had just gotten my first paycheck. I opened it and thought, "Oh, this is all I get". This person I was having the conversation with started brainstorming ideas for me to make more money so that I could support a family someday. She sputtered off, "maybe you should open a yoga studio and contract someone to manage it during the school year", or, "maybe you can open a tutoring business", and finally, "maybe you should just quit teaching altogether and go into something that will make you more money". Wow. Those all sound like really fantastic ideas that are really not me. Anyone who knows me knows that I do not deal with money. My budgeting is to make sure I don't spend more money than I have. So, while my (very meager) teacher paycheck can be limiting to my ambitious goals, it really does not bother me because I love what I do and could not have picked a better profession for myself because I am motivated by the intrinsic rewards; not the monetary funds.

Last week, my aunt came to visit us. We had a long conversation about life and one of the points she brought up is that we often think that making more money will make us happy. We sometimes have this mentality that, "Oh, if I could only switch jobs and make more money", or "If I could only marry rich, then I would be happy", or, "I want to go into the oil industry because there is a lot of money there". We think that money brings us happiness because it allows us to go anywhere we want to, buy anything we want to, eat anything we want to, entertain guests in anyway we want to—and basically, prohibit us from 'suffering' in anyway possible. We think it will be a safety net.

But what ultimately happens is money becomes a band-aid for our loneliness, our insecurities, our voids. We think, "if I can have this nice house and drive this nice car, then it means I am a happy person". We become greedy. Yes, we have money to take that vacation, but we don't because we could potentially miss signing a really big client. Yes, we live in a nice house, but we are so busy working and making money that we never invite anyone over to enjoy it. Yes, we can shop at Whole Foods and buy organic, but we are so tired at the end of the day that we don't want to cook and we eat out anyways.

We forget to take care of the individual. Money can buy many things, but money cannot buy forgiveness, non-judgmentalism, self-worth. My boyfriend can buy me flowers after a fight I, as the individual, still have to forgive him. Money cannot buy emotions and certainly cannot buy love.

So, this week, I have been contemplating how to define happiness. I think, especially as young people, we get ourselves caught up in wanting to live these lavish lifestyles, wanting to be rich and famous and known, that we don't necessarily look at the disadvantages. Yes, being petroleum engineer makes a lot of money, but they make a lot of money at an expense: they have to travel, often live in the middle of nowhere, where cost of living is high (I, for one, am happy living in the suburbs, making my teacher's salary, where I have my CorePower yoga right next door). We let ourselves get sucked into dysfunctional relationships because we don't respect ourselves enough and haven't taken the time to truly dissect happiness.

I have been contemplating this idea of 'happiness' all week and am still not sure I have any solid conclusions (other than singing Disney songs makes me very, very happy).

October 27th, 2013: My Happy Playlist

A few weeks ago, I posted a playlist of songs that I often listen to when I need a good cry. This week, I thought it was only fair to post a playlist of songs that I listen to when I need a pump up. I think music has a unique quality to speak, through melodies and lyrics, to us and change our entire ambiance. This tradition started when I was in high school, thanks to my high school dance coach, and I have slowly added songs since. As a superstitious athlete, I had a routine where I would go sit in a corner by myself and listen to some of these songs in a prescribed order. Each one had a special purpose that helped motivate me. When I began interviewing for jobs, I listened to an updated playlist. And now, I often listen to these songs on my way to school in the morning to energize myself for the long day ahead. Of course,

I update this playlist; I delete songs when I have heard them too often and they lose their special meaning and I add songs if I have a special connection. And, when I know of a co-worker or friend needing a pick-me-up, I go straight to my iTunes and burn them my Glee playlist.

My Happy Playlist

Texas Was You by Jason Aldean: *I really just love singing to this song (of course, only in my car, by myself, where no one else can hear me...)*

All Kinds of Kinds by Miranda Lambert: *Miranda just reminds us that we all come from different places, different experiences, different perspectives, but that we have to remember we all are people.*

Walking in Memphis by Lonestar: *On the plane to nationals one year, I for some reason got this song stuck in my head. But, of course, I had all the lyrics incorrect. As we were getting ready to perform in finals, this song came on and I immediately knew it was a sign. And, we ended up taking 4th place that year. So, it has a little bit of a superstitious quality to it.*

Wake Me Up by Avicii: *I just like to sing to this one. It has been the first thing I listen to on my way to school for the last three weeks.*

Everything by Michael Buble: *I always love a little Michael Buble: romantic, optimistic, and festive. He reminds us of the kind of love we deserve to be in, has a beautiful voice, and lightens up my mood every time I hear this song.*

The Blue Umbrella by Jon Brion: *Ok, so if you saw Monsters University, this was the song in the short at the beginning, with the blue umbrellas. I think the song itself is refreshing.*

Let's Go Crazy by Prince: *As my dad says, everything Prince sings about is dirty, but I happen to think this song gives off energy and I always find myself doing huge facials as I sing along (Yes, I am probably that girl you laugh at). It's all about having a good time and enjoying yourself.*

Taking Chances by Céline Dion: *The song is about taking a leap of faith. As a person that always wants to be in control and find the logic behind every-thing, this song reminds me that sometimes we do not know the answers to everything* and that sometimes we just have to let life take it's course. Plus, any Céline Dion song is fun to belt out those long, powerful notes.

Autumn's Fading Sun by James Egbert: Ok, I am not one for EDM music, but I went to James Egbert's concert one time, and it was awesome. I appreciated the experience the music is able to give the listener; I can certainly see why people are attracted to it. James' music, in particular, is very uplifting; the sounds are very happy, as a dj, watching him jam and move to his music is jovial, and the people around are generally in a good mood, which puts me in a good mood (Unlike some of the biker bars I have been to, no one got kicked out for fighting). The way you dance to EDM is kind of just walking around, bobbing your head back and forth to the beat, a move available to anyone (I thoroughly appreciated the fact that I didn't have to worry about someone trying to grind on me because it's not really a grinding environment).

Will You Be There? by Michael Jackson: This is the song from Free Willy, which used to be my sibling and I's favorite movie when we were growing up. Likewise, I am not really sure what the lyrics of the song ever says, but there are just a lot of sounds and "oooooh"ing, which alludes to a very happy song.

November 11th, 2013: How I (So Far) Survived My break up Part II

About a month ago, I posted a blog about how I (so far) survived my break up. After sharing and talking with so many inspirational people, I wanted to add a couple bullet points. All of this is really a matter of perspective: I can choose to dwell, get emotional, be lonely, or I can choose to learn, accept, and move forward in my life. And, I for one, am too busy to be dwelling on something that I can't change.

(So, if you haven't read the original blog, I would recommend you do that first).

8. So many people have been asking me, "Are you really sure you are OK and not in a state of denial?" Yes, I really am OK. You would think after dating someone for six years, especially the six years from age 17–23 that are so crucial to your development, I would be a mess. But, the truth of the matter is, when I look back on the relationship, I regret nothing. If I were to do it over, I would do everything the same.

I was always loyal, never clingy. I did cute girlfriend-y things, like attempt to sew him pajama pants when he had nose surgery and made scrapbooks and wrote really nice, thoughtful anniversary cards. Despite my busy schedule, I found time to support him, such as traveling to sit in 30 degree weather while six inches of snow piled on my lap to watch him play his last lacrosse game. Yes, I had my flaws and yes, I had my moments, but in the end, I know that I could not have possibly done anything else.

Because I am an analytical thinker, I tend to take a long time to make decisions because I want to make the most informed decision possible. Even picking out a restaurant can be a taxing ordeal because I have to consider all factors involved: price, flavors, people, atmosphere, etc. So I have been trying to remind myself that some things in life cannot be controlled and cannot be perfect, so I just have to go with the flow and accept what happens.

From the people I have talked to, sometimes it takes people years to get over relationships and I think it is because they constantly go back and wonder, "What if I did this differently?" But, "what if" is exhausting. I think we all need to remember this—that life is not a series of fixated cues, but rather of fluid ties. Every experience we have allows us to learn and grow as people, especially in relationships. One of the things we always fought about was communication. So, now I know that, when I am in a new relationship, I will take those things with me.

9. Probably the most difficult thing for me to accept when we first broke up was how strong our relationship used to be (used to be is the key word). I remembered getting butterflies in my stomach every time I drove up to his house and I remembered how painfully I missed him when I went to Europe last summer. I remembered how he used to pull me closer whenever another guy looked at me and the one night I asked him to buy me a box of tampons and he bought me the biggest size possible (ok, I will stop with the corny stories). At first, I didn't understand how we could have fallen out of those passionate feelings. I struggled because it was evident that he had the ability to be everything that I needed and wanted—he was that before—but I had to accept that things had changed and, although he had that ability, he was making the choice to be something different.

But then, I had to (and keep having to) remind myself that we are the not the same people we were when we started dating. Yes, those moments existed and they were absolutely wonderful and charming. Then college graduation happened, the real world sunk in, families got involved, lifestyles, viewpoints, and goals started changing. We grew apart; he wanted to go into the business world to make money and I wanted to save the environment. He wanted to start thinking about having children and I wanted to go back to school to get another degree. I had to realize that was the course our lives were taking and, while the six years we spent together can never be erased, we had fulfilled the purpose in each other's life and it was time for something bigger and better. While I can cherish those memories, I have to remember those are in the past and things are different now, which is perfectly acceptable and absolutely part of what it means to be human. Although it may not be clear right at this moment, all of this means we are both destined for something bigger and better and I am ready to discover whatever that might be.

November 19th, 2013: ...Is It Thanksgiving Break Yet?...

It has definitely been a struggle to get up and go to work the last couple of weeks. There is something to be said about the human circadian rhythm; Thanksgiving break is a week later this year and I can definitely feel the anxiety and jittery-ness in the air. The kids all give me blank stares, are engaging in behaviors I have never seen before (and probably never want to see again), leaving stuff all over the floor (why does it have to be lame stuff, like candy wrappers and broken pencils, and not something cool, like a $25 gift card to Starbucks?) and have no concept of "We are watching a movie today because I don't want to talk to you so please don't come by my desk and ask me a million questions. And in fact, I am not even going to grade the worksheet I gave you today so I don't really care how much you write on it."

I know that we all have weeks like this (for me, it has been the last two weeks), so today, I thought I would post a few things I have been doing for myself to make it a little more bearable.

*1. **Blast pump up music on my way to school**: Yes, just like an athlete, I created a playlist of music that will pump me into a better mood. I crank that bass and roll into the parking lot in style. The playlist varies every day. A couple of weeks ago, I woke up to a very degrading text message, so I turned on some Michael*

Buble, who is so carefree and joyful. Last week, I put Avicii on repeat and this week, the trend has been Dixie Chicks. It is a natural caffeine.

2. Admire the majestic views (also on my way to school—I have really had to motivate myself these last few weeks): I live about 30 minutes away from school, which can seem like a drive at some times. But, luckily, I only hit traffic on the mainstreet (which takes me approximately 4 minutes to get through). My entire drive to school is looking at the mountains that are slowly beginning to be dusted with snow. And, when I leave at 6:30, the sun is just coming up, so my drive to work is watching the pinks and oranges fade into blue.

3. Pack myself a really delicious lunch: There is nothing more delightful than spending the morning, anticipating what I have to eat for lunch. Lately, it has been pizza rolls, which, although probably very bad for me and not nutritious at all, have definitely gotten me through the morning. And, the lunch room is often my favorite part of my entire day. My colleagues are some of the best forms of entertainment for my day. I often leave with my stomach muscles hurting from laughing so hard.

4. Wear something I feel good in: Some days (which has been more often than not), I have resorted to wearing jeans. Some days, when I know it is going to be a really miserable day, I might wear a cute skirt or top or super sparkley necklace to perk myself up. Superficial, yes, but these days, I have to take whatever I can get!

5. And, when all else fails, know that there is a very great probability that **I will be coming home to my sister in her cow print footie pajamas.** Or, multiple pictures of my other sister's dogs, dressed up in Halloween costumes. Or, my roommates having a competition to see who can make the fireplace hottest and having our living room 88 degrees.

...Is it Thanksgiving break yet?...

Step Five: Abolish the Anger

And, then there came a time that I got angry. I raged. Steam blew out of my ears. I stomped my feet. The turbulence glowed red and hot. Anything related to Kent, I despised: lacrosse, the college he went to, Qdoba, the Ford Escape he drove, even saying his name. Anything that reminded me of him made me sick.

It tipped off one evening that my roommates and I were having a conversation, someone mentioned Kent, and Logan said, "You know Britany, Kent used to make comments all the time about how much he got laid. He would walk up to your room, wink at us, and say, 'I am about to get lucky.'"

How dare he say this to my roommates and my sister about me because if he was saying those things to them, he most certainly was also saying them to his team mates, his friends. How dare he taint my reputation! After all the lacrosse games I uncomfortably traveled to with his mom, the papers I wrote for him, the time I sacrificed to drive to see him on the weekends.

How dare he think of me as his object of desire. And, how dare I let myself be in that position. I flashbacked to all the times he presented those obviously chauvinistic ideals that everyone else caught onto, except for me: the time he refused to take me to dinner until I put on a skirt to show off my legs; the times he would ask me why I never wore any lingerie for him; the times he would tell me, "Coach says releasing your testosterone levels makes you perform better.." At the time, I thought this was my role as a girlfriend; I "loved" this man so my job was to take care of his needs, whatever those may be.

But, it turns out this isn't true, and the comments Kent made about me behind my back enraged me. How dare he take advantage of my innocence, of my devotion to making him happy, no matter what, and how dare he spread untrue rumors about me.

I got mad at Kent's mom. It is true that we are all products of our environments. We learn from observing interactions, and I was mad that Kent's mom (a) would believe these were a woman's role in her family, and (b) would teach her son these corrupt, oppressive, patronizing ideals.

I got mad at my parents. Of course, the only reasons girls like me stay with guys like Kent is because we don't value ourselves enough; we don't think we are worth anything better than that. I looked at my friends who had successful, healthy relationships, and I blamed my parents for not instilling that self-worth in me. Since my parents divorced when I was ten years old, my perceptions of a healthy relationship were skewed. If only I had learned at an early age that I was worth more than that, and my role is NOT to be a sexual object, then I would never have dated Kent in the first place and I wouldn't be undergoing this emotional turmoil. If only my parents would have taught me better...

And, I got mad at myself. I was mad that I didn't see his pompous attitude before. I was mad that everyone else saw it and I never listened. I was mad that I devoted six years to someone who just kicked me to the curb and didn't respect me enough to dump me in person. I was mad that I let Kent control me; I let him distance me from my friends, my family. I was mad that I never stood up for myself, that I continued to drive to his college every weekend, excusing the fact that he never came to see me by just saying, "Oh, well I enjoy hanging out with his team more than my own friends." I justified it when he didn't call because "his cell phone ran out of battery," and I stupidly believed him. I was mad that I didn't break up with him first, that I let the relationship drag on. I was mad that I let his mom demean me, and then threw myself at her to ask for her forgiveness. I was mad I let my own job remain in limbo while I "waited for him to decide his future."

I was mad that, despite all my denial, just like his sexual comments, Kent had been doing things behind my back that I was too naive and ignorant to recognize, and that there was, in fact, another girl. For a long time, I refused to believe that there was another girl involved. How could Kent have been dating me that whole time, perhaps started feeling something for another girl, and I was completely clueless? Whenever anyone brought this up as a possibility, I brushed it off. No, that could not be true. He would never do that to me.

But, as it turns out, there probably was another girl. (As my friends told me much later on), within a few short weeks, there were pictures of him on Facebook with another girl. We knew this girl, she lived out in New York, and probably hung out with him when he visited for his job interviews, and that was why I didn't hear from him when he first returned from his job interview.

I was angry. So, I did what I thought would be the best way to abolish my anger: pick up some supplies at the store, invite my friend over, and hit Kent-inspired golf balls into our pasture. There is something to manifesting our emotions in physical ways, and whacking at golf balls felt so, so good.

January 3rd, 2014: Where Have All the Good Guys Gone: A Call to Action

This 17 day holiday break has been a very magical time for me. I have spent a lot of time reconnecting with old friends, reminiscing on my past, and rethinking what I want out of my future. As you may know, I have been on a dating/relationship research project. My goals have been to interview as many people as possible to figure out rules of dating in your 20's (which, it actually turns out, there aren't very many rules at all), what makes a successful couple, and what ruins relationships.

A conversation I had with my roommates this week made me very angry. I tried to let it go, but the more I think about it, the angrier I get. So, before you continue reading, I want to warn you that this is a rant about how we, girls, allow guys to treat us. And, I also want to establish a little bit of credibility for myself as well: part of the reason I am angry is because I allowed myself to be subjected to this same kind of treatment.

Recently, I have been very interested in how societal values have changed. I will tell you that girls are frustrated at the lack of quality men that are out there anymore. My friends are always harping on how there "are no good guys out there anymore"— guys don't hold doors open for us, they don't walk in the way of oncoming traffic, they don't buy us flowers just because. My friends are always saying that guys are getting lazy—they text us to ask us on dates, expect us to chip in with the bill, ask us to drive.

While I completely agree with most of these accusations, I also believe that part of this has stemmed from what girls have allowed to be acceptable. I think part of the reason is because, as girls, we are insecure about ourselves. Society tells us that we need to be blonde, stick thin, super stylish all the time, college educated, gregarious, crafty, be able to whip up a Thanksgiving dinner in a heartbeat, etc.

So when we look at ourselves, and realize we are NONE of those things, we start hyperventilating and comparing and settling; "Ok, so my boyfriend never takes me out with his friends, but that is ok because I have small boobs so he shouldn't want to anyways", "He told me we were exclusive and then posted a picture of another girl on his Facebook, but that is ok because she is waaay prettier and makes more money than I do", "He makes me rub his scaly feet all the time and never offers to rub mine, but that is ok because I am very socially awkward so that is my way of giving back". But, as young women, we need to learn to value ourselves. As said in 'Perks of Being a Wallflower', "we accept the love we think we deserve". So, when we don't value ourselves, when we are insecure, when we don't realize that God made us all different for a purpose—we let ourselves get taken advantage of. (And, again, I am totally saying this because I, too, was in a place that I did not value myself and my attributes and, now that I look back on it, I realize I deserve SO much more—and you do too). YOU are great just the way you are—who cares if you are nerdy and spend all your free time reading books? Who cares if you love jamming out to Celine Dion? Who cares if your life goal is to own your own water polo factory? We are all different and diverse and that is the beauty of life. Embrace yourself—you can't be anyone different.

Here are a few common responses I hear from people (and, of course, my response to those as well):

"I know I am his last priority; but that is ok because we are both busy"*: Stop making excuses for him. I was totally guilty of this in my last relationship. I was always saying, "Oh, no it's fine that we haven't hung out in four weeks because I know he is busy with school but it will be better when this semester is over", and, "Oh no, it's fine that I wasn't invited to his family birthday dinner. They just wanted exclusive family time", and, "Oh I don't mind I always have to go visit him and he never comes to visit me. I enjoy going to the gas station every week and filling up with my own money that I don't have because I am a poor college student/ graduate". (Oh, and actually, things never got better when the semester was over, the birthday thing became a huge wedge, and me driving everywhere caused one of my cars to blow up...)*

Now, I believe there is a difference between both being busy and putting each other as last priority, and being busy and making time for each other. Being last priority might look like forgetting to call each other frequently, choosing to hang out with your long-lost high school enemy instead of your significant other, playing Candy Crush and Zombies while on a 'date'. Both being busy and putting each other as first priority might look scheduling time to call each other and both making sure you have time to talk, putting your cell phones away and committing to being present when you are spending time together, sporadically letting each other know you are thinking about them. Stop making excuses for him. If he isn't doing it now, he probably will never do it.

"I don't really like that he stays out all night with his friends, but I am just worried that I won't find someone better": You will. He does exist. You just haven't met him yet. And, if you are still dating that dead weight, then you certainly are not going to meet this strapping young fellow. I certainly felt this way; I would tell myself, "Oh I am dating him because I love these qualities and haven't found someone else who fits me as well" (except now that I think about it, I don't even know what those qualities even were and I am pretty sure I found someone waaaaaaay better already). You just have to open yourself up to the possibility and be confident that there is indeed someone that is a better fit for you. Oh, and be patient, which is sometimes the hardest part, but I believe it will be worth it. There are still plenty of great guys out there who will treat you with respect. I have seen it in my sister/roommate, my married friends, my single friends, my friend's parents, etc. It does exist. Don't let yourself settle because after all, you are looking at the rest of your life together. Why make yourself miserable?

"My friends/family just don't like him because they are jealous. They don't know what we have": Actually, your friends and family probably know you waaaaay better than you know yourself. Outsiders are always able to pick up on things that you are too naive or immune to see. If they say he is looking at another girl with elevator eyes, he probably is. If they say he treats you like crap, then he probably does. If they say he will be a terrible father, then he probably will be. Listen to your friends and family (and your dogs—if they run and shake and bark from under the bed and hide in the pantry, it is probably not a good sign). They have your best intentions in mind; listen to them.

"Relationships are hard and can be so much work": I remember having a conversation with someone a couple years ago, and she shared these same words of wisdom with me. At the time, since she was older and had been married a while, I thought she was exactly correct. But, when I take a step back, I realize that, no, actually relationships should not be work at all. After my last boyfriend and I broke up, I suddenly had a burst of energy; I was staying up late, getting up early, going to more social events and coming up with more innovative ideas than I had in years. I didn't realize how much work I was putting into it that was a just more of a hindrance on my life. Yes, in order for it to work, you will both need to compromise. You will have to change some of your habits and so will they. But, it shouldn't be work because you should want to make those compromises and changes to make that person happy. As one of my favorite ballet teachers once said, "It should be easy; your lives should just co-exist together".

"We fight about the same thing all the time": Good. Get rid of him. Don't let yourself be subjected to a monotonous, unwavering argument because it will just turn to bickering. If you are constantly fighting the same battle and neither of you is changing, then it is going to become a battle that you fight for the rest of your life. We were constantly fighting about him 'forgetting' to call me; his excuse was that 'he didn't like to talk on the phone'. I even got him a car charger with a picture of my face on it to remind him to call me. Did it work? Of course not. Is it worth it to go through that much stress? Probably not. There are way more important things in the world to worry about.

"We got in a big fight last night but it is ok because he sent flowers to my work so I forgive him": Don't let yourself be bought. Money has never bought happiness. Is he really sorry, or did he just send you those flowers because he knew you would tell your co-workers about the tiff and he didn't want to look bad?...

"I don't know if we are going to get married or not. We will see": So, if the whole point of dating is to look for a potential spouse and you cannot even see a glimpse of a future with this person, then why waste your and their time? Being 23, I am relatively young, but I also know that, if Prince Charming doesn't show up in the next few years, I might have to start accumulating a lot of cats so I don't go out like an old maid. Life is too short to just be frivolously dating and spending time with people you don't see staying in your life. Trim the fat. Cut your losses.

After a lot of examination of myself and the girls around me, I get very angry when I hear about the disrespectful things guys do and say to us. The truth of the matter is, we need to look out for each other and we need to tell guys this kind of behavior is unacceptable. What ever happened to the times when our parents grew up, when the boy ran to the side of the car to open the door for a girl and held out her chair for her? When the guy asked the girl on a date in person? When the guy, oh I don't know, actually called when he said he would? In part of my research, I have been asking the wiser (not the older...) about their perceptions of these changing societal norms. Most of all agree that, while there were certainly scummy guys twenty years ago, part of the change is because (a) girls wear skimpy clothes that sends off a promiscuous message and (b) social media has caused people to forget their manners. Where have all the good guys gone? Well, the slutty girls chased them off.

Regardless of if it works out for you and whoever you are dating or not, I believe it is our responsibility to other women to not let ourselves be treated so poorly anymore; if I allow a date to treat me poorly, he is going to think it is acceptable, and most likely use those same moves on the next, and the next, and the next, until someone finally gives them a nice, sturdy kick in the rear, or they find a girl with a complete lack of self-esteem that she bends to their every beckoning call.

So, do yourself and the rest of the female population a favor: stop allowing men to treat us like garbage. Each of us deserves to be treated like a princess and don't let yourself settle for anything less.

(....but I should also add that, as women, we should not necessarily take advantage of this kind of treatment, which will be in a future Blog post...)

Step Six: Finding Forgiveness

The next step in this 'healing' process was to find forgiveness; to forgive Kent, to forgive Kent's mom, and to forgive myself.

Forgiving myself was definitely the most challenging part of this step, so I decided to save it for last and to start somewhere smaller: with Kent's mom.

Let me contextualize for you and go back to the fall before "the dreaded phone call." The story with Kent's mom and I is very similar to many other mother-in-law's-not-thinking-the-daughter-in-law is good enough to date her son. Because I grew up in a dysfunctional family, I always respected her strong family values and always tried to learn from her. One Christmas, she taught me how to make a piecrust; another she taught me how to make her famous meatloaf. Whenever I needed help decorating a room or picking out a wine for a social function, I would call her and she would come to my rescue. When my own mother kicked me out of the house and June offered for me to move into the basement, I was ecstatic because I could finally observe on a day-to-day basis how to she orchestrates her family.

At first, we were best friends. She helped me buy a new car, we went shopping together, made dinner, talked about the local town gossip. It was really fun and even though Kent was busy with school and lacrosse, I still felt close to him because I was learning how he grew up and about his family dynamics.

However, as two women living together often goes, about two months in, things started heading south. And quickly. One weekend, Kent had an away lacrosse game. I, feeling very over-whelmed as a first year teacher and feeling very exhausted from a sinus infection, decided to stay home from the game. June came home, upset that I did not travel to the game and support him.

Suddenly, I began seeing June in a different light, which was very uncomfortable to me. I cannot deny that June is an amazing mother to her children and I must honor her complete and utter self-sacrifice towards her family. However, it became apparent that we had a clash of views. While I thought my role in Kent's life was to be his girlfriend but still hold my own separate life, June expected that I replace her and do exactly what she would do. Being 22 years old at the time, being a wife was not some-thing I was ready to do and I still wanted to live my own indepen-dent, carefree lifestyle.

June and I had a few typical female moments. One day, on my way home from visiting Kent, she called me and lectured me on how she was afraid *I would end in divorce like my parents* and that *I needed to look into hormones to regulate my mood.* I felt completely betrayed. This lady that I had so much respect for was now tearing down my character, challenging everything I worked so hard for, pointing out so many flaws that I was trying to correct. Another time, I walked into the kitchen while she was gossiping about me on the phone with Kent. Finally, she pulled me into the office one day to tell me she felt I was ungrateful, selfish, and unaware of how I impacted their family. So, I packed up my stuff the next day and moved in with my sister.

The next few months were incredibly tumultuous. Because it was still lacrosse season, I continued to drive to games and sit with his family, although there was obviously some tension. He would tell me that *I burned the bridge between me and his family and he wasn't sure it could ever be mended* and that he couldn't *believe that I moved out* and that *it was all my fault and I needed to apologize*. And, I took all the blame because I did not know any differently. I loved Kent and was willing to do whatever it would take to stay together because I thought that was my role. I continued to call June, to write her apology notes, to invite her to get our nails done, and eventually to just meet up to duke it out. She was always "too busy" to meet me, but I still continued.

My experience with June taught me about forgiveness. I blamed her for driving a wedge in between Kent and me, for feeding him thoughts about how I would not be a good wife or a good mother, I was angry for her not willing to meet me and to ask her to see my side of the story, and I was hurt that she would think of me as a weak person.

In September after "the dreaded phone call," I sat in church and the passage was from Mark 11:25, which says, "And when you stand praying, if you hold anything against anyone, forgive him, so that Your Father in heaven may forgive your sins." I believe what the Bible instructs in these passages is that forgiveness cannot be sought; although there are things people can do to repent and express their guilt, forgiveness cannot be forced. Forgiveness comes from the within the person accepting forgiveness. There is really nothing anyone else can do to make you forgive them. Yes, they can show you ways they are sorry. They can do something nice for you. They can compliment you. But, much like sorrow and anger, forgiveness is an internal state that we must overcome ourselves.

We are all sinners; we all act in impulsive, self-assuring, immature ways. So, how can we hold someone else accountable for standards we ourselves do not follow? It sounds hypocritical. It would be like me calling out my co-worker for complaining about the same person that I do. None of us are perfect people, so we must learn to forgive others for their shortcomings as well.

I think not recognizing these two very important pieces about forgiveness cause crutches in our lives. We find ourselves saying, "I will only forgive her if she apologizes to me," or, "I will never get over it until he shows he has changed." But, the truth of the matter is, we cannot control other people. We get ourselves hung up on things we think other people should do. We assert our beliefs and perceptions on them when, in reality, their beliefs and perceptions could be completely different. You can't wait for people to say they are sorry; you have to learn to forgive on your own.

Yes, there will be times in our lives that people do not apologize, even though they surely should. There will be times in our lives that people disappoint us, betray us, use us. They will say malicious things about us, talk about us behind our backs, start untrue rumors. But we must forgive them on our own and move on. If we wait for people to reach our expectations, we may be wasting our time because there is a good possibility they will never accomplish what *we* think is appropriate.

Forgiveness must occur within ourselves. I began to go back and re-think the situation with June to begin forgiving her. What I realized was that I could not expect her to apologize for driving Kent and me apart. I could not expect her to call me and tell me how wrong those hurtful things she said about me were. Instead, I tried to put myself in her shoes and try to understand why she might have said those things to me.

For one, I believe that actions are projections of jealousy and insecurities within our own self. When Girl A picks on Girl B for "being a brown noser and a suck up," I always remind Girl B that Girl A is probably just jealous that Girl B is getting some kind of attention. When Girl C makes fun of Girl D for "being too skinny," it is most likely that Girl C is just insecure with her own weight and it is easier to make fun of Girl D instead of confront her own issues. I began looking at the situation with June in this same respect and asking myself why she would have felt the need to say those hurtful things to me.

I went back through each comment I could remember and examined each for projections of jealousy and insecurities:

You are just ungrateful: When I lived with Kent's family after my mom kicked me out of her house, I felt very indebted to their kindness. Being a little embarrassed that I had to live with my boyfriend's family, I never wanted to draw attention to my disposition of not having a place to live. I wanted to do things to say 'thank you' to them, but I never wanted anyone to know. So, I would stay up late, once everyone was asleep, and I would clean the kitchen, unload the dishwasher. Whenever I went to the grocery store, I would buy treats for the family, and wait until everyone was out of the kitchen to put them away. But because I wanted to do these things unnoticed, it appeared as though I was doing nothing, and that I was taking without giving back. When I looked at it from this perspective, I had to fault myself for not bringing those things to light. How *could* June know I was doing those things if I never said anything about it? Of course I would appear ungrateful.

I am just afraid your parents didn't set a good example for you: While this was the most offensive comment someone could ever say to me, I tried to look at it from June's perspective and understand why she might say that. It is true that she quit her career to be a stay at home mom and take care of her sons. She devoted her entire life to raising her boys, so this comment probably stemmed from her being afraid that I was going to erase all of her hard work. So, perhaps this comment came more out of fear of losing something she held so much pride in, rather than me.

What it all came down to was June was in a crisis and I just happened to be the item for displacement: June felt like she was losing her son, someone she quit her job for and devoted the last 23 years of her life raising, and realizing that her purpose in life was no longer raising children—what she knew best—she freaked. She pushed Kent away from me because she saw me as competition, she saw that I was not going to do things her way. For that, I felt sympathetic towards her—sorry that she lived in such an isolated world, sorry that she was not so much aware of how her own insecurities were coming out, sorry that she was in a crisis. After that realization, a switch flipped and suddenly, I forgave her. It became a thing of the past, something irrelevant to my present, and a really beneficial lesson in forgiveness for my future.

Once I found forgiveness and understanding for June's behaviors, my next task was to work on Kent. I started by pinpointing my feelings of anger and dissecting the cause of that. I felt most under appreciated by him.

I had made so many sacrifices for him and now I feel like those went for nothing: Can I let you in on a little secret that I have not told anyone? A few months before we broke up, Kent got invited to tryout for a professional sports team. I was so excited for him. I spent the whole weekend he was away stalking the training camp, stalking the other players, looking at their schedule and scheduling how many games I could make it to, figuring out what his likelihood of signing with the team was. I started anonymously e-mailing all of the local news agencies and newspapers to give them his name and his statistics so that he would be Google-able to other teams.

When he dumped me so suddenly and so heartlessly, I felt very unappreciated, as if all of those sacrifices I made for him went for nothing; I made those sacrifices to keep our relationship together and as it turns out, it was going to fall apart anyway.

I had to remind myself why I did those things in the first place: because I cared about him. And, I had to remind myself that I couldn't take credit for doing nice things for people if I want some kind of reward or affirmation in return; then it becomes an entirely selfish act. If I gave Kent a foot massage because I wanted him to take me to dinner, then that was not an act of kindness but rather a business transaction. If I bought Kent a really nice birthday present because I wanted him to buy me a nicer one in return, then I cannot consider myself a generous person.

Coincidentally enough, this was a topic at church one week. We talked about this idea of joy; we often *think* that joy comes from doing things that we like to do: reading books, making cookies, going shopping and buying stuff. As our pastor described, this kind of joy is surface level and superficial because we are doing something on the surface, that we think we desire; these activities are about what makes *us* happy and what *we* want to do. The truth of the matter is, to really feel joy, one must think outside of the self; joy is connecting to something bigger than just us.

We have to be careful, however, that we are not doing 'selfless' things for people for selfish reasons; that we are not buying co-workers gifts so that they nominate us for 'employee of the month,' or running errands for people so that they are obligated to run errands for us at a later date, or listening to someone's sob story so that we can share that information with someone else later on. My little sister is perhaps the one person I know who exudes this quality of utterly selfless actions. For example, I will come home and she will have done my laundry for me; not because she wants me to do hers one day in return, not because she wants me to buy her something for doing it, not because she even enjoys doing laundry, but she does it as a genuine action, simply because she wants to do something nice for someone else. I think it is an anomaly to find someone like her, who does not have a hidden agenda or motives; she is my role model and I am learning to be a better person because of her.

And, as it turns out, letting go of expectations is also freeing. Have you ever seen someone skip that seems like they are in a bad mood? No because there is something innocent and freeing about skipping. Sure, you look silly, but it is letting go of your pride, inhibitions, and ego that allow you to feel this deep-rooted sense of joy. I think that so often we are so concerned with how other people perceive us that we spend our lives trying to suppress those actions that will lead us to pure joy. I can attest—one of my best friends also happens to teach at the same school that I do. Last year, we were chaperoning prom together. When we left, we were so concerned about the kids seeing us that we took off running. I ended up losing my shoe right in front of large group of kids and, embarrassed, had to go back to retrieve it.

The Greeks even have language for this. Dionysus, the god of wine making and ritual madness, symbolizes this idea of ritualistic and sensual behavior. The Greeks held Dionysian festivals, which included a performance to capture the sensual and almost animalistic qualities of female life. Think of the term *ecstasy*: it was about singing and dancing in an almost trance like state—and by letting go of inhibitions and purging the soul of this stuck energy, a new female composure and joy was found. Now, I am not saying that I think we all need to dress up and run around in circles like madmen, but I do think this is something healthy about freeing yourself of societal constraints.

While this is an everlasting process, I am trying to embody some of these qualities so that I can find some of this deep-rooted joy in my life. I am learning to give without expectations of receiving, I am learning to think outside of myself, and I am learning to revel in the moments with people rather than the material items. Yes, this is definitely one of those "easier said than done concepts" and yes, I will probably never be perfect at it, but it's about the journey, not the destination.

This sermon was actually very enlightening because while my whole life I thought I was a very nice person, it turns out I was quite selfish. So, I began figuring out how I could sift the selfishness out of doing nice things for people. I first started by finding ways I could be helpful without expecting recognition. I would wake up early or stay up a little later to unload the dishwasher or clean up the living room. I would stay a little later after a party to help clean up. I would stick a small gift or trinket in someone's mailbox without putting my name on it. I had to teach myself to be nice just for the sake of being nice.

And doing nice things for other people reminded me about the joy I got from doing them for Kent in the first place, and when I recognized that I did nice things for him just to do nice things, I suddenly wasn't angry about "sacrificing my time" anymore because it really wasn't a sacrifice.

In addition, he also significantly bruised my pride by dumping me on the phone. I felt this lame phone call and lousy explanation was kind of a slap in the face. When I dissected it, however, I thought about Kent, sitting in the front seat of his car, desperately telling me things were not working out and begging me not to cry. I remember he could not look at me. And, I began to feel sorry for him as well. At the end of the day, he realized he could not be the man I needed him to be; he could not stand up to his mom, he was not going to be the star lacrosse player; he did not get the amazing salary he desired. And, revealing that you are a coward, that you did not have the strength to even do this in person, must be incredibly degrading your ego. And for that, I forgave him as well because he did not have the strength or the noble character he always thought, and that must actually suck to realize that about yourself.

And, perhaps the hardest reality for me to face, I had to come to terms with the fact that he did have another girlfriend, someone who was "filling my shoes." There were a few things I had to remind myself of.

First of all, I was back on the dating market as well. So, when the time comes for me to get another boyfriend, he can get angry too.

At times like these, we tend to blame ourselves; "I must not be pretty enough," "I must not be smart enough," "I must not have blonde enough hair." But, the truth of the matter is, something in Kent changed that did not fit me anymore. It was his change, not mine. And I certainly would not want to be with anyone who was pretending to date me. If he decided one morning that a small, skinny, June-Cleaver blonde who cooked and baked everyday would work better for him, then so be it.

Yes, it is painful to know that he probably moved on very quickly, but I also reminded myself of the kind of boyfriend she was getting. I refused to know anything about her. If he was talking to her while we were together, I did not want to know. Where they met each other and if I potentially knew her, I did not want to know. When they started officially dating, I did not want to know. I did not even want to know what she looked like in the event I saw her in public somewhere. This was a very difficult urge for me to stifle, but I knew that if I stalked her Facebook, I would probably find out something that would hurt me, and I was on the road to recovery. It did not matter anyway.

Forgive Kent for not recognizing my good girlfriend-ness: Check.

Forgive Kent for having another girlfriend: Check.

Forgive myself for dating Kent: -------. Forgiving myself, however, took a little more introspection, a little more acceptance, a lot more time.

At first, I was mad at myself that I did not see the relationship ending. When I looked back on it, it was perfectly clear that things were not going to work out. Slowly, he started talking to me less, we started hanging out less, he started not getting along with my friends.

I started counseling the summer before we broke up because, at his mom's request, I wanted to look at myself from a different perspective and wanted to fix some of my "broken family" tendencies that she so kindly pointed out to me. And, while in counseling, the topic always came back to Kent. My counselor kept telling me that if we were going to have a successful marriage, he would need to figure out how to stand up to this mom. Of course, I never quite saw it in this way. I just kind of brushed it off and would tell her, "Oh, but he is changing. We are working things out. Things will be different once he is away from his mom and he is far, far way in New York."

The truth of the matter was I was working things out; he was not. Remember that scene at the local town fair? Ok, perhaps my snarky comment of, "it is nice to see you are home from your vacation" was not the best for the situation. Kent hurled around and stomped off. I followed him, begging that he would talk to me about what had just happened and instead, he just turned around, and walked away. We eventually talked about how he was going to start standing up for me in front of his mom and how he was going to talk to her about trying to work things out with me. That never happened.

About a month later, we were on our way to a friend's wedding. After the ceremony, the couple handed out CDs to the guests to listen to on the way to the reception. As we were driving to the reception destination, I put the CD in his CD player, and it got stuck. I remember him slamming on the brakes, pounding the steering wheel, and yelling at me, "Why don't you ever listen to what I say? I told you to not put that CD in. Now it's broken." I remember driving in silence the remainder of the way. Of course, it was not about the CD, but rather about his frustrations and his anger. Had he lost control, that could have been me that he hit, not the steering wheel.

I was mad at myself for not catching onto these tendencies earlier. I was mad at myself for not standing up for myself, and for letting myself be taken advantage of. I was mad that I allowed his mother to control our relationship, mad that I let her say so many horrible things about me, and most of all, mad that I did not break up with him myself sooner. I wished I would have noticed how disrespectful he was towards me two years ago and dumped him in some really dramatic, really public way. As a teacher, I have to be assertive with my students and I cannot let them take advantage of me, so it made me feel inadequate and weak that I let someone do that to me.

I often thought to myself, "What was I *ever* thinking?" I resented myself and felt embarrassed that I would ever put myself in that position in the first place. Why did I stay with him for almost six years? I honestly had no idea. When I would meet people who also knew him, I would say, "Yes I dated him, but please don't judge me," because I was embarrassed to have been associated with someone so disrespectful and so immature for so long.

But, if I was going to heal and move on, I had to learn to forgive myself. I told myself two things: first of all, I reminded myself that I did not know any differently at the time. At the time, I thought he was it; I thought I would never find anyone who was as charming and who fit me as well as he did. I had to forgive myself for my ignorance.

What finding forgiveness taught me was how to look at people as fluid creatures, rather than static entities. This actually occurred to me as I was teaching *To Kill a Mockingbird* that fall to my freshmen students. Dr. Phil has a quiz on his website called "Love Languages." The core concept is that we all give and receive messages of love in different ways; some of us require quality time, some of us require small gifts, some of us require word of affirmation. While I am not sold on the validity of the test (since it is just 25 very ambiguous questions), I think the concept relates back to what Atticus Finch teaches us: that we all perceive things in different ways. When Scout takes up cussing, instead of punishing her, Atticus calls it, "a phase she is going through," because he understands that cussing does not define Scout as a person, but rather is a symptom of her development.

When I first started dating Kent, I would spend hours writing him sentimental cards only to receive a Hallmark card with only his name signed in it. To me, I would rather someone use words to express their affirmations rather than buy me gifts whereas he is a man of few words. As Dr. Phil would suggest, we just have different love languages. Or, as Atticus Finch would preach, we just have to crawl around in someone else's skin to understand their motives. Had I known this earlier in our relationship that sentimentality was not Kent's strong suit, I probably could have saved some tension, disagreements, and phones that were thrown out of frustration.

As adults, we forget that people are living, growing, learning creatures. We are quick to judge, quick to punish, and quick to sculpt a fixated schema about people. Of course, as a human species, this is a natural tendency because we are bombarded with so much information at once that our brain organizes it into schemas. However, we must be aware of this process. So often, someone says or does one thing that we automatically prescribe "ungrateful," "boorish," and "malicious" to their personalities and we decide we will never like them again; we forget that everyone is growing, learning, and reflecting just like ourselves. I am guilty of this all the time when I see old high school classmates back around town. I remember what I thought about them in high school and forget that, like myself, they had the opportunity to grow up and are probably not the same people. I know that I, for one, go to bed a completely different person than I woke up because throughout my day, I encountered experiences that change me, if only in small ways; I am different.

Teaching caused me to view my life in stages of two. I could craft the most brilliant lesson plan and I must allow myself a run through before I can call it perfection. So many things occur during the first time you teach a lesson that you could not possibly ever think about. These could be simple things, such as activity order, when and how to pass out papers, or how much time to allow on assignments. It is always the second time that I teach a lesson that it comes to life. I am now taking this approach with everything in my life; I must experience a situation two times before I pass judgments because inevitably, like teaching, the first time is a run through and gives me the opportunity to reflect, learn, and grow as a person before the second. It is like driving. The first time I got in a car, I almost killed my dad and myself by running into a curb and then proceeding into a tree. However, being a fresh driver, the first experience allowed me valuable lessons and to this day, I have never made that mistake again. I practice this with my students all the time. As a new teacher, I am prone to making many mistakes. So, when my students forget to put their name on their paper, do not double space their essays, or answer their phones in class, I remind myself that this was the first run through and I make notes to change for next time. What this requires is patience, which, in our busy lives, we are not prone to accept.

When thinking about my relationship with Kent, I had to remind myself that I, too, was a fluid, not static, creature, and that every experience I gained from him and the break up would influence the person I am today. So, while I might perceive those experiences as "a waste of time," and I might wish that I had dumped him myself three years earlier, I also had to remind myself of the lessons I gained. And for that, I couldn't be mad at myself.

Secondly, I had to remind myself that, while I did spend a significant amount of time with him, I could take steps to ensure I would never end up in that position again, which brings me to my next step. After I realized what a terrible match he was for me, my greatest fear was that I would default back to my original intentions, and I would marry someone just like Kent, so I wanted to put work into making sure that would absolutely not happen.

Step Seven: Understand Why It Wouldn't Work

*I*n the beginning stages of a break up, there is always this kind of gray area about whether you will get back together or not. There are so many stories of people who date for some period of time, break up, run into each other ten years later, and end up rekindling their love for each other (such as *The Notebook*). Noah and Ally's love story is highly romantic and I am so glad they ended up together, but I personally think it is kind of pathetic that Noah lived in some rural, beat-up farmhouse, waiting for her return. What if she never returned? Then he wasted a big chunk of his life. These are really cute love stories and all, but I did not want to be the girl that just remained stuck. In order for me to move on, I had to realize we were never getting back together. And, in order to do that, I had to realize why it really would have never worked out in the first place.

First, I thought about what my life would have been like had I moved to New York with him like I originally planned. No offense to you who live in New York, but I am from Colorado, which is the best place in the world to live. I can't help but feel so fortunate to call this state home. I feel so fortunate every day on my drive to school. The road I take sits above a hill and as I get into town, it releases into a valley. In August and September, I get to watch the sun rise from the horizon and admire the pinks, oranges, and light blues. In the winter, I get to admire the crisp snowfall that folds across the mountain ranges in the distance. Some mornings, I see the valley enveloped in fog. It is an excellent way to start my day (I often think about taking a picture to capture this majesty, but then I remember that picturing and driving is probably more dangerous than texting and driving...)

For one, Colorado also has so much to offer. I can hang out at Cherry Creek and LoDo's on the weekend to get a spice of the hipster life, or I can hang out at the Grizzly Rose and swing dance with some guy from Western Nebraska who came to buy groceries. During the summer, I can mountain bike, hike, and raft in the same exact spot that, during the winter, is powdered white, fit for skiing, and ripe for snowball fights. I took a trip to California last spring and was amazed. My friend and I went on a stroll. The weather was about 75 degrees and there was not another soul in sight. In Colorado, it could be 50 degrees and sunny and people are still outside, mowing their lawns, washing their cars, or playing with their kids.

Another advantage to living in Colorado is the changing seasons. We do have four seasons, although sometimes we may see summer in winter, winter in the spring, and fall in summer. In the fall, my Facebook will blow up with statuses about pumpkin spice lattes, making homemade banana bread and chicken noodle soup, and wanting to curl up in a blanket and read a good book. When fall runs into winter, everyone will be talking about the holiday season, decorating their houses, the excitement of the first snowfall, wearing boots and sweats, and the wonderful apple cinnamon and evergreen scents. When winter runs into spring, everyone will be complaining about how they are tired of the cold and excited for the nice weather. As spring runs into summer, everyone is excited about staying up late, spending days outside, bbq's, good friends and good memories. Colorado gives us this unique opportunity to experience this rolling change. When we get tired of the heat or tired of the snow, we can expect that, in just a short amount of time, the weather will change. It never stays too constant for too long. This change reminds us to break out of our patterns and routines, try something different. Just like the weather, we are never too stagnant for too long.

Now, there is still a likely chance that I will end up in New York someday, and also a likely chance that I would have actually enjoyed the life out there. But, in order for me to get over Kent, I had to rationalize and make myself believe that it would have been miserable. No thank you, this life I have in Colorado fits me just perfectly.

Once I realized I did not want to live in New York, I began thinking about all the things we fought about, and all the times we disagreed about something. For example, about a month before "that dreaded phone call," we were at my roommate's parent's house for his birthday. Kent, who graduated with a degree in business, was talking about fracking and how much money Kent could potentially profit from starting up a business in this industry. My roommate's parents, who live in a rural area, discussed their concerns with the possibility of fracking behind their house and how it would depreciate their home value, what they worked for their entire lives. After going back to re-think this scenario, I recognized a huge discrepancy in Kent's and my values: he was attracted to the money and I was attracted to the quality of life (being a teacher, you kind of have to accept you will never be able to afford a custom built house). The issue was not about the fracking--but rather where we placed value in our lives--and in realizing this difference, I realized how different our viewpoints on the world really were, and how, had we gotten married, we would have been battling each other for the rest of our marriage (because, had we gotten married, we were sure to also get a divorce).

Additionally, we did not really carry the same lifestyle choices. One of my friends asked me, "So what did you guys do for fun?" I took a long minute to pause because we did not really do anything for fun. Our lives basically consisted of going to Kent's lacrosse games, going to dinner, taking a nap, going to a social event, waking up the next morning and watching T.V., recovering from the lacrosse game, eating, doing homework, and going out again. As a person, I am very adventurous and always up for new experiences such as going to concerts where I don't even know the band name, visiting places I have never heard of, trying out new foods. With Kent, we were always watching t.v., watching lacrosse, taking naps. He always suggested that we do fun things, like go snowmobiling, but we were always too busy with lacrosse to go anywhere. I was happy to do those things with him, but now when I think about it (and the insurgence of my ADHD), I know that I would have been miserable spending my weekend, glued to the couch, relaxing and watching T.V.; I need to be out, exploring, climbing trees, hiking mountains, and shooting bow and arrows like Katniss Everdeen.

The style of marriage we wanted was also completely different. Kent needed someone to wait on him and make him the center of her world; basically, take his mother's role in his life. Since he was moving to New York and his mom was staying in Colorado, he needed someone to replace her, which is great because some girls really love to fulfill that role. I am not one of them. I need a man who can do his own laundry and cook his own meals because I barely even have time to do that for myself. I remember when I acquired my very first teaching job. Kent was the first person I called and I was bursting at the seams with excitement. His response was, "Cool. I need to get back to studying." I felt crushed because I wanted him to be just as excited and proud of me as I was for myself. But, this instance very early on proved that we were on very opposite wavelengths. We would have spent our entire marriage arguing about what I should do and what he should do and that would not have been enjoyable whatsoever. No thank you.

I accepted that what had happened was in the past, and that those moments can never be taken away, but that it was time for something different in the present and future. Part of my turmoil and uneasiness was trying to figure out if I thought Kent would come back and, if he did, would I want to take him back. We broke up a couple times before (mostly out of immaturity, an occasional hormonal overload from me, and exhaustion) so I was not completely set that he would never come back. And, if he did come back and realized he had made a mistake, I wanted to make sure I was prepared with an answer.

After the guy-wrenching incident at LifeTime, I distinctly remember waking up that next morning, and then making it to lunch, and then to dance practice before I realized that Kent had not even crossed my mind. Realizing that we were absolutely, positively never getting back together and that we were terrible, horrible matches for each other alleviated some anxiety because

I knew he would never stand as an option again. I would never go back to him and I actually hoped to never even talk to him again. It was quite liberating to know that I would not be tied down to Kent any longer and that something much, much better would be waiting for me.

Step Eight: Living and Learning

One problem with doing all of this analysis and introspection is that you have a lot of thoughts that come up. And, thoughts often come up as word "vomit." I wanted to appear as though I had gracefully survived this break up. However, when I ran into people who would ask me about it, I first would spill much more information (that was potentially damaging to his reputation) than I wanted to. It has never really been my style to let someone know they are controlling me (I am very oppositional defiant like that; it might be a Dutch trait). So, I began to train myself to respond in a nonchalant way. When asked the question, "How is Kent?" I would practice responding, "You know, I have not spoken to him in a while. I think he might be in New York or Norway, but I hope he is doing well." And, when they looked at me astonished that we had broken up, I would just smile and say, "Yes, well, we broke up last summer, lots of things happened, but that is ok."

And when I mean *practice*, I mean I had to practice this for months before it felt semi-natural. Being a very social person, I obviously had way more things to divulge, but I also knew he had a reputation to uphold and he could probably run around telling everyone I am his "crazy ex-girlfriend."

Yes, it was true: Kent had now moved his way into being my "ex-boyfriend." Except that term somehow felt unnatural to use. As our favorite childhood literary character, Alexander, taught us, "what a terrible, horrible, no good, very bad" word. I always refer to someone I dated-and-then-broke-up-with as "a guy I dated" or "the boyfriend I once had," never as **MY EX-BOYFRIEND.** It just never feels quite right.

I think calling someone your **"EX-BOYFRIEND"** is a very charged, immature, and completely unfair term. For one, **EX-**references a lot of anger. Even *saying* the word itself brings up some really dark, negative emotions. It gives me this image of some crazy girl, yelling, throwing stuff on the lawn, breaking plates and televisions while her **"ex-boyfriend,"** some big, burly guy with tattoos, sits in his car and laughs at her while fondling his new girlfriend and has absolutely no feelings or sense of attachment to the crazy girl out in the yard. Sure, anger is a natural emotion when you first break up. You feel lost and confused, under valued. When Kent and I first broke up, I was most angry because I felt used. I saved his life on more than one occasion, wrote the resume and cover letter that got him a job, sacrificed my own needs to accommodate his, and I felt all of that went unappreciated. However, letting that anger simmer and bubble is never healthy, so I had to find ways to deal with it. Referring to someone as an **"EX"** continues to perpetuate that vicious emotion of being angry and ain't nobody got time for that.

Referring to someone as an **"EX-"** also insinuates that there is something terribly wrong with them. Who knows, maybe there is. Maybe your ex-boyfriend turned out to be some roid-popping, test-cheatin', woman beater. Maybe your ex-girlfriend ended up smashing your car windows, draining your bank account, and marrying your best friend. Maybe those kinds of people deserve the term **'EX.'** The majority of relationships, however, end because the two people just aren't a good fit for each other. Sometimes, that presents itself in an extremely emotional way, where people are crying, snotting through tissue boxes, spending endless hours listening to sad songs and eating chocolate cake while sobbing in the bathtub. Sometimes, it is a gradual breakdown where you slowly start to drift apart and one day, you don't really have anything to talk about anymore. Sometimes, it is just two people consensually agreeing they are on different pages in their lives and it isn't going to work. We are all human, we all make mistakes and have flaws, and sometimes, it could just be that two decently moral people just shouldn't be together. When I run into people we both knew, I always have to remind myself that Kent still has a reputation to uphold, I don't know who he still talks to, and that people have different experiences with him than I did. There certainly are bad things he can say about me too, but overall, we are not bad people; just really not meant to be together (or really in the same room ever again). I trained myself to say, "You know, I have no idea where he is right now, I don't really care, but I wish him the best and hope he is happy with his new girlfriend."

Much like calling someone an 'expatriate,' referring to someone as an **"EX"** means you want to ignore absolutely all association with them, as if that time in your life is erased and never existed in the first place. However, if you invested some amount of time and energy in this person, there was obviously something slightly intriguing and gratifying there. Yes, I will probably never talk to Kent ever again. But, I can't ignore the six years we spent together because those years were as much about me and my development as they were about him. Pretending those years didn't exist and pretending that I had absolutely no association with him is ignoring a huge part of who I am today. I learned so much about myself and about relationships from both the positive and negative aspects that came out of it. And not just him, but any form of a romantic relationship, no matter how short or insignificant it may have seemed, I have ever had taught me something and made me a better person. One guy taught me to appreciate the blood, sweat, and tears that go into our transportation systems; another guy taught me how to drive a motorcycle. One guy taught me what it feels like to be cheated on, another taught me the importance of time, communication, and setting priorities, and what it's like to lose your best friend. One guy taught me what unrequited love feels like; another taught me that bad kissers are the worst. And, I know that all of those little bumps in the road are preparing me for the real thing, so I have to give credit to those I've met along the way. They can't be **"EX'S"** because they offered some form of enlightenment to me, whether it be through something that was really distressing or something that was really wonderful.

Word connotations are so interesting because at surface level words seem so trivial, so arbitrary. However, as rhetoricians suggest, words become engrained in our consciousness and alter our perceptions of the world. So be careful the next time you refer to someone as your **"EX"**; with it carries bitterness, carries pain, carries un-dealt with emotions.

The good news for anyone who slips into the "I've Dated Britany" category is you will never be an **"EX"** (unless, of course, you do something completely crazy and irrational, and then you might just fall into the restraining-order category, and then I am probably changing my phone number/place of residence/ blog address).

When looking back on all of the things I had to do to overcome the break up, I feel very empowered. I would never consider him my "ex-boyfriend" because so many great things came out of that relationship: I learned how to be a girlfriend, I learned what a bad boyfriend is, and I learned a tremendous amount about myself. A year later, I have proven to myself that I can, in fact, survive and that I am ready to propel my life forward. While sometimes going into another relationship seems daunting, I am liberated by knowing that I do have the tools to survive a break up and that I have the choice, the agency, to date someone or to not date someone.

So, Kent became "the guy I once dated," or "my long term boyfriend." I decided I would devote my energies towards dissecting what happened in our relationship and learning from it so I do not let it happen again. As humans, it is also natural for us to default back to "what's comfortable," which is why we have the saying, "you turned out just like your mom." I see it over and over again—people date the same kind of person and wonder why they always get treated the same ways. I had a fear that because the Kent-type was my comfort zone, I would then regress back to a Kent-type relationship, which I absolutely and positively did not want; once was enough for me. So, I began to go back to pinpoint those dysfunctional tendencies that I had not noticed before.

Here is how the process works: first, you have to let yourself grieve. For some people, this looks like getting really, really drunk and making out with a bunch of random people. For others, it means having a cry fest and watching chick flicks at your best friend's house (probably also drunk). I personally like to write on my blog and plan big, extravagant trips. Next, you have to take a step away from the situation and not think about it for a while. Distance allows you to filter out the emotions and prepares you to use that objective lens; you meet some new people, gain some more life experience, learn new things about yourself. And, when the time is right, something will trigger you back to those memories. You will re-visit them in your mind, you will use your new life experiences, you will begin to understand situations in different ways, and you will realize why things happened the way they happened.

Although experiencing these inconsistencies, revelations of how selfish people are, and unforeseen heartbreaks will never not suck, understanding the process makes it easier. I am able to recognize that there are ultimately three stages I will go through (the grief, the distance, the re-visitations), and by the time I have completed the last stage—when I can look back on the time we spent together, the deep conversations we had without getting butterflies in my stomach and without feeling a longingness, when I can share stories and talk about him without any feelings attached, I will be ready to move on. Sometimes "moving on" means meeting someone else; sometimes it means getting a promotion and setting new goals for yourself. In each case, it depends.

Of course, I knew how to engage in this cognitive shifting because I had practiced it before. The first person I did this with was my dad. My dad was my hero. I called him three times a day, went over to his house after work every day. He did my laundry, made my lunch, cooked me dinner. I raved about him being my Atticus Finch to my students. And then, he got a wife. And this wife did not fit my schema of who my father was. I went into a mental turmoil and started questioning every relationship, every decision, every perception I had about my childhood. It was another identity crisis. So, in counseling, I started going back through some of my memories of my father—the time he went to watch me at nationals, the time we went to North Carolina, the time we went to that New Year's party. I had to look at them from a different standpoint: maybe my dad had different a different personality, maybe he made flawed decisions, maybe things did not happen the way my mind remembered. I always thought my dad was lonely, and wanted to invite him to my social activities, but perhaps he actually enjoyed being introverted and spending time alone. Although my relationship with my dad is not the same as it was, it has blossomed into something a little more adult, a little more mature. I don't rely on him to make every decision for me anymore. I don't call him everyday, I can make my own lunch, I can choose my own car insurance by myself—and that is healthy (but, he *does* still pay my cell phone bill...).

I think as humans, when thoughts and memories are painful, we have a natural tendency to run away and avoid them. We busy ourselves with work, we tell everyone we are fine, we do not bring it up in conversation. It is much easier to brush it to the corner of our brains, let it corrode in the recesses, and pretend it never even happened.

However, eventually those painful thoughts and memories grow so large in our subconscious that they start to surface. Sometimes, this presents itself through bad habits such as drinking. Sometimes, this presents itself through bad relationships such as expecting dysfunctional tendencies. Sometimes, this presents itself through physical symptoms such as headaches. Or, like myself, sometimes this presents itself through anxiety; I always get those dreams about my teeth falling out.

So, as I learned from trauma training, the more effective way to get past those painful memories are to re-experience and re-visit them over and over again until suddenly there is no emotion attached any longer. As painful as it was, I forced myself to go back through my relationship with Kent and to re-visit the good, the bad, and the ugly memories together. Actually, my entire relationship, everyone always asked me why I was dating him and I always responded, "I just haven't found anyone I liked more." So, I started replaying events in my head to try to see them from everyone else's perspective. I remembered this one time we were listening to the radio. "My Best Friend" by Tim McGraw came on, and being the old-fashioned sap that I am, I started thinking about what our first dance song would be. I asked him and his response was "Crazy Bitch" by Buckcherry. Now, at the time, I thought he was just being playful and sarcastic, but looking back on it, that was actually his perception of me (which no one should think that about their girlfriend—no one). I thought about the time he 'forgot' to get me a birthday present or got too busy to call me or that time he hugged that girl, "just as a friend." I learned to re-frame these memories to fit my new and improved version of 'Kent'.

I was very fortunate that Kent moved far, far away and I would not have to worry about running into him. We grew up in the same hometown that we both moved back to after college, and that I had these physical, geographical boundaries. When we go through traumatic experiences, we tend to avoid whatever reminds us of the pain and suffering. Pay attention to what you are avoiding. Is it a song that had meaning in your relationship? Is it a popular coffee shop that you spent so much time together at, gazing into each other's eyes? Is it a movie, a video game, a group of friends? Of course, there is a time and place to avoid, to repress. Sometimes, you have to do that to survive because it is just too painful; it took me about nine months to be able to fully recover. But at some point, you have to confront it to prove to yourself that you are ready to move on. Being a teacher, I had the luxury of spending my summer processing, reliving, and learning. My roommates would often come home from work to me lying on the couch, "resting my eyes," but what I was really doing was healing, thinking, processing, learning.

Don't let some break up stop your life; you may need to pause it for a little bit, but you are only making yourself stronger in the end. When I felt ready, I forced myself to go back through the "dreaded phone call" and break up talk in his car. At first, it was extremely painful. Emotionally, I could only get myself through the first line of "It's time we start seeing other people" before I started welling up. But, each time I re-visited the memory, the previous part became easier to handle, I could get myself a little further, and I cried a little less. A few weeks later, I tested myself by driving past his house. I was a little jittery, a little anxious as I approached the driveway. And then, I whizzed past. I looked down to see if I recognized anyone's car and I felt nothing.

Absolutely nothing.

I did not throw up from nervousness.

No feelings of anger or frustration flooded back to me.

I actually didn't care if it happened that his car was parked in the driveway.

And, my heart certainly did not break. It did not even skip a beat.

That is when I knew all the work, the cognitive shifting I had been doing worked.

I felt nothing. There was no grief, no sadness, no nostalgia. My life was going on.

When I look back on it now, I absolutely needed to go through each one of those stages. I needed to be a zombie for a month, to be in fight-or-flight mode. I needed to get angry and catapult the golf balls. I needed to cry, to rationalize my feelings, to forgive. As I went back to reflect on the break up, I also began uncovering some of my inherent values that were buried because there was no need to pay attention to them at the time; my values of selflessness, of compassion, of adventure and diversity. I started by looking at my frustrations with how Kent dumped me: I was frustrated that he took so much of his mother's advice without consulting other people. I was frustrated that he held my family against me, even though I am a perfectly functioning adult. I was frustrated that he did not come at this as a discussion, but rather as a finite decision, and therefore, did not leave me an opportunity to defend myself. By recognizing that these were, in fact, some of my views of the world, I was able to conquer the world more confidently.

I remember Kent telling me, "If we are meant to be together, then we will end up together." And, I remember thinking to myself, "Um, well, if you are in New York, and I am in Colorado, then how is that going to work?"

Throughout the break up, I learned a few things about growing up. I learned that sometimes, you have to date other people to figure out what you want. I re-watched a whole season of *Boy Meets World* a couple weeks ago. Granted, it is just a fictional television show, *but* Cory and Topanga do split up for an entire season and they do end up back together. We have these foolish perceptions in our heads that we are going to run into Prince Charming, fall in love, and get married, and never break up, never have any disagreements, never doubt being together. But, like our parents, relationships are always flawed and sometimes you have to walk away from one and date a few other people to realize you wanted the original person in the first place. Everyone has stories about, "Well, we dated for a while, then broke up, and five years later, something brought us back together and we realized we were in love," or "Well, I dumped him for this other skeezy guy whom I found out was cheating on me anyways, and then I realized what a great thing we had going." Being a 20-Something is about making mistakes and bad decisions so that we learn from these decisions and be appreciative of the good things. I know that I will never get back together with Kent, but everyone else, I am not so sure. You never know how the winds might blow....

I learned that old people give the best advice. The median age of employee at my school is like 102. Actually, probably more like 38. But, I could not have survived until 24 without these wise souls. I look at some of my friends who work with people around their age—and while their jobs sound like a hoot and a holler everyday—their personal lives are a mess. Whenever I have a crisis in my life, I always seek out their counsel. And, they all tell me the same thing: "Oh, I remember when I was your age and that same thing happened to me." It makes me feel less isolated, less alone. I am comforted to know that all of these crisis' happen to everyone else. They are just developmental milestones, and since all these old people are still kicking and haven't died yet, I think I will survive. Making friends with old people is the best!

I learned that you don't have to attend every single social activity: When I was in high school and even in college, I always felt it necessary to attend every single social event. When graduation party season came, my friends and I prided ourselves on the 30+ graduation parties that we attended. It basically was—drive, eat cake, say hi to the person, and leave (unless the party consisted of a bouncy castle, and then we stayed). On my weekends, we would have social activities planned for Friday night, Saturday afternoon/Saturday night, and Sunday afternoon. The idea is that if you miss out on a social event, you would miss out on the inside jokes, and be isolated. But, as I get older, I realize that my friends have so many things going on in their lives that if I miss one social outing, it won't be a detriment to my social standing. It's ok to do different things and hang out with different people.

I learned that perhaps it's not about finding someone you love, but finding someone you can see spending the rest of your life with. The fact of the matter is, when you get married, you are supposed to deal with that person for the rest of your life. So, I marry someone with stinky feet, and I will have to smell their stinky feet for the rest of his life. Up until this point, I have kind of been focused on who I *like*, rather than who I see a future with, which completely alters the way I look at dating.

I learned that everyone has issues: celebrities, your best friends, your parents, teachers, significant others, etc. *Everyone* has issues. There is no such thing as being perfect and being perfectly put together. Even those people who appear to grow up in perfect families and have a perfect lives have issues that stem from that "perfectness" (like, for example, being too attached to their moms or not knowing how to handle stress). And, on the other hand, people who grow up in imperfect families and live imperfect lives have issues that stem from the imperfectness (like, for example, attachment issues, trust issues, money issues, etc.) Whenever I suggest to people to go to counseling, the first thing that comes out of their mouth is, "Well, counseling is for people who have problems. I don't have any." Well, actually, we all have problems; some of them are just more severe and life altering than others. The human condition is structured so that we experience insecurities, inadequacies, and incompleteness to build resistance and strengthen our characters. So, it's not really fair to judge someone based on the fact that they have issues because we all suffer from some kind of issue. I, for example, have severe anxiety issues (probably stemming from my imperfect family). It's bad, like borderline psychosis diagnosis. But I think part of growing up is accepting that everyone has issues and learning to deal with your own issues so they do not significantly impact your life. I am well aware that I am an anxious mess so I try to do everything I can to keep myself from going off the deep end; I yoga, write on my blog, write checklists. I try to confront my issues and don't let them hold me back.

I learned that it's about learning to cope because bad stuff still happens. In a conversation with one of my friends this weekend, she said, "I am afraid I am just becoming numb to everything." I am not sure if 'numb' is what is happening, but rather perhaps just learning better ways to cope. I believe our twenties are designed to throw as much crap as possible at us so that we learn to be resilient and will be able to coast lazily into our later years because we already learned to triumph earlier. It is like starting a new job; at the beginning, it is extremely challenging. You stress about it, there is a huge learning curve, and you aren't sure if it's for you. Once you spend some time and figure it out, everything becomes smooth sailing. Or, like graduating college: part of college is designed to throw so much stress and so much knowledge and so much work at you just to see if you can handle it. And, once you prove that you can, we throw you into the work force, which perhaps is a little less stressful than college. We need strong, resilient people in our society. But, we must go through that learning curve to enjoy the smooth sailing part.

I have learned that bad stuff is always going to keep happening: your Catalytic converter unexpectedly breaks and you have to shell out $800 to pass the emissions test, your grandparent falls and ends up in the hospital for a month, your dog runs away, your best friend goes to jail, your shower breaks, someone loses his job, etc. Bad stuff will never stop happening because that is the nature of being an adult. But, with each obstacle, we learn how to overcome a little better each time until finally, bad stuff doesn't affect us as much anymore because we have developed so many tools to cope.

I learned that life is a series of cycles: One of the reasons I enjoy living in Colorado is because the seasons serve as cycles; when you get too tired of the heat, fall rolls in, with scents of pumpkin spice and apple cider. Then winter comes, a time to sit in front of the fire and eat hearty meals. Spring brings excitement and renewal and summer means backyard bbq's, lemonade, and late nights. As humans, we need change in our lives to add variety, which is why so many people move back to Colorado (it usually goes like this: "I hate the snow and I hate Colorado so I am moving to California," and they move to California, and realize that everything is the same all the time and that feels wrong). Sometimes, we go through cycles that are fabulous; we are on top of the world, the life of the party, everything is going well. And, sometimes, we go through cycles that are really, really rough and we want desperately to be back in the previous cycle. The fact that life does cycle is important because it means we will never be static and we will always be going somewhere different. And, there are so many different kinds of cycles we can go through. We might cycle from being a health nut to a sugar addict; to wanting companionship and then wanting extreme singleness; to staying up late with our roommates, telling childhood stories, wanting to read books alone in our rooms. It's a natural Circadian rhythm. I think part of growing up is recognizing that things do cycle and that, while we may not necessarily be in the cycle we want to be in, we are there for a reason and have all the power to cycle out. I would label myself a very emotional person; I thrive on listening to super emotional music, watching super emotional movies, and being in super emotional states. Heck, I cried last week in front of my freshmen class while reading *To Kill a Mockingbird* when the balcony stands up for Atticus as he walks out of the courtroom. But, for some reason, I cycled out of my emotion-ness, and it wasn't until someone pointed it out to me that I realized I was drifting away from that piece of me I value so much. At the time, it was probably necessary for me to cycle out of being so emotional and I have since reverted back to thriving on emotion (and feeling the need to write everyone love letters and crying and all that good stuff). So, being in 'funks' or cycles is not necessarily a bad thing because it induces change, and in change, we can find introspection and growth.

Most importantly, I learned that the break up was much less about losing him, and much more about finding myself.

Next stop, finding my real "Prince Charming"...

Part II:

My Existential Crisis

My Identity Crisis

There is no doubt that being a 20-Something is HARD: The moment you have been waiting for has finally arrived. You graduated. You took your last summer off to do things you always wanted to do. And, now, as you begin your new career, you are suddenly feeling empty, void, uncertain, and insecure. You are having an identity crisis. And it happens to everyone.

I suffered my first identity crisis when I was a junior in college. For as long as I could remember, I defined myself as a dancer. Everything I did revolved around being a dancer: the workouts, the stretching, the meals, the clothes, the physical appearance, the volunteering, the presentations and performing. But, the time came that I had to give that up. I felt like my identity was stripped. I defined myself as a dancer for so long and devoted so much of my life to it that I had no idea where I would go from there.

So, I started exploring myself. I took up a new hobby, I introduced myself to new friends, I entered a research internship, devoted myself to my teaching program, bought a new car, strengthened my relationships with my family, and learned to love this new version of myself. It took me some time to pick myself back up, reflect and distance myself from the situation, and re-invent myself. It was not an easy process but in the end, I am proud of what I had become: while I used to be Britany, the Dancer, I was now just Britany, the girl who dances. I had to learn to separate myself: dancing was what I did, but not who I was. I could still be all those things that dancing taught me: presentable, classy, professional, confident, creative, innovative, athletic. I just had to find other avenues to do it. In fact, my life brought me back to dance as I coach my own team. It is funny how life works out. Sometimes, the things we least expect and most want come back to us at the seemingly most random times.

I see so many of my friends going through this same identity crisis. We have devoted so much of our lives to athletics, to school, to always reaching the next step, that when we graduate we find ourselves lost, bored, and uncertain. I think that is why so many people go to graduate school right after college; the unknown is uncomfortable and we want to go back to structure, to people telling us what to do and making decisions for us; the familiar class schedules with the homework and scheduled breaks. We want to go back to a time that we can see an end—just one more semester, just one more test—that the workforce does not allow. We want to have answers, but sometimes, we just have to accept that life is about obstacles, challenges--it is about changing, growing, finding, replacing, and reinventing yourself.

Throw a break up on top of that, 20-Somethings are bound to experience some anxiety. Especially being a teacher, and being expected to be an adult role model, I often have to go into class, pretend like everything is peachy keen, when in actuality, my life is in shambles and I'd prefer to be whimpering in the copy room and have my mom patting my back. No one ever prepared me for the immense amount of challenges I would face post-college. Between the time I graduated college and now, I have moved five times, gotten two speeding tickets, been rejected from three jobs (but obtained one), watched my dad get re-married, and been dumped. That is a lot.

But, what I have also realized is that, while these times are very tough, I am being prepped to handle the future. Life will never NOT be difficult; but through these trials and tribulations, we just learn to deal with the difficult aspects in a better way. During-Kent, had I gotten that speeding ticket or watched my dad get re-married, I would have been a complete disaster. Post-Kent, those things did not even phase me because I learned so many coping skills through the process.

What I find the tendency of 20-Somethings to be is, we work really hard at school, work really hard at finding a job, get a job, and then stagnate because we accomplished everything we worked towards for the last 22 years of our lives. We spent 17 years studying, studying, studying, pulling all nighters, writing papers, attending office hours, taking naps in the middle of the day, getting up early to go to recitations and practice. Then, suddenly it stops and we are working a 9-5 job. We get home, eat dinner, and end up with a couple extra hours where we have nothing to do. This feels really unnatural because we just spent the last 17 years of our lives being insanely busy and having too much to do and we really want to take advantage of having nothing to do. Now, we feel "burnt out", spend the rest of the evening watching reality television shows, wake up, and repeat that cycle again. Unfortunately, the average person lives to be 82 years old, which means we have 60 more years of our lives to go to work, come home, and sit around watching T.V.

Seeing so many of my friends getting stuck in this rut, I decided to reflect upon my own quality of life; certainly, working and sitting in front of the t.v. for the next 60 years of my life did not seem very enriching. Now that I was Kent-free, I had the opportunity to make my life whatever I wanted it to be. I did not see this period of my life as the pinnacle of everything I had always worked towards, but rather an opportunity to finally have the means to get what I really wanted out of life.

The Importance Of Setting Goals

First, I created a to-do list of things I had been avoiding. For a while, I powered in *survival mode*; I only had enough energy and emotional capacity to do the bare minimum, which meant I let a few slightly important tasks slip. This included, but was not limited to: showering every day, going to the grocery store, doing laundry, responding to parent e-mails, picking out my dance team's costumes, getting a cavity filled, and calling my grandpa back. Luckily, my sister and roommate are awesome, so I did have clean clothes and food to eat, but I needed to start getting my life back in order.

After accomplishing those nagging tasks, I started setting new goals for myself. When I was in high school, my poms coach forced us to write short term and long-term goals at the beginning of every season. We would spend a week coming up with goals and printing them on fancy, decorated paper. She would store them for the season. Mine usually represented a typical high school girl's dreams: get a solid quad, make a new friend, pass my driver's license test, grow my hair two more inches, run outside once a week (ok, maybe once every month?).

Out of habit, I continued this tradition into my college career. This time, these goals changed again: play on an intramural sports team, hike the Flatirons, try a new restaurant, make five new social friends, pass my classes and graduate. After I was accepted into the teaching program, I focused my goals on getting a job, since I had heard how tough the job market really was. I found things to build my resume, such as participating in a research internship and tutoring, I signed up for networking events, and took advantage of career services by attending their resume and interview workshops. I even started preparing a backup plan and a third back up plan in case I didn't find a job and had to live with my parents another year. I immersed myself in fulfilling my goals. In April, after four years and a lot of sucking up to the right people, the moment finally came and I was offered my dream job of teaching high school English and inventing/coaching their poms team.

Phew. I could finally breathe a sigh of relief. All of that work finally paid off.

When I went into my new teacher orientation meeting, my principal asked what our goals for the year were. I confidently said, "I am just hoping I survive being a first year teacher". So, the year passed. I had some good teaching moments, but mostly bad ones. I got myself to fall break, and then to Thanksgiving break, and then to holiday (not Christmas) break, and then to spring break. I was so relieved when May came around and I could confidentially say that I survived and reached my goal (only a few kids were left a bloody mess on the ground, but hey, you can't save them all).

In July, someone asked me what my goals for myself were. I looked at her dumbfounded. My entire life had thus far been centered around setting and achieving goals for myself, and those goals especially catering to Kent. I realized that, once I had a teaching job, I hadn't set any meaningful goals since. I had plateaued.

Goals are important for us to set in our lives because they prevent us from being static; even if we do not necessarily achieve all of our goals, they allow us to continue reaching, striving, being innovative, and making ourselves better people. For example, one of my goals is to try out for a professional dance team. Even if I never achieve that goal and never actually make a team, setting the goal becomes my main motivation to keep myself in shape and from completely chopping off my hair. Goals also cause us to reflect upon ourselves, to figure out what inconsistencies and inadequacies we have and then, make a plan to correct those things. Time seems dangerously endless.

This teaching year, my goal is to no longer just survive, but to make myself a better educator, coach, roommate, and friend. I set a goal to cook or bake at least one thing a week (my family always gets on me about not being domestic, which is slightly true, so I am trying to combat that). In my classroom, I am working towards instilling more intrinsic motivation and doing a variety of more meaningful/less busywork activities. I set a goal to wear less of the white t-shirt/cardigan duo (which, I actually accomplished until last week when I lost all motivation and go-go juice). In my relationships, I am trying to listen more, talk less about myself and ask more questions about others, be more empathetic, more giving, less judgmental. In my personal life, I hope to travel to more places, experience more things. These goals are not necessarily earth shattering. I am not looking to be the first female on Mars or make my way onto *Good Morning America*. But, by setting small goals, I find myself more motivated in my life.

And, as I was forced to do on my high school dance team, I write all of these goals down on a fancy piece of paper and hang it in my room, so that every morning when I wake up, and as I am brushing my teeth, I can walk by and be reminded about the path I am electing to take to make myself a better and more informed person.

Back when I first graduated college, my goals included: apply to graduate school, make a new friend, market my blog, cook one new thing for dinner a week, visit a new place once a month. Today, my goals involve finish graduate school, finish my book, learn to play guitar, market my blog, continue to learn to cook one new thing a week, work on my flexibility in the classroom, build better relationships with my students. There is always something we can work on.

Goal #1: Stateside, Beachside, Or Mid-West Side?

I knew I also *needed* to travel, experience other places, other people, other things, and explore myself. I needed to know whether or not Colorado was authentically me, or if the authentic me belonged somewhere else. Traveling did a few things for me. First of all, very superficially, it allowed me an excuse one weekend a month to halt my search for "Prince Charming". I felt a lot of pressure from my friends, my co-workers, my family, society in general to constantly be on a search for "Prince Charming". Like, if I was not out every Friday and Saturday night scoping out the bars for potential eligible bachelors, then I was dooming myself to be the crazy cat lady for the rest of my life. But, I also knew that I was not ready to jump into another relationship and it would not be fair for me to date someone else without figuring myself out too.

The first thing I did was book a trip to Detroit to visit my best friend from college. I grew up in Colorado, went to college in Colorado, and now work in Colorado, so I needed to see what the rest of the world had to offer. The weekend I went would have been Kent and my official, "6 year anniversary", so I wanted to go away for the weekend to avoid sitting in my room with the curtain drawn, sobbing on my bed, eating boxes of chocolate, and feeling sorry for myself. This new chapter of my life was about ME, and was about discovering what I, an autonomous agent, wanted. I flew into Detroit, went to dinner with my friend and her family, spent the weekend exploring the city, watching Animal Planet 101 videos, and visiting Ann Arbor.

I brought back a few new understandings from Detroit:

What I found was a little different than the stereotype suggests. Yes, there are burnt down, abandoned houses. In fact, I saw many landmarks that had full trees growing through the centers, indicating that these houses had been singed for a very, very long time. Yes, there were bumpy roads full of potholes and neglect. Yes, there was graffiti sprayed around many old, barred up windows. It was an incredibly humbling experience. My life saw a lot of petty drama compared to the everyday, decades long of struggle and strife some of these people go through and going into the city helped me to remember to put the break up in perspective: my life wasn't over; it was just beginning.

It is very depressing to think that Detroit, during the first half of the century, was the "Paris of America". You can see this throughout many of the old buildings—the marble Pewabic pottery work, the glass and gold interfaces. At one time, Detroit was a flourishing city that everyone wanted to go to, just like Denver, Seattle, and San Francisco could be today. Then, the race riots began. The rich, taxpayers decided that they did not want to raise their families in this environment and moved out to the suburbs. By the rich people leaving and not paying taxes and the auto industries re-locating to places like California and Tennessee, the city of Detroit went bankrupt.

And let me tell you—the suburbs of Detroit are beautiful. There are streets of redbrick, ornate, Gatsby-style mansions, tucked away in the woods. There is water and lakes, factories and museums. One of my favorite places we explored was the Heidelberg Project. When the artist, Tyree Guyton, returned from the military in 1986 to the streets of Detroit, he found that people were afraid to even walk outside at night. So, with the aide of his grandfather and local neighborhood kids they began collecting stuff--trash, old records, stuffed animals, shoes, car parts--around the city and decorating the houses. The most interesting house is the stuffed animal house, in which there are hundreds of stuffed animals nailed to the house, signaling the need for comfort in this dangerous city.

What I learned from visiting Detroit is what Debra Marquart discusses in her piece, "The Horizontal World". She suggests that the Midwest is plagued with stereotypes—bugs, humidity, cloudy skies, flat, plains, endless roads. But, in reality, those who are privy to growing up in the Midwest know the hidden treasures that surface—the slower pace of life, the friendliness of the community, the strong family values, and the calming sounds of the cicadas at night. Even in the city of Detroit, people like Tyree Guyton, police officers, and some government officials, are trying to bring the city back up. There are pockets in some of the worst neighborhoods that new development sprouted.

I think Detroit is an excellent example of why we need to take care of each other. The rich, wealthy car factory owners moved out of the city because 'they didn't want to pay taxes to help the lower classes', but now the city of Detroit has been branded as one of the worst cities in America. If you take the time to explore it, it really is not that bad and offers a different cultural perspective. Getting out of our comfort zones is good for us every once in awhile. Leaving gives us insight into how other people live and also makes us feel fortunate (or unfortunate, however you want to take it) of the lives and places we live. I, for one, feel very fortunate to live in Colorado, where even our worst parts are not nearly as desolate, forgotten, and demolished. Last week, the biggest issue in my freshmen class was the iOS7 upgrade—one kid literally cried when it came out because he had been stressing about it all morning. And, in the grand scheme of things, implanting ourselves into someone else's life allows us to recognize some of these self-fulfilling behaviors within ourselves.

I asked myself three questions:

Do they have a yoga studio I might like? Yes.

Did I like the people in Detroit? Yes (except that creepy guy at the club)

Could I see myself living in Detroit? Potentially, but I might have a problem with the rain.

And this trip sparked a travel bug in me. I would encourage any 20-Something to travel because travel allows you to gain so many life experiences that you miss out on by staying stationary.

So, I went places. I went to Chicago, I went to Los Angeles, I went to Las Vegas. And, once on these trips, I not only learned about the place itself, but also about the people I went to visit.

As soon as I got on my flight and sat next to a very friendly Polish couple, I knew I would love Chicago. The friendly couple bought me a drink, we chatted about their homeland, their sons, and their love for skiing. I am intrigued by culture and society and therefore my favorite part of traveling is to learn how other people live in other places. I love to learn the history, to hear the stories, to see how the people adapt to their environments. The official Chicago things we did included walking through Boystown, taking the architectural ferry tour, eating Chicago style popcorn, Chicago style pizza, and at DMK (BEST hamburger I have ever had in my life), taking public transportation, and meandering around Wrigley Ville and the surrounding city blocks. My other adventures included epically failing every time I scanned to go through the train station and getting stuck in the rotating counters, losing my cell phone, having my elbow caressed?, watching hours of *Boy Meets World*, and engaging in incredibly nerdy discussions about books, the new DSM, crime rate, human physiology, current research, etc. (I love that my friends are just as nerdy as I am).

One thing I love about visiting other places is the conversations I can have with other people who have similarly traveled to the same place. Unlike most aspects in life, land is static. Yes, some buildings may be demolished, some restaurants may go out of business, but overall, the streets, the landmarks, the waterways, the train stops are relatively unchanged. If you are reading this and have been to Chicago before, you automatically start mentally going back to your own experiences and visualizing the same streets, intersections, restaurants I mentioned and probably start remembering your own stories and adventures in that same place. Before I left for Chicago, our lunch conversation consisted of everyone sharing their horrible experiences flying into Midway (which made me very fortunate to sit next to the nice Polish couple on the plane), which then turned into a conversation about disastrous family road trips.

Travel binds people together in so many different ways. For a while, I was very reluctant to leave Colorado because I had built an entire empire here; Kent was there, my friends are here, my family is here. And, as my friends started getting jobs in other places, and I stayed stuck here, I felt a little bit of anxiety and loss, as if everything I had ever known was leaving me. I could no longer call Lisa or Aimee on a Friday night to just hang out because they were a thousand miles away.

But, what I realized is that, just like with Kent, once those friendships and memories are established, they will exist forever. Sure, some friends you will lose touch with. Some friendships end up in huge blow-ups. But the experiences you share will never go away. I recently met up with an old childhood friend that I have not seen for at least ten years. And, while today we have completely different jobs, completely different interests, and are at completely different stages of our lives, we still share that sacred bond of friendship. It is very scary to think that I might have to "start over" and that everything I once knew might be no longer. Traveling allowed me to accept and welcome some of those very uneasy aspects of being a 20-Something.

And, I realized that sometimes, visiting people makes you closer to them than actually living in the same city. A strange phenomenon occurs when you live with someone else for a weekend. First, you are exposed to each other's little habits. I brush my teeth at least seven times a day, Lisa is a really deep sleeper. These are things we would not normally have learned about each other. You are also forced to breakdown and submit to natural human needs, such as going to the bathroom, eating, sleeping, taking a shower, snoring, etc. When you only see someone for a few short hours at a time, you can sometimes hold these things back. And, you tend to value time together a little more because you know as soon as the plane lands, time is ticking. You feel the need to cram a lifetime of catching up and fun into one short weekend. As soon as I stepped off the plane, even though it was 11 PM at night, word vomit just came out of my mouth as I caught my two friends up on my job, my dance team, who recently got engaged, which boys I was talking to, etc. So, by the end, you are exhausted, but the ride was well worth it.

Do they have a yoga studio I might like? Yes.

Did I like the people in Chicago? Yes. It felt like an intelligent city.

Could I see myself living in Chicago? Potentially, except that the people dress up way fancier than I ever like to.

If I were to rank them, Chicago would be my first choice, and then Detroit. However, I knew I needed to expand my horizons than just these two Midwest cities, so I began thinking about popular places 20-Somethings move to, and started to visit to determine if it is a place I could handle.

I went to Los Angeles to visit a dance friend. I came home with some bad habits: a fouler mouth, a re-surfaced addiction to sugar, and a really nasty cough (probably due to the dense amount of pollution).

When I travel, I want to know if the people are outdoorsy, environmental, intellectual, use public transportation, friendly, etc. I try to turn on the local news. I investigate the history of the city and why people flocked to it (and, why are there so many psychics and palm readers?...)

The city of Los Angeles is very stimulating, fast-paced, and brandized. The artwork is vibrant and glitzy. Every shop you walk into has a scent that matches the theme, a name that matches a theme, merchandise that matches a theme, and an interior design that matches a theme. It is all about the ambiance and the appearance. We went to a juice shop, Nekter. Of course, the names of the juices were all brandized: "The Buzz", "The Cure", "The Glow". The interior is designed with native succulent plants, and clean, modern lines. The employees are totally hip and, of course, the juice is expensive. There are fitness gyms up the wazoo, fashion stores, and various sweet shops lining every corner. I couldn't decide if the people of L.A. actually support this very green, healthy lifestyle, or if they are just supporting it because clean eating/drinking out of mason jars/doing yoga/being crunchy and earthy is so fad right now.

And because L.A. is the place people flock to be discovered, no one is really that friendly. I held the door open for someone one time and I think he almost peed his pants from astonishment. It's all about competition. As my friend pointed out, everyone has a dog because they are lonely and don't have friends. And, people are not really looking to be tied down and get married (so don't travel or move to L.A. looking for a future rich husband because he isn't interested). It is a dog-eat-dog-world and no one cares about you. Even the dance class we took enforced these same values; the instructor walked in, burped, threw a few cuss words, taught an incredibly vulgar dance (part of the choreography was flipping the audience off), AND she purposely forgot to put my white-girlness in a group because she had no purpose for me since my awkward, gangleness was never going to be cast in a music video. I might as well just give up.

I could see why Los Angeles is one of the largest cities in the U.S.; the mild, consistent weather means that your daily schedule need not change because of rain or snow or a potential tornado (unlike here in Colorado, where your entire Mother's Day plans go out the window when a surprise blizzard inches through). So, you can continue being your competitive, fit, juiced-out self no matter what.

Now, I know I am being critical, but I really did enjoy my time in L.A. It was full of L.A. things: dancing at one of the best

studios in the nation, doing some yoga, eating at In&Out, playing on the beach. I basically dated my friend all weekend; we had
long walks on the beach and talked about having children/our
futures, we enjoyed a nice, Italian, candle lit dinner, and we held
hands as we gazed into each other's eyes at the Field of Lanterns
(ok, it didn't go that far, but we did enjoy a nice Sprinkles cup-
cake together). And, it truly is a unique experience to look into
Hollywood Hills and know that so many rich people are so close
(yet so far away). Who needs a 'Prince Charming' anyways?

Do they have a yoga studio I might like? Plenty.

*Did I like the people in Los Angeles? No. I met a guy at a wedding one time; he
was cute, we were making eye contact, he came over to talk to me, and when he revealed to me that he worked for the Los Angeles Police Department, I knew right away
it wasn't going to work out.*

Could I see myself living in Los Angeles? No.

For a friend's bachelorette party, I also went to Las Vegas.
We came home on a Monday, and by Wednesday, I still felt like I
was in "party mode"; all I wanted to do is dance, play my music
loud, tell jokes/funny stories, and stay up really late. For someone conscientious and Dutch like me, Las Vegas is not necessarily on the top of my destinations, but the company I traveled
made it all worth the while.

In case you have never been to Vegas, there is a *way* to do it.
The system kind of goes like this: fly in, get a cab and check in
at your hotel, eat, sight see/get your name on guest lists, go back
to your hotel to eat/nap/get ready/slutty, hit up the clubs until
who knows what hour of the night, stumble back to your hotel,
maybe do a little gambling, go to bed, wake up at 10-11 AM, eat,
go to a pool party, come home to eat/nap/get ready/slutty, and do
it all over again. Of course, in between and during all of these
activities, you are engaging in some special beverages. It takes a

little bit of pre-planning (which can be challenging), especially scheduling which clubs you are going to go and when. If you don't get your group on a guest list, you might find yourself waiting in line for two hours to eventually pay $99 to get into a packed club (Luckily for us, my friend at Tao was able to help us out!).

Everything in Vegas is an illusion. For one, time is never a concern. You have NO idea that you stayed out dancing and gambling until 6 AM and end up rising at 11 AM and really are under the illusion that you got plenty of sleep (although, as soon as you get on the flight home, you realize just how exhausted you are). You eat whenever you are hungry and don't really pay attention to the $35 buffet because those crab legs and limitless drinks look oh-so-appetizing. How much money you spend becomes an allusion; the metered $9.70 cab ride turns into a $15 adventure, after your driver adds in the fees and you throw in a tip (or, a $7 In and Out meal turns into a $20 meal plus round trip cab ride). The resorts and casinos themselves are an illusion; I don't know how many times we got lost trying to find the elevators, despite the flashing signs and arrows because everything is designed in a pinwheel shape (and, those of us from Colorado didn't have the mountains to determine west).

Even the people in Vegas are an illusion. The waitresses, the hotel employees, the cab drivers, bouncers all act like everything is peachy and fun all the time. We had one waitress who reminded me of Barbie: fake blonde hair, boobs, eyelashes--the whole shebang. And, when she greeted our table, she literally bounced up and down to jump for joy of how excited she was to be there. We had another cab driver who gave us his whole life story about playing college lacrosse and retiring from the police force to Vegas where his daughter is about to graduate and go to Princeton (he even threw in a fake Southern accent when we told him we had family in the South). Vegas is fun; it is lights and glam, outrageous fun and limitless activities (not, however, a limitless pocketbook), interesting people and loud, fun music nonstop.

The entire atmosphere of Vegas is an illusion. We forget that many of these waitresses and cab drivers probably moved to Las Vegas because they were on the poverty line somewhere else and saw this as "a golden opportunity" and that they probably are still making minimum wage, working 12 hour shifts, four days a week, with no insurance (but hey, now they can sign up for Obama-Care!); the people we meet don't actually care about us (I will save my opinions about the strip club for later, but that is all an illusion as well...) We forget the school systems in Las Vegas are struggling, impoverished, and a popular destination for Teach-for-America candidates. We forget that, underneath the illusion that is Las Vegas, in a short amount of time, we will have to go back to our own lives and face some of the decisions we made.

I give major props to whoever created the concept of "Vegas"; someone took one of the worst parts of the country and made it into one of the most popular and lucrative Spring Break desti-nations. People flock to Vegas to forget about whatever problems and dilemmas they are facing in their daily lives. While those issues will probably still be there when they return, Vegas gives the illusion that, for just a short time, life can be different than what it is.

Do they have a yoga studio I might like? I am sure it would cost a $25 cab ride.

Did I like the people in Las Vegas? No, it is a little too fake for me.

Could I see myself living in Las Vegas? No, I am not even sure I want to visit again.

What all of this traveling to larger cities did to me was make me value just where I was. Sometimes, I feel a little inadequate for living in the same town I grew up in. When I tell people, they sometimes give me funny looks, as if I am not pursuing great enough dreams. Maybe living in a big city is for you; I love visiting big cities, but I learned that it is not for me. There is nothing more comforting than flying over the Rocky Mountains and knowing that I am going home. Kent can have New York.

January 7th, 2015: Why I Think Every 20-Something Should Travel

1. Travel forces you to solve problems: *There is nothing like being stuck in a country where you don't know the language, you don't know what a celebration hamburger is, your cellphone doesn't get any service, and the bathrooms are gender neutral. So, you pick up new skills that your ordinary life would never permit: how to read a map, how to follow people's hand gestures (because you can't understand the language), how to estimate the time of day based on sunlight and to be extremely descriptive and on time about setting meeting spots, and you bring these newly acquired things home.*

2. Travel gives you opportunities to connect with other people, both home and abroad: *Before my trip, everyone who had ever been to Paris wanted to tell me about their experiences, and give me advice on what to pack, where to go, how to navigate the metros. And, upon my return, they wanted to hear about my experiences, compare their own, listen to the different things I did, and how they can't wait for their next trip. They wanted to talk about Picasso, and about the very crowded Louvre, and if I would recommend Disneyland Paris, about the weather, the magic of the Eiffel Tower sparkling, and their own international travel horror stories.*

And along our travels, we met many different people we would have never crossed paths with. Sitting in the cafes and riding the metros, I always listened for a familiar American accent. We encountered many other American tourists, of which we talked about where they were from, and what they were doing in Paris. I not only learned about Paris, but also about Washington D.C, about this couple's magic proposal at

Tiffany's on Champs Elysees, about traveling to Morocco for an oil company. I met a couple Parisians, who were able to explain the school system to me, France's perception of Obama, and which neighborhoods to avoid. Listening in to other conversations, I was able to get a glimpse of life and customs in England, Australia, Brooklyn.

3. Travel allows you to appreciate what you often take for granted: *On our 12-hour layover in New York City, my travel companion and I decided to ride the subway into Manhattan. We sat down next to a resident and asked her how much she thought a cab would cost to take to the airport tomorrow morning. She said, "Oh, pretty expensive. Probably about $35". In my world, a "pretty expensive" cab ride would be $100, not $35, and it made me realize just how fortunate my own life is.*

And, being away always reveals which relationships are the most important to you. When I booked my ticket to leave on Christmas Eve, it didn't even cross my mind that I would miss my family for Christmas. And, as I sat at the gate to board our plane, and I thought about the fact that my family hasn't missed having some form of Christmas together for the last 24 years, I realized how much I would miss them, and how much I do actually love them, and how excited I was to return home to them.

Of course, I noticed myself missing other things as well: vegetables, ice, my Corolla, yoga class. And when I got home, I couldn't wait to bring those things back into my life. It is true: you never really know what you have until it's gone. The fortunate thing about travel is, it's probably still there when you return.

4. Travel helps you learn stuff about yourself: *Fun fact, I am actually an introvert. I didn't really know this about myself, because I am actually pretty outgoing and I talk a lot until I spent 12 days with my travel companion.*

I read somewhere that the difference between introverts and extroverts is that, once extraverts think of something, they feel like sharing it with everyone, and once introverts think of something, they don't see the point in sharing. One time, I was accused of being "hard to read", "having a wall built up", "digging a moat, plagued with sharks, and leeches, and other sharp objects that people have to somehow find a way to swim across" (pretty sure I found the moat at Chateau Vincennes though). I honestly was kind of offended by this, because I personally thought I shared lots of things about myself. But, it wasn't until this trip that I realized that this person was actually right: I am on lock down, and I can't really get mad at people for not acknowledging my needs or for not knowing things about me if I don't tell them.

And, since it turns out I actually am an introvert, there is a likelihood I won't tell them anyways.

Travel teaches you a lot about things you like (citron macarons), and things you don't like (duck confit—never again). It teaches you how you react in stressful situations, such as when your bag is the last one on the carousel, or you miss your flight. It teaches you what kind of people you get along best with, what kind of aspirations you have for yourself, how rigid or flexible your personality is, that you way over pack, how much sleep you can actually function on. And, the good thing is—traveling as a 20-something, you can always change any of those things that you learn and don't like.

5. Travel causes you to break habits: Last semester, I worked on a project for my grad class about power structures, and was on this huge, unhealthy kick about how people try to manipulate and control situations to gain power positions. I started seeing some unnerving and corrupt power structures in my everyday world that I did not like. And, I couldn't stop it. Everywhere I went, people's power plays jumped out at me, like I was looking at one of those book fair hieroglyphic bookmarks. And then, I went to Paris, where my brain was occupied with travel-related issues (such as connecting the written French words to the spoken French sounds). And, suddenly, the presence of power structures floated away.

Perhaps some of these other habits are eating too much sugar, skipping the gym, not following through with engagements. In our lives, we need constant; we need to wake up at a constant time, so that we don't get sick. We need to work a constant job, so we aren't constantly re=inventing the wheel. We need to eat at constant times, so that our bodies know when to expect nourishment. But we also need change; without change, we become static, monotone, robotic. I think travel gives us a natural affordance to re-vitalize, re-align, and re-set ourselves.

6. Travel shows you the world is much, much greater than yourself: As humans, we are innately selfish and narcissistic. We want what is best *for OURSELVES, and we want OUR desires met. The longer we stay in one place, the more ethnocentric, and egocentric, we become. I found myself wondering what makes me 'better' than any of the other 2.3 million people in this city that I would deserve special treatment. Why do I have the privilege to push and shove through the crowd to make sure I made this train over someone else? What makes me a better person that I deserve that last seat over someone else? Even though I don't live in one, I always love visiting big cities, because it reminds me of just how expansive the human population is. Paris alone has a population of about 2.3 million people, which means that 2.3 million other people also need to feed themselves, to get themselves to work, to use the bathroom, to dress themselves, to take care of their families. I am really no better than anyone else.*

*7. **Travel teaches you really are also no different than anyone else in the world***: *Of course, cultures have their own little nuances. In France, they eat a gillette cake for New Years, and whoever gets the bean is supposed to have luck for the rest of the year. In New Orleans, they stick a baby in a cake for Mardi Gras and whoever finds the baby is supposed to have a good year. During Thanksgiving, whoever gets the wishbone is supposed to have their heart's desire granted. But, all of these traditions have relatively the same purpose: to give us the false illusion that good things will happen to us.*

As I walked around the museums (and, let me tell you, Paris has PLENTY), all I could think about was how, since the beginning of time, humans are relatively the same creatures. Humans have always searched for something to explain the unexplainable, whether it be through sacrificial ceremonies, diagramming the constellations, or praying to a god. Humans have always strove to make their mark on the world, whether it be through elaborate castles with dazzling halls of mirrors, or building large and impressive tombs, or tattooing themselves in a snake pattern, forking their tongue, and swallowing a sword. And, humans have always needed a find to way to feed themselves, to cloth themselves, to shelter themselves, to communicate with each other, and to entertain themselves, whether that be through catching fish with their bare hands, or dining over an exquisite pot of fondue, wearing animal fur and beads, or factory-made plastic heels, digging a hole and living in the ground, or building a stone castle with secret passageways, to speak in French, or English, or sign language, to watch operas and ballets, or movies and video games.

Across cultures, while we may represent them differently, the root of who we are as people is the same. And, for that matter, as long as no one is getting hurt, I can't judge people for living their lives in different ways than I choose to live mine, because while these gender neutral bathrooms and absence of queue lines and words that certainly don't look like they are pronounced may seem strange to me, other people might think it's strange that I shower every morning, that I pollute the earth by driving my Corolla by myself everywhere, that I like to drink cold beverages and could carry a gun with me if I wanted.

8. Travel enhances your illusions of the world: Before I left, I told my sister, "You know, I have been experimenting with reading books. Like, I might read two books at once, and compare themes, or I might re-read a book I read when I was a kid, and think about how my connection to it has changed, or I might read a book set in Paris, while I am in Paris. It really enhances the reading experience" (ultra nerdy, I know). So, when people asked her why I was going to Paris, she just replied, "I don't know? Something about a book?" Although not my only reason for taking the trip, seeing Paris will inevitably change my experience of reading books, and watching movies, and buying products that are anything related to Paris. While my comprehension of 'The Sun Also Rises' by Ernest Hemingway was in no way subdued or inhibited, actually seeing the monuments, and understanding how cafes work changed the way I was able to visualize the characters, understand the conflict, and interpret the messages. We can always look at pictures, and we can always watch videos, but actually being in places—actually walking up from the subway to Notre Dame rising in majesty above you—is a completely different thing.

9. Travel gives you a lifetime of enjoyment: One of my favorite parts of going on a trip is catching up with everyone upon my return. Especially going somewhere like Europe, you are so inundated with information, history, culture, people, lack of sleep, etc. that you do no necessarily realize the full impact of the trip, and appreciate all the super cool opportunities you had until you are able to go back home and ruminate on it. When you look back on a trip, your memory never focuses on the stomach pains you felt from ravage hunger, or how miserably cold you were while waiting in line for Crush's Coaster, or how badly it hurt because you had to go to the bathroom but didn't want to pay. Instead, you think about how funny it was that you threw away your boarding passes and had to hurdle a wheelchair to retrieve them. You remember standing at the discotheque, and retrieving your fork from the trash because you can't understand French, and realizing that you can see over everyone's heads. You remember the awe of the Moulin Rouge, or the magic you felt when Ana and Elsa drove down Mainstreet at Disneyland Paris.

And, it's always a pleasant reminder when you find a ticket stub in your coat pocket, or come across an unspent euro (and you remember the time you were scrounging up 6,70 euros at the airport to buy those last minute presents because your shuttle came an hour earlier than planned), or when you see something that reminds you of your trip. The trip certainly doesn't end when you arrive home, but rather exists forever in your memories.

10. Travel inevitably always changes you: I always love the anticipation leading up to a trip, because inevitably, I know I will come out a different person than I started. When I start the trip, I am not sure what that change will be, but I know that I will never be the same. Experiences change us. After climbing the 14er this summer, I was somehow more at peace with The Unknown. After going to Iowa over Labor Day weekend, I somehow gained the ability to analyze a situation, and then compartmentalize it after I drew my conclusions so I wasn't such an anxious mess all the time. After re-reading Gone With the Wind, I was somehow able to appreciate and revel in the suffering we undergo on a daily basis.

And, of course, it's not always immediately evident what those changes might be, but they will subtly infiltrate the everyday behaviors and perceptions. I can't tell you just yet how exactly I have changed since returning home from Paris. I can tell you that I now understand how food can be a form of entertainment, and not just nourishment. I picked up a few new French words, perhaps a slight accent, and some extra pounds from eating so much bread. I know that I really value my time alone, iced drinks, and my Corolla.

But, the other slightly more meaningful changes—the ones that will change and alter my soul forever—the ones that will alter my perceptions of and interactions with the world—I will just have to wait and see.

Money always finds a way to replenish itself; experiences can never be bought. So travel, see the world. Learn about people, learn about cultures. Learn about yourself. Be changed.

My Spiritual Journey

I also realized that I needed to dissect my values, to figure out who I was in this world. The best way I knew how to do that was to call up my good friend, The Spiritual Master, and start going to church. I took a Bible as Literature class in college and decided that, even if the whole heaven–hell, angels and demons thing turns out to be fake, the lessons learned in church about how to live are important.

Sometimes, I think we need to get away from our faith for a little bit of time to re-appreciate its power in our lives. We often get so stuck in routine because we think "being a good Christian" is going to church every Sunday, dinner group Wednesdays, volunteering every Friday. But, sometimes we get so mired in routines that we lose the meaning of what we were doing in the first place; it becomes monotonous, sometimes feels like a hassle, but we keep doing it because "that is what good Christians do". My family raised us Catholic. We did the whole religious education classes on Tuesday nights, the rituals of reconciliation and communion. My mom brought home Holy Water from the church every week and adorned us with St. Christopher medals and rosary crosses. After an experience at a wedding, I stopped going to church, and am now re-gaining that faith, stronger than ever. I am beginning to question my own beliefs, experience religion in profound ways, and am learning to pray for grace, for strength, for patience. Sometimes, we need to go away for some time to re-evaluate and re-appreciate.

Religion works in interesting ways. We live in a very big, very complex world. People are drawn to religions because religions put some of those complexities and anxieties back into someone else's hands; it's not you controlling the universe, but rather some bigger force, and in many situations, that is comforting. One of my favorite units to study with my students is Greek mythology because we discuss how, in all religions, there is a code for the afterlife, a code for how to live a moral life (for the Greeks, it was all about being sturdy and blonde and athletic and having lots of lovers), a code for who controls the natural elements (Poseidon, Hades, Zeus). Like, when we make a mistake, it is really comforting to know that perhaps that mistake was supposed to be made, OR that is was probably just Zeus and Poseidon fighting over Athena, and therefore, as the believer, I do not have to take personal accountability because there is just some god disagreement in Olympus.

Interestingly enough, my spiritual journey first began after my counselor suggested I see a psychic, just for fun. And, it was fun. When I first sat down, she warned me, "Now, just so you know, this is how your future looks right now, but if you make different decisions, it could turn out differently". I immediately thought to myself, "Of course, I am going to make different decisions". She talked about how she sees my future in moving pictures; she would stop, ask me a very ambiguous question, watch my response, and then start blabbing on. She told me:

- I will be fully committed to someone by 27, although she was unable to see exactly what that would look like (I asked what kind of man it would be, but apparently my soul didn't speak strongly enough for her to pick up the waves—she closed her eyes and moved around her hands and couldn't come up with anything—I was expecting something like, "He is tall, dark, and handsome" or "He is someone you already know" or "His name is Dave" or "He will come in on white, shining horse and sweep you off your feet" or even something like "He will come to you when you least expect it" but I was offered no consolations in that department...). I think I could have told her that myself. I have never seen myself being married at 23. Besides the fact that I want to wait for my wedding guests to buy me great presents, there are so many other things I want to do with my life: get my Master's degree, do more traveling. I want to win a state championship, be rated a highly effective teacher, buy my own house. I have always known that marrying young was not my style; I am too much of a 'blue' or logical/rational thinker.
- There is someone out there who is in competition with me, that despises me, and spends a lot of time trying to put me down (wow, that is sure comforting) but to recognize that is an insecurity within themselves and out of my control (I assumed this was Kent's mom the psychic was "seeing").
- While I have a sturdy foundation, there are some aspects in my life that are "bouncing around like ping pong balls

in a ping pong table" that are still waiting to settle. They "are like a caged puppy, being let into the big city, not knowing what to do and begin running through traffic" so it is difficult to see parts of my future until those things are decided. And, those things have the potential to make choices, so it depends on what choices they make.

- When people are stuck in their chakras, they begin experiencing physical symptoms in those places.

- We have difficulty letting go of people in our lives because we believe they hold some kind of historical map of our lives; they represent who we are, where we have come from, and what we have overcome. But the truth is, as soon as those memories happen, they are forever embedded in history. While we may not be able to have a conversation with those people and bring up those memories, we can always re-visit them in our minds. Like, if I ever wanted to feel those butterflies of Kent dropping me off at my dad's house in high school, and walking in with blood all over my face because his nose started bleeding, then I could.

- Creating visual mind bubbles of what you want/what you want to say to someone will help communicate our thoughts and feelings to people, although we may never physically say those things, the universe will relay the message and our intended audience will respond.

- We must take a step back and look at our lives from an outside perspective: explore through observation, not through perception. When we look through our perceptions, we tend to only notice those things we want to see: we notice characteristics in people, tendencies in people, feelings in people that may not necessarily be accurate.

When we look through observation, we see things at face
value. We must clinically look at other people's relationships (those we do not have any stake in) that will help us
make determinations about ourselves.

· There is travel in my future (already booking my flights!)
and some kind of extra training (maybe this is the clairvoyance classes she said she was offering...)

Overall, I am not sure if I am 100% sold on the ideas of psychics and energy and destinies; I am not sure if it is the kind of
thing that you pay attention to what is true and discard the other
90% that is not true (for example, she told me I was very angry
that my "soul is throwing daggers and breaking panes of glass").

But, I think the purpose, much like with religion, is to give
people confidence in the unknown. That is one of the most difficult parts I have found in this journey is surrendering my life
to the unknown. I like things to be controlled: I like to know
how I would react to any situation. For example, I have a template for how I react when a student drops the F bomb, I have a
template for how I react when someone cuts me off, and I have
a template to how I react when someone questions my integrity.
Throughout this whole process, I spent a lot of time and energy
trying to make templates for the unknown scenarios. And, I realized that there are just too many unknown scenarios: too many
things that are out of my control, too many other people's decisions it could rely upon, too many choices that are still up for
grabs. So, people use things like religion and psychics to make
themselves feel more in control, to give them something to look
forward to, and to help put their conscious minds at rest.

Perhaps for you, your faith is not going to church every
Sunday. After Kent dumped me, I needed to go because I needed

to hear lessons about forgiveness, self-lessness, and hope. I needed to hear that we were not supposed to be together and, if I just have a little bit of faith and some patience, something bigger and better is waiting for me (even if the psychic herself could not predict it). It took some of the stress and anxiety off of me. My focus in going to church is how I can learn to be a better person; if this concept of heaven turns out to be a bunch of hoopla, oh well.

Re-Evaluating at the Self Level

On top of traveling and churching, I also starting re-evaluating myself. Since I spent six years with Kent and so much of our lives became intertwined with each other's, I had to figure out who I was independently. Not to bring up this traumatizing statistic, but 50% of modern day marriages end in divorce. I believe this is for a variety of factors, but there is a 50% chance that I may get married and then get divorced someday, which means that I needed to learn how to pay my student loans off and tackle the world by myself.

I first began by thinking about what aspects of my life I did not like, and then creating a plan to resolve those inadequacies. The good/bad news is research suggests we undergo the most personality change between 18-25, so now is the time to fix those things before we become too old and rigid.

One thing I did not particularly like is my attachment to my technology. What actually did it for me was one day, I was playing Candy Crush, and I was thinking about what the game was.

Basically, I just touch a screen and move my finger. It technically is supposed to be a strategy game, but most of the time, I just try random moves to see if they work. I spend the entire time trying to reach the next level, I have an adrenaline rush when I actually do, and then feel defeated again when a new much more challenging level pops up. It's a vicious, never ending cycle. The same thing is true with social media: I waste so much time, scrolling through the same exact status updates and pictures that were present the last time. So, I started a list of things I would enjoy doing more than monotonously playing with my technology. I could read a book, so I went to the local used bookstore and stocked up. I now keep a heavy supply of unread books in my room that I can start reading at anytime. I could ask my roommate to teach me about cars and help me change my oil and air filters. I could write letters to my grandparents.

And, I realized that there are in fact some limitations to goals and aspirations, particularly within the aspects of time, money, and ability. When you are younger, they always tell you to, "Shoot for the stars!" and, "Dream Big!" Well, it turns out I can certainly jump as high as I want and I can sleep as long as I want, and some things will actually never come true for me. For example, singing. I am a terrible singer. One of the reasons I go to church is to in fact work on my vocal chords. I practice singing a lot. I listen to lots of music. And, I ask my friends who are singers about how they get better. And unfortunately, there really is no hope for me. No matter how hard I try, how much money I spend on singing lessons, how much practice I do, I will never, ever be able to sing the National Anthem at the Super Bowl, and that is just a limitation I have had to accept.

Check: I need a guy who can handle my poor singing.

....And Then There was Simon...

And, then there was Simon.

If I was the Damsel in Distress, locked away in the highest tower on the tallest mountain, Simon was the Knight in Shining Armor who swam across the moat and rescued me on his silvery horse (literally, he rode in on a horse).

As I began re-discovering myself and re-defining what I want in a relationship, I would often relay my findings, my anxieties, my insecurities to my good friend, Sarah. And one day, she exclaimed, "You have got to meet my brother. I think you would get along really well." I inquired a little more about him: listens to country music (check), has a cool mom (check), designs stuff for a living (probably doesn't hang out with sports celebrities and brag about it: check), is 32 (older and hopefully more mature: check), lives in San Francisco (could be worked around).

How girls bond: over boys. When you like a boy, your friends tell you how cute he is and how he clearly likes you too because he can't keep his eyes off you. When you are dating a boy, your friends tell you how perfect he is for you, how much better he was than your last boyfriend, and how they can't wait to be in your wedding. And, when you break up with a boy, your friends tell you how ugly he is, what a scumbag he is, and how you are so much better off without him.

(Now, I should preface this by saying that I think this is especially true in your adolescent-college-early twenties-years. I obviously haven't been married yet, so I am not sure yet what married women bond over—maybe sharing cooking recipes and laundry secrets?).

In bonding with your friends, it is one of three scenarios: the first scenario is that you just broke up with a boy or some boy was a jerk to you. So, you call all of your friends to talk about the situation, mostly to get confirmation that you are waaaaay better than he is anyways. Then, you go over to your friend's house to stalk him on Facebook or check his e-mail accounts and in some situations, decide to print off a picture and pin it to a dartboard.

The second way you bond with girls is when you like a boy. Usually, it is a friend of yours who either (a) wants to hook you up with someone she knows, (b) is dating the boy you like's best friend, or (c) is the boy's best friend (which sometimes turns out kind of awkward). So, leading up to the date, you and your friend talk all the time: what kind of interests does he have? how often does he go to the gym? ....what has he asked about me? Then, you, of course have to talk about what you are going to wear to the date, what kinds of topics are appropriate to bring up and what you should stray away from. You might shop together, get your nails done together, get ready together prior to the date. Then, you go on the date and she is constantly checking in to see how things are going. And then, of course, after the date, you have to spend a day or two debriefing: did he hold your hand? what did he say when I walked away? do you think you will hang out with him again?

The third scenario is that you hang out with all your single friends all the time, accompany them on awkward blind dates, or go man hunting together. You spend time sending each other pictures of outfits so you can make sure you are dressing equally hot. You scope out the prospects the bar together and play games of who can find the hottest guy. You spend the night at each other's house and debrief what happened that night and see how many phone numbers you picked up. You are constantly looking for concerts and events that you think will have a large man population at. You make a list of non-negotiables together, and ask each other about dating rules (do I pretend I don't see the bill when it is put down? at which number date is it ok to ask about his previous relationships?).

Post-date friendships work a couple different ways: the friendship may fizzle if (a) the date goes well and you start expending your energy on your new boyfriend, (b) the date doesn't go well and you don't have the need to keep your new friend around anymore, or (c) regardless of how the date went, you found a new best friend because you have discovered you have more common interests and needed each other more than you anticipated.

It is kind of like a dinner scene in books and movies: eating together represents communion because people bond over food because food gives people a common element to discuss. The conversation might start with, "My neighbor claims he saw an alien last night" and then someone else might say, "My cousin got abducted by an alien and said they were green", and then someone else says, "Do you remember watching that great Disney channel special, Xenon: Girl of the 21st Century growing up?"....and the conversation takes off from there.

Since I was so wrapped up in a relationship during these crucial adolescent-college aged girl-bonding times, it was not really
a priority for me to create close girl relationships because I (a)
wasn't going through a break up and (b) wasn't trying to find a
man. As my friends started getting married, I realized that I was
not sure who I would ask to be in my wedding because I had let
those potential bridesmaid relationships slip. Now that I am the
one everyone wants to set up with her brother or her husband's
best friend or their co-workers, I find myself finding those girl
relationships again and am so fortunate for their influences on
my life. I enjoy having people who want to go shopping together,
get nails done, watch chick flicks together. I am learning more
about myself and about people through these relationships. Boys
are bringing us together.

So naturally, through Sarah wanting to hook me up with her
stud of a brother, we became best friends and wasted many, many
hours talking about him.

NOVEMBER: THE AWKWARD BLIND DATE

The plan was to pick Simon up from the airport, go to dinner,
and then to the local country bar for a concert. Since this was
the first blind date I had been set up with since Kent, I was extremely nervous. I spent the whole week leading up to it updating
my dating habits with Sarah: do I tell him about Kent? do I let
him open my door? what happens if he doesn't ask for my phone
number? (Because, of course, I hadn't done that since high
school and dating in this modern world is completely different).

Then, Wednesday finally came. I blocked out my entire day
to prepare for 'the date'. I made sure I got plenty of beauty rest
the night before. I worked extra hard in my yoga class to acquire
tone muscles. I actually shaved my legs and straightened my hair.

The first meeting was actually very awkward. Since we were picking him up at the airport, we (and by 'we', I mean 'I'), spent the majority of the car ride figuring out how the first meeting would go: Would we all pile out and hug Simon, Sarah first, then her husband, and then me? Should I not hug him? Would I just sit in the car since I didn't really know him? Should I shake his hand? Would we just do a drive by, slow down to five miles per hour, and have him jump in the back? Maybe we should just not pick him up at all.

I am not really sure what actually happened because the airport was a cluster. Everyone kind of jumped out, jumped in, and I met Simon as he climbed in next to me, shook my hand, and told me he had my name tramp stamped on his back. Immediately I knew he was my kind of guy.

Dinner was awkward, to say the least. We probably sat about ten feet away from each other and made eye contact once. I accidentally dropped my napkin and debated for about five minutes how I pick it up (what did my research on new dating laws tell me? I didn't even anticipate this scenario!). Luckily, when we got to the concert, the music was so loud that no one could hear anyone else anyways, so we just stood, swayed, danced a little, and enjoyed the music.

There is no denying that blind dates are AWKWARD. It starts with—your friend wants to hook you up with one of his/her friends. You are initially flattered that someone is going to take the time out of his/her busy schedule to think about you. All you can talk/think about is this blind date that you have coming up.

And then, it is an hour before you are supposed to meet the person and suddenly, your brain crashes and goes into hyper anxiety mode. The more you think about it, the more you don't want to even go. What is the first thing you are going to do when you walk in because they could potentially not even be there yet and then you have to awkwardly wait alone for them to come. Or, they could already be there but you have NO idea what they look like so you have to wander around aimlessly until you catch someone's eye. And after that happens, how do you greet the person? With a hug? A handshake? A grunt? What kinds of topics do you talk about? Who pays? How long are you expected to stay? How are you going to get out of it if it sucks? And suddenly, after all of this analyzing, you determine that maybe this blind date is not really worth the energy and anxiety you are going to put into it because after all, how often do they really work out?

Ok, so say you actually decide to go on the blind date: what could it hurt anyways? Blind dates are awkward because, what you would probably do in a matter of a week or two, has to be condensed into one potentially short afternoon. First, you have to decide if you are physically attracted to the person. Sure, you probably Facebook stalked him/her, but we all know that pictures can be deceiving. If you go the traditional route of non-blind dating, you have probably already approved and gotten past this step. Next, you have to determine if this person is compatible with you, based on the one answer they give you to your question. If you knew this person ahead of time, you probably already know a few of the nitty gritty details, so you have already prepared yourself for some more in depth conversations. And then, at the end of the date, you have to determine if this person is worth a second shot. In a normal dating situation, you have probably been flirting with this person, which is why you asked them out or they asked you out: you already know you like each other.

And, if you are on a group blind date, it's especially awkward because you feel like you are in a fishbowl. You and the person you are being set up with KNOW you are being set up and that your friends are watching your every move. So, you try to be especially sly and chill so they don't interpret you as being really awkward.

So, all in all, blind dates are awkward because you have to do so many things in such a short amount of time. You have to determine if there is (a) physical chemistry, (b) emotional chemistry, and (c) screen to make sure they don't have any pervy qualities.

This was exactly the situation with Simon. We were thrown into a gauntlet, with everyone studying our moves: very unnatural. After the concert, we went back to Sarah's apartment and hung out for a little longer. Don't worry I am leaving out the mushy-gushy details because even I am too immature for that. But, what I will say is, when I returned home, I was in a daze that did not wear off for the next two days. There was something magical, something attractive, something so different about Simon; despite the fact that I only knew him for a few hours, I felt so comfortable, so myself around him. The more I thought about him, the more I uncovered the awkwardness from the blind date, the more items he checked off my list, the more I liked him. He texted me that next afternoon, said it was really nice meeting me, and that he would call me when he returned home to San Francisco.

And, of course, being me, I started over-analyzing everything and my anxiety started rising again. So, I set up an appointment with my counselor. She said, "Britany, you are so used to working hard for everything you have in life—your family, your career, your relationships—that it feels uncomfortable when something is given to you on a silver platter".

She was absolutely right. Because I survived my last break up so far, I decided that I was stronger than I imagined and that I would let this relationship blossom.

A few things I liked about Simon: he called when he said he would. He went hunting with his family the next day, but did call me as soon as he landed in San Francisco (literally, I am pretty sure he was walking off the airplane when he dialed my number). We talked for about two hours. I told him about my favorite memory of being invited into the V.I.P section of the Disney Princess parade when I was 20 years old, and he told me about the time he took a two week backpacking trip, solo. We set some parameters: he would call me every Wednesday and every Sunday night. I really loved this sched-ule and anticipated his call every Wednesday and Sunday: it was just enough time for me to think about what I wanted to say to him and how I was going to say it. And, we would go on our first official date when he came home for Christmas in four weeks.

DECEMBER: THE ROMANCE BEGINS

The week Simon came home for Christmas was perhaps the most romantic week of my entire life. He flew in on a Friday night and our date was set for Saturday. I was house-sitting Friday night and could not delay our connection any longer, so I called him, said I was really scared of being in a big house by myself, and invited him over. He snuck out, borrowed his dad's truck, and drove over. I felt like a high schooler, which I suppose is how love is supposed to make you feel: giddy and awkward.

Saturday, he picked me up at 6:00 for our date. Despite the fact that our houses are at least an hour apart, he insisted on driving all the way to my house (I was skeptical at first about let-ting a blind dater know where I lived, but I figured if anything happened, I could blame his sister). He came to the door, told me how beautiful I looked, gave me flowers, met my roommates, and took me to dinner. Ladies, if you ever dreamt of a more perfect, more *Leave It to Beaver* type date, this was it.

He came back to my house Monday to ride horses. Since I am an amateur at this, I just stood back and let him saddle them up. I offered to make him a frozen pizza, and since my style of cooking is to just heat the oven and let it cook (aka not be patient enough to let it pre-heat), the pizza turned out not so good and we went to Chick-Fil-A instead. He was going on a ten-day vacation to Mexico in a couple days, and since we were not technically dating, instead of giving him a relationship-defining Christmas present, I gave him my favorite book to read on the beach, *The Poisonwood Bible* by Barbara Kingsolver.

Wednesday, perhaps my most favorite memory of dating Simon, was Christmas. Since it was Christmas, and we were not really that serious, we intended to spend time with our families. As I was leaving my dad's house for dinner, Sarah texted me and said they had an odd number of people at their Christmas celebration and needed another player for games. Naturally, I ditched my brother on the curb, told him to get his own ride home, and raced to their house.

It was clear that the family enjoyed a few bottles of wine as the very competitive game of Catch Phrase pursued. And, when "Wagon Wheel" by Darius Rucker came on the iPod shuffle, Simon pulled me off the floor. As the Christmas lights glittered, the laughter of the family faded in the background, it became just Simon and I, clumsily two-stepping around the house. I know this was the moment I fell in love with him. He whispered sweet nothings in my ear, *"you are just supposed to be a figment of my imagination right now"*, *"why can't you come to Mexico with me?"*, *"I thought about you all day"*, *"even when you are not here, you torment my thoughts"*, *"Britany, what am I going to do with you?"*

We stayed up all night, talking and giggling (like high schoolers). The next morning, I dropped him off at the airport, a little heartbroken that I would not be able to talk to him for at least ten days, but so, so much in love. With Kent, anytime I envisioned our wedding, I could never quite get past walking down the aisle. When I would lay in my bed and daydream about what it would look like, I would get stuck: I would come out in my old-fashioned lace dress, and then the image would dissipate. In order to retrieve that dream, I would then try to imagine who we invited to our wedding, or what colors we would pick, and I could never quite get there. Simon, on the other hand, made me think about things I never thought of before. He would ask me questions about how I wanted to raise my children, and I decided they would be raised without T.V. He would ask me questions about what kind of wedding I wanted, and I decided I probably wanted just a big party in my backyard.

I remember taking an afternoon snooze on my couch one December afternoon and waking up with a vision of a modest diamond ring. Unlike Kent, Simon caused me to think about the actual marriage part, not just the wedding, and he forced me to consider how I wanted my future to be shaped: did I want to be a stay at home mom, or a mom that worked to support her family? Did I want my children to share rooms with their siblings to build those inseparable bonds or did I want only one kid? What kind of places did I want to travel to and what kind of adventures did I want to go on before I had a family? Or, did I want a family right away?

While Simon was away, I had a lot of time to think about him, to think about myself, to think about Simon, and to think about Kent. And, I had a lot of time to think about how I was going to make this work. Simon offered me so many unique things that

I had never met in anyone else. He made me think about things (marriage and raising a family), he made me feel things that even Kent never brought out. I just put it back into the universe and decided I would do whatever it would take to make it work, despite the distance.

To be honest, I never quite understood why people would start a relationship long distance. I thought long distance is only for desperate, divorced people who are online dating and can't find anyone else in their near surroundings. It is one thing if someone moves away for a short period of time, with the intention of moving back, or the other person moving out, but to completely start off being far apart never quite made sense to me until I met Simon. After experiencing a short period of it on my own and interviewing some of my close friends about their long distance relationships, I do believe there are some definite benefits that you cannot get when you live an immediate distance.

- Because you cannot see each other every day, you are forced to be a little creative with getting to know each other. With the development of technology, this is completely do able. You can call each other, you can text. You can Skype or e-mail. You can send letters and postcards. When I started missing Simon I thought about creative things I could do, such as write a sonnet or "love" poem. And, I really enjoyed putting together care packages to let him know I was thinking about him.
- Seeing each other becomes "An Event" (or a Google calendar event if you are dating me): This was actually one of my favorite parts of "dating" long distance because the anticipation the week leading up to seeing each other always made the actual seeing each other that much more

exciting. I loved spending the week prior cleaning my room, doing laundry, getting my hair cut, shopping for outfits, washing my car, telling everyone where I was going this weekend, planning out what we would do, etc. It caused me to do things out of my ordinary weekly routine and look at how I could make myself better, which is never a bad thing at all.

- And, when you do see each other, you spend quality time together. I notice that, with some couples, when they spend so much time together, they lose their sense of quality engagement and conversation and often default back to their technology. This was totally Kent and my relationship; I remember being at dinner one night, and he spent the entire time, on his phone, trying to beat me at 'Words with Friends'. But, when you know you only have one weekend to spend together a month, you tend to put away your cell phone and spend time actually building a relationship.

- You are able to still have your own life: I am very independent and very busy, so I really enjoyed being able to still do my own thing and then hang out. I could still hang out with my friends on the weekends, I didn't have to worry about someone randomly showing up at my house. I could still grade papers whenever I wanted to, sleep in my own bed by myself, buy whatever I wanted to eat. Especially being so young, there are so many things I wanted to accomplish. So, living my own life but then sharing those details with someone else was perfect. Long distance really forces you to plan things way in advance, so I always knew what my schedule was going to look like and could plan my busy life accordingly.

- Even though you do buy plane tickets, you spend less money when you are together because you aren't going to dinner and a movie every-single-weekend-of-the-month. And, you try to think of more elaborate things to do to make the trip more meaningful, things you would not have done otherwise.

- With our scheduled "date" nights a week, he would call me Sunday and Wednesday, which I really liked. For one, I wasn't anxiously waiting by my phone every single night, hoping for a call that might not come even happen. And two, in between calls, it allowed me to think about what I wanted to tell him and which questions I wanted to ask so our conversations were actually meaningful and not forced. I also had time to think about things that might have made me upset (because, let's face it, girls do have a tendency to over-react).

Yes, the disclaimer is that long distance relationships are HARD. I think, in order to be successful, there has to be some kind of timeline when you know you will be together "for good". These relationships require trust, honesty, respect, and a whole lot of emotional strength. For me, I gathered my strength from my military wife friends; I was CHOOSING to be long distance, whereas they may not have necessarily had that choice; if they could do it, then I could too. There are undeniably some differences from short-distance relationships. For example, it takes longer to get to know each other because you have to do everything at planned intervals; you may not meet their friends and family, ways they handle stress, or how they interact with co-workers right off the bat. So, your relationship might progress at a slower pace and you definitely have to practice some patience.

I would say a long distance relationships is not necessarily impossible, especially in this high tech world. It is just a different kind of relationship where you have to look at things in a different kind of way. But, at the time, Simon was perfect.

JANUARY: SAN FRANCISCO BOUND

When Simon came back from Mexico, I knew, for myself, I had to go visit him in his natural habitat. I am a visual learner and I had to see where he lived, what his natural scenery was, and if I saw myself fitting into it.

One day, while checking my e-mail, a flight itinerary just popped up. My jaw dropped. Without really saying anything, he had bought me a plane ticket. And, I was on my way to San Francisco ten days later.

If Christmas was the most romantic day of my life, traveling to San Francisco was the most romantic weekend of my life

As I waited for him outside the terminal, I was kind of nervous that I would not recognize him. I mean, I had only seen this guy maybe twice in my life and there is a good possibility that I had forgotten what he looked like. But, as he came racing around the pick-up line in his black Dodge, my heart began to flutter. He drove by, I hopped in, he pulled me over in the seat, rubbed my hair, and we continued to his apartment.

The weekend itself was nothing too extravagant. We went hiking, had a picnic and a competition to see who could find the largest rock to throw off a cliff. He took me around his work site, educated me on the project he was working on, drove me by his office like five times. We went to the beach, had lunch and ate fudge, saw who could find the largest oyster shell to jump on and break. On our way home, we talked about life philosophies: the benefits of hiring athletes, nicknames, the struggle between balancing work and private life. On Monday morning, he went to work and then came back later to take me to the airport. I barely made it home. In fact, my flight took off six minutes after I got on the plane. Perhaps my most favorite memory of dating Simon was this morning. He went to work, I stayed at his apartment, and he came home to pick me up. He walked in the door and said, "I was just thinking, 'Ug it's Monday again', and then I remembered Britany is at home! And I got excited!". And, we sat on the couch as I made excuses not to leave, watching the time tick. Here I was, traveling 1,300 miles to visit some guy I hardly even knew. It required me to cancel practice with my dance team, to modify my laundry schedule, and to beg my sister to drive me to the airport. Now THAT was completely out of my character. But then again, love does funny things to a person.

But it was the thoughtfulness and respect that he put into everything that really captivated me. One of my anxieties of traveling to see him was that we would probably have to sleep in the same bed (unless, of course, I insisted on someone sleeping on the floor). Kent was the only other guy I had ever shared a bed with, and it took me about a year to get to that point. But, being a gentleman, Simon offered to sleep on the couch. In addition, he had also taken the care to buy me my favorite foods, to make me breakfast and dinner each night. When I went to take a shower, I was actually surprised that he left me alone the entire time (and never came in to turn off the lights or throw cold water on me like Kent would do). That meant a lot to me that he was taking so much care to make me feel comfortable.

I came home from San Francisco completely SOLD on him. I think my friend picked me up from the airport and I spent the rest of the day, laying on my bed, not being able to do anything or think about anything else but him. Like, in a daze that I could not get back to normal functioning for at least a week. Is this not what love is supposed to do to you?

To thank him for sending me out to San Francisco, I chartered his address from his sister and sent him a box in the mail. It included an old-fashioned CD of all the songs we sung together on our trip to the ocean, a t-shirt in his size to support my dance team, a pair of sunglasses, homemade banana bread, printed pictures of our time together, and a thank you card. I was so excited for him to get it that I probably checked the tracking status of the package more often than I checked my social media page.

Despite the long distance, I realized that there were so many other ways I could continue to fall in love with Simon besides just seeing him.

I could fall in love with him by learning about his favorite activities, such as hunting, fishing, hiking, and camping; he could learn about me by watching my favorite movies, reading my favorite books.

In addition, I could spend time with his family, learn about the kind of role models he had growing up, hear stories about him taking apart the lawn mower and then putting it back together. Because I worked in the same area he grew up in, I could learn about him through his old teachers and coaches.

As I began to overanalyze the trip, a few anxieties came up. First, since he was so much older than I, I might have to adjust my timeline a little bit. If we were going to be married, it might happen sooner than I (and my psychic) originally planned. This caused some anxiety because, being extremely analytical, I originally wanted to know every single thing about a person before I married them; Kent and I dated for six years until he decided it was not going to work. However, what I realized was that because

I was attracted to the person that Simon was NOW, and because I believe experiences make up a person, I could wait to fill in the blanks. And because he was 32, not 22 like Kent, that meant he was pretty set in his ways, so his probability of a large personality change was a small margin.

I think it works this way: when you are young and start dating someone, you need to spend a significant length of time with him or her before you decide to get married. You change so much between the ages of 18 and 25 that you need to make sure you can change together. This is how my sister and her boyfriend are: they have been together since they were 17 and have definitely grown together, and marriage will be an easy transition. Kent and I clearly grew far, far apart during this time. However, I think when you get older, you stop changing and know yourself better, it's not as crucial to spend years dating someone. You just need to know enough to know it will work. With us being long distance, I knew I would not be able to learn every little thing about him, but I realized that, if we were to get married, I would have the rest of my life to do those things—it would add to the excitement. I made a list of all the things I needed to know about him (or any guy for that matter) before I was ready to make an official commitment:

1. **We would need to experience at least two arguments:**

Arguing and working through conflict is a natural part of life. When you think about the concept of marriage, it is actually very unnatural. You are asking two people, who come from completely different backgrounds and have completely different experiences of the world to co-exist and live together. Eventually, someone is going to get mad about something. Of course, the first argument could just be a fluke, so you might have to give yourself two arguments before you make an official determination.

2. We would need to enjoy adult beverages together:

Let's face it. Alcohol is a part of American culture. Some people are completely different when they are drunk. Sometimes, that is when the suppressed, depressed self comes out and you spend the entire night, consoling them out of suicide, pulling their hair back, and watching them puke in the toilet. I spent so much time in college with friends doing this and do not want to be with someone for the rest of my life that I have to worry about. When I drink, I become a social butterfly. I love dancing, standing on things, making new friends. I need someone who would complement that side of me.

3. We would need to see each other stressed out:

Simon already saw me stressed out when we were on our way to the airport in San Francisco. When I am really stressed, I tend to close down and get super, super quiet. But, I would need to see Simon stressed out as well. Does he become angry and violent? Does he shut down and disappear from the world? Does he find little projects to do and mow the lawn (that could actually be a very beneficial style to be partnered with)? Because life is often stressful, and being in a marriage, you are expected to support the person, I would need to know if I could handle Simon's style of stress.

4. We would need to see each other angry:

I am not really interested in marrying the kind of guy who throws stuff, breaks stuff, punches walls, etc. I do not get angry very often, but when I do, I go to the gym and run really, really hard on the treadmill. That is my style of coping. I do not want to put myself in a potentially dangerous situation, so I would like to know these things prior. Kent, for example, got heated when something angered him (perhaps this was the testosterone from being an athlete). He never quite expressed his anger on me, but would often do that to items within reaching distance—his phone, his steering wheel, his homework. And, I would always think to myself, "what would happen if he completely lost control?" One of those days, it could have been me, even if it was on accident. I did not want to be with someone that had those kinds of tendencies.

5. **We would need to see how each other handles kids (or, if not available, dogs would suffice):**

Raising a family is not only stressful, but also brings out the differences that couples have in family values. Some parents might want to discipline their children with a spanking, other might want to use time out. Huge arguments and disagreements often erupt based on these discrepancies. In addition because I want to have children someday, I would want to know if Simon had fatherly-instincts. Whenever Kent would come over to my house, my dog would run, hide, and shudder under the bed (that should have been my first indication that he was bad news bears). Dogs always know best, so I would want to find out these things about Simon, too, before we got married and had kids.

And, I knew that I needed to just give these things time; I could not *force* an argument to occur "just to see what would happen". I could not push his buttons "just to incite some anger", and he probably had his list going about me as well. I had to be patient, but sooner or later, we would find these things out about each other.

FEBRUARY: HANGING OUT WITH THE FAMILY

We continued our scheduled Wednesday and Sunday night dates. Simon sent me pink roses, delivered to school, for Valentine's Day. A man after my own literary heart, he even researched which color roses to send me; pink, which means affection (red means *affection*, which for us, might have been a little too soon).

About four weeks after I flew out to San Francisco, Simon came home to spend the weekend with his family. The plan was for Sarah and me to both leave work early, pick up her husband, and drive to Vail, where Simon would be awaiting my arrival with his parents.

That morning, I woke up extra early (of course, I probably did not even sleep the night before). I made sure to shave my legs, exfoliate my skin, pluck my eyebrows, straighten my hair. I beamed with excitement to see Simon. The whole way to school, I belted our "love song" playlist in my car (but of course, I turned it down once I drove into the school parking lot in case any students might see my very immature, infatuated behaviors). I counted down the seconds, the minutes until I could leave school and be on my way to see Simon (there is a slight possibility that I let my class out a little early so that I could make that meeting happen sooner).

The two-hour drive to Vail was treacherous. I spent the entire time, nervously fidgeting, knowing that every second, I got closer to my Prince Charming. When we arrived, I ran into the house, jumped into Simon's arms, wrapped my feet around his waist, and squeezed him like I would never let go. I had never been so excited to see anyone in my life; not even Kent when I returned home from Europe.

We spent that night playing board games with his family and when it came time for bed, I went to my bunk, he went to his abode upstairs, and sometime during the night, I snuck up to make sure he was still awake, waiting for me. We stayed up, giggling about sweet nothings, talking about how much we missed each other and all the things in between.

At about four o'clock in the morning, I snuck back downstairs, fell asleep, and waited for someone to wake me up to go skiing. When we woke up, we ate breakfast, packed our gear, and headed to the slopes. Not being much of a skier myself, I relied upon Simon to teach me some new tricks, and by the end of the day, I could ski down a blue like no one's business. Before I knew it, Sunday arrived, and Simon needed to return to San Francisco. I dropped him off at the airport, stepped out of the car, jumped into his arms, and started counting down the moments until I would see him again.

Even though I *knew* I was so in love with Simon, I never mustered up enough confidence to tell him. For some reason, we are all afraid of that dreaded "L" word.

I actually ran a Google search, asking "When is the right time to say 'I love you'?" because I was just curious what "the experts" were saying. *Men's Health* magazine reports that you should say "I love you" when you feel comfortable with the person. You should ask yourself, "Can you list the relatives he/she likes least? Can you list his/her three favorite books/movies/songs? Do you know her birth date, middle name, and where she was born?" Excellent. I am adding these to my list of questions to ask on a first date. If we get these things out of the way, then he is free to express his undying love for me at any point in the relationship.

e-Harmony reports that men are more likely to start thinking about saying, "I love you" in the first two months of the relationship, while women may take about five. This is also really great to know because if a guy professes his love for me after two months, I have about another three more months of leeway to decide if I love him back or not. And, if he doesn't profess his love within two months, then I can just assume he has ulterior motives and can send him packing.

How Stuff Works suggests 'testing the waters' before dropping the L bomb. You should ask your significant other things like, "Do you feel like we are a good match for each other?", "Do you see this working out in the long haul?", "Do you picture a future together?" Perfect. So, if I feel like I am in love with someone (and most likely this will be after 5 months, as e-Harmony reports), all I need to do is ask a few simple questions about our future together. If we are not on the same page, I can just keep that tiny little secret to myself until one day when we magically end up on the same page (On a side note, I got an "I almost love you" one time and now I am seeing that as a method to 'test the waters').

One report says, "The guy should totally say it first because if the woman says it first and the guy hasn't had time to process his emotions, it could put too much pressure on him". Another report says, "Woman should say it first because men are often scared and need the courage to say it back".

I think one of the reasons we are so fearful to use that dreaded "L" word is because it carries many other charged terms, such as the 'commitment' word and the 'marriage' word with it. If I profess my love to someone else, it means that THIS RELATIONSHIP IS SERIOUS and it could have serious long-term consequences, such as getting married, that I am not ready to deal with yet.

I think another fear is that the other person will not reciprocate those feelings back. Here I could be, baring my heart and soul to you, and to not hear it back could "damage my confidence and derail the relationship completely" (or, so CNN says). So basically, not hearing it back from someone else could hurt my feelings, so I might as well just keep it to myself so I don't have to experience that feeling of disappointment and regret.

I think the Greeks had it right when they devised different words of love for different situations. A *platonic love* is a kind of love for a friendship, *agape* is a selfless, unconditional kind of love, *eros* is a sexual-passion love. In English, however, we do not necessarily have this kind of language to delineate the different ways we can feel about a person. We can say, "I am infatuated with you", which I would say means, "I feel very affectionate towards you and am on the road to 'Love' but want to make sure this isn't just the honeymoon phase'". And then, you can just say, 'I love you", but that is about it.

We are afraid to be vulnerable. In my sophomore's vocabulary books, it means, "open to attack; capable of being wounded or damaged; unprotected". However, in our culture, I believe the world 'vulnerability' has a much more negative connotation (just like the word 'bossy' apparently does as well). To be vulnerable means that you have a weakness, an insecurity, a problem. It means that you have to admit you are capable of making mistakes, that you might have to rely on other people to accomplish tasks, that you might have to expose something that you have locked away for many years, deep inside your psyche. In our very competitive and capitalist society, I can see why vulnerability would be a detrimental thing to show. If you are running a business, the moment you show that you are second-guessing yourself, other business people will eat you alive (which is EXACTLY why I am not in the business world). If I am trying to sell someone insurance, the second I question myself about rates, I lose my credibility and probably my client as well, which then could also mean my job, my family, my dream vacation to Tahiti...

If you haven't watched the TedTalk, "The Power of Vulnerability" by Brene Brown I would highly suggest it. It could change your life. In her presentation, she talks about her research on relationships. Basically, she wanted to know about connection and why we, as people, have an undeniable desire to feel connection. She says, "When you ask people about love, they tell you about heartbreak. When you ask people about belonging, they share the most excruciating experiences of being excluded. And, when you ask people about connection, the stories they told me were about disconnection." She realized that, through this research, these negative stories stem from shame: the fear of disconnection. After dissecting thousands of interviews and journal entries, she came to the conclusion that there is one difference between people who feel a strong sense of belonging and of love, and those who do not, and that is those who feel a strong sense of belonging and love BELIEVE they are worthy of belonging and love; ironically, the one thing that is keeping us out of connection and love is our sense of self-worth. She calls these people "whole-hearted".

After watching this TedTalk, I began looking at how I see vulnerability in my own life. As a teacher, I believe it is important to create a welcoming classroom environment in which kids feel safe to make mistakes. As adults, we are so quick to judge and point fingers at kids that we forget they, too, are the same living, growing, and learning individuals that we once were. Lord knows I have made my fair share of mistakes. This means that I have to make myself vulnerable in front of my students, which means I have to open up a little bit of myself, such as sharing the story about getting my speeding ticket after that "dreaded phone call" (of which, three of my students saw me pulled over and two of them testified in traffic court with me....awesome). The way I see it, if I can make fun of myself, I can distract their insecurities and they can feel comfortable to share an incorrect answer, to make a mistake, to be vulnerable. I like to share stories from myself at their age, like how it took me four tries to pass the permit test, the time I ran away from my house for a week, the time my high school boyfriend gave me a break-up note, the time I ditched my poor date at homecoming to dance with someone else, my irrational fear of fish. I think that, by opening myself up, they can see me as a human—not as an unrealistic version of a 'perfect entity' as we often see our elders.

In her TedTalk, Dr. Brene Brown discusses the idea of courage. She defines *courage* as, "to tell a story with your whole heart"; that people who tackle life with courage understand they are imperfect, that they will make mistakes, have insecurities, battle obstacles. But, that people are also able to establish an authentic connection because they are able to let go of, "who they thought they should be in order to be who they are". In what is probably my favorite part of the interview, she says, "They fully embraced vulnerability. They didn't talk about vulnerability as being comfortable nor did they really talk about it being excruciating—they just talked about it being necessary. They talked about the willingness to say, 'I love you first', the willingness to do something without guarantees. They're willing to invest in a relationship that may or may not work out. They thought this was fundamental".

Let me just kill the mood and say that the older I get, the more I realize just how corrupt and selfish people are. I believe this is partly why our divorce rate is so high. It is uncomfortable and very difficult to deal with our insecurities and feelings of shame, disappointment, and guilt, so we just put up a front and displace those emotions. Why tell your husband you had an affair because you can't handle your insecurities when you can just sign a piece of paper and pretend it doesn't exist? Why admit that you made a mistake and probably should not have texted that ex-boyfriend when you can just move out and never speak to each other again? Why accept that you have really strong, intense feelings for someone when you can just tell them it's not working and go back to your work? As Dr. Brown discusses, these are all ways that we just medicate ourselves; we suppress the problems, pretend they don't exist, distract ourselves, cover them up. At the end of the day, they are still there. We just numb ourselves. Technology is an excellent way to protect ourselves. Anytime you are in the line at the grocery store, waiting at the doctor's office, sitting on public transportation, take notice at how many people are on their cell phones, and how many of them appear to actually be doing business, or just scrolling through old text messages. It is uncomfortable to not be focused on something. Someone might engage you in conversation, someone might sit down next to you, someone might ask you a question you aren't prepared for. So, it's easier to protect yourself than to leave yourself vulnerable. Of course, even though I knew I was in love with Simon, I never told him for all of these reasons.

My current personal philosophy is, if you love someone, you love someone, and you might as well just let them know. If I were to go back and change one thing about my relationship with Simon, it would be to have told him sooner how I really felt. But, of course, like most people, I was scared. I feared rejection, unrequited feelings, and vulnerability, especially after Kent. Life is too short to hide secrets and beat around the bush and 'test the waters'. To me, a relationship is always about serving the other person. And, if I love you, I want you to know that I love you because I want you to know how special you are to me; I want you to know that you are valued, thought about constantly, and important. If you are not sure if you love me back or not, or you just aren't ready to say it, then that is fine too because what I am sharing is for YOU to feel good about yourself, not me. Once I changed my perspective on the purpose of saying, "I love you", it made it much easier to grasp that, and it was not about rejection, or something being wrong with me: it just wasn't a good fit.

MARCH: THAT SECOND DREADED PHONE CALL

As it turns out, we actually would never see each other again. On the way to the airport after Vail, Simon told me, "You are like a guy. I have been trying to figure out how to get you to open up to me. It's like you are locked away in the castle and I have to swim through a moat to get through", which, now that I look back on it, was completely true. So, I, being the hopeless romantic, immediately sat down at my desk and wrote out an old-fashioned love letter, confessing my undying love to him, saying that I never expected to meet him as soon as I did, how, when my other boyfriend broke up with me, I realized how much freedom I had, and that Simon made me think about things I never thought about before.

Simon called me one day, said some stuff about, "things not working out", "losing the connection", "we stopped getting to know each other", and "still wanting to stay in touch and be friends". It was a three-hour phone conversation, and by the end, I told him I did not see the point in us continuing to stay in touch if he was in San Francisco and I was in Colorado and we were never going to hang out. So, that is where it was left.

His famous closing line was, "I just don't want to be the reason you quit your job and don't stay in a school district for a long time for me because my job requires me to move around all the time".

I really love this phrase, "I just don't want to hurt you". Like, WTF does that even mean?

Of course, it comes in other forms as well: "I just don't want to be the reason you have to leave your job", "I just don't want to turn out like all those other guys you dated who were jerks to you", "I just don't want you to wake up one morning and decide you don't want to be with me anymore".

So, what, we are just going to halt the progression of this relationship because you are afraid of my feelings?...

Well, newsflash: If I am choosing to date you, I am perfectly aware that the odds are NOT in our favor and there is a VERY slim possibility that things are not actually going to work out between us. And, I am VERY aware that, with investing my time and my energy into you, I am also setting myself up for heartbreak in the near future. Um, there is a reason it didn't work out with the other guys who "hurt me", there is a reason I am attracted to you, and I would never be blind sighted to the fact that one of us might have to quit a job to be with the other person.

But, you know what? For whatever reason, I see enough value in you that whatever time and emotional energy I expend on you in the present moment is worth whatever heartbreak I might deal with later on. There is obviously something I like about you enough that I am willing to not date anyone else, to consider a sacrifice in my career, and to spend the time deciding if I think I would enjoy you long term. It's not really all about you. There is a reason I am willing to be vulnerable to your charms so saying, "I just don't want to hurt you" is actually not a valid excuse for being sketchy.

Now, if you know you are the kind of flighty guy who is always running away from commitments and you know that you will never be able to keep up a serious relationship because that just doesn't fit your personality, then by all means, please let me know so that I stop wasting my time liking you. You "not wanting to hurt me" would mean that you recognize within yourself that you are a stud, but that you have some kind of tragic flaw that causes you to get cold feet, and so you are actually doing me a favor by telling me to stop falling for you. If that were the reason, then I would say thank you, and let's be on our separate ways. And, you should probably stop talking to all girls in general just so that you don't feel guilty about "hurting" their feelings, too.

That is really awesome. I would never fault anyone for admitting they want to just be selfish because that is a humbling realization to admit. Sometimes, I feel the same exact way. Right now, I could think of nothing more restricting than having to share my bed with someone every night. Right now, that sounds terrible and I very selfishly love sleeping by myself.

I never understand why guys can't just be honest about their feelings. It is perfectly acceptable to want to be selfish and I never understand why guys can't just say that straight up. But you beating around the bush and trying to make me think, "this is all out of consideration for you" is actually very unfair. What kind of ends up happening (in Girl Land), is I think to myself, "But we are so perfect for each other and I think he is totally into me sometimes and if I can just plug a little bit more, I can get him to open up to me". And, from his end, he is probably thinking, "I'd like to keep her around, but I am not quite ready to open up to her because it is scary and I'd rather just keep being a bachelor", which in the end, actually ends up hurting more because in girl land, we think there is still a chance, and in boy land, you know there is not.

I would much rather prefer an honest, seemingly selfish answer than an answer that I have to spend time deciphering and decoding. No, this has nothing to do with YOU not wanting to hurt ME because when you do break up with me, you are probably going to be out of the picture anyways, so you won't be experiencing any of that hurt I am suffering.

So, thank you for pretending to be concerned about my emotional well-being, but I can actually see through it all. I think if we were all just a little more honest with each other, this dating game would be much more enjoyable and much less taxing on everyone's collective energy.

What I really think this very clique phrase, "I just don't want to hurt you" really means is, "I want to keep you around, but I am not quite ready to give up my bachelor status yet. I really like being unattached to someone, don't really want to be responsible to call you every night, and want to be able to pack up and go at anytime I please, so I'd rather just keep you around, but not really make any official commitments to you". I think, in the case of Simon, it was fear, but it was also sensing that I was not ready to be in a relationship; that I still had some self-exploration to encounter, and he did not want to stifle me. The thing about break ups is...

1. **Is it better to be the dump-er or the dump-ee?** There are pro's and con's to both sides of the situation. It is probably easier to get over when you are the dump-er because you are the one making the ultimate decision. But, usually the way it happens is the dump-er has to look like the jerk ("I can't believe he said that to you! He is so ignorant/immature/selfish"), even if you are doing it out of the kindness of your heart. The dump-ee can always play the victim card and get a lot of sympathy from people. But, being the dump-ee sucks too because you end up looking

like the idiot who didn't see it coming and usually end up having to defend yourself.

I have accepted the fact that I will probably always be the dump-ee, for a variety of reasons. First of all, I am an idealist and like to see the best in every situation, so when things don't feel right, I tend to overlook them. Second of all, I like to be a solution maker, so when things go wrong, I try to find ways to fix them. And, lastly, I had a terrible experience being a dump-er that will probably prevent me from ever doing that again. Basically, when I was in high school, I tried to break up with this boy. It was a really awkward situation. We "dated" all summer, but then didn't talk for about a month, so I figured he was in the same boat I was in. I was wrong. I told him it wasn't working out. He wept, begged for me to change my mind, etc. It was embarrassing for him, awkward for me, ruined whatever chance at friendship we had.

2. Would you rather have a big explosion-break up, or a slow, gradual, anti-climactic falling out? We have all seen examples of those vehement, big-explosion break ups on television, where the girlfriend flings the guy's clothes out her window, she finds out he is cheating on her and slaps his face, they have a big screaming fit at each other and vow to delete each other's numbers and never, ever talk again. These usually end in feelings of resentment, bitterness, and hatred (Something Jerry Springer-esque).

Then, there are those types of break ups that end in none of this. It is one person, calling the other to just simply say, "Things aren't working", you have a casual conversation, and hang up the phone, and that is it. Or, as life drifts on, you slowly stop finding time to talk to hang out with each other, talk to each other, text each other. And, one day, you realize you haven't even thought about them in a week. In this kind of break up, you are probably left with some things unsaid, left with feeling confused, and feeling like some strings are still attached. This was Simon.

While I have definitely experienced both on a certain level, I am not really sure which situation is better to be in. Kent's break up was a big explosion (I am surprised his windshield in his car did not break from the tension surmounting between us). Simon's break up was a very nonchalant conversation, which in some ways, felt very anti-break up ish. On one hand, bitterness, anger, and resentment is NEVER a healthy feeling to have towards a person. However, the fervent fight probably allows you to release some emotions and provides you some immediate closure. On the other hand, ending a relationship in an anti-climactic way means you still have some respect for the person, but it probably leaves you lingering and hopeful for a little bit longer.

3. What is the standard procedure about birthdays, celebratory/tragic life events, etc.? This is a perplexity that many of my friends have had recently and I haven't quite distinguished the social protocol. When their birthday comes around, do you say "Happy Birthday"? On one hand, if you have been with someone for a significant amount of time, it might be appropriate just to let them you know are thinking about them and hope they have a good day. On the other hand, it could stir up some old feelings or lead them to believe you want to get back together that you might not want to go down that route. Or, if he or she gets engaged or married, do you wish them well or do you pretend you don't know anything is happening? If his or her favorite pet dies, do you offer condolences because you know how devastated he or she probably is or do you let them have their space and grieve without your influence? (On a side note, has anyone else been dumped multiple times on their birthday? I think it's just because birthdays mean gifts, and the size of the gift means the extent of the seriousness of the relationship, and especially in the beginning stages, that is really scary).

4. What do you do with all of their stuff?...This is often confusing, especially if it is nice stuff that you actually use. You have a few options. You can (a) put it in a box and mail it back to them, (b) burn it in a campfire, (c) donate it to someone else, or (d) keep it and use it. If you choose options A-C, then you are eliminating their influence on your life, but that kind of sucks because you won't have memorabilia to look back fondly on the relationship one day. If you choose option D, then it is nice because obviously the stuff was still gifted to you for a reason and can still have practical purpose in your life, but then you might end up in the awkward situation when you are dating someone else and you have to explain where your college lacrosse t-shirts came from...

...and what do you do about those Facebook pictures that your hair obviously looks VERY good in?

The thing about break ups is...they suck. No matter how it happens, who does it, how they do it, when it occurs, break ups always come at the worst possible moments and have more lingering effects than you ever want. Just like starting a new relationship, when ending a relationship, you have to be very crafty and careful about the moves that you make.

Having recently encountered this same "dreaded break up phone call", I went back to my steps.

STEP ONE: SURVIVE THE SHOCK

The same thing happened as before: I tossed and turned in bed all night, analyzing, trying to get a grasp on what had just occurred. Because I did not know Simon as well as I knew Kent, I had to learn to accept that there were some things that may never make sense.

I got up, drove to school the next day (also got that speeding ticket) and tried to conduct business as usual. I told the most important people what had happened and let them know I would talk about it when I was ready.

STEP TWO: CLEAN SIMON OUT OF MY LIFE

This step was relatively easier this time. I just deleted Simon's phone number, sent his e-mails to my archives, unfollowed him from InstaGram. Social media, unfortunately, adds a whole other dimension to relationships that our parents never had to deal with. It is really, really tempting to just type his name into my search bar to see what he is up to, but I also know that I am probably not going to find anything I want to see. It's kind of like snooping on your boyfriend: if you find something questionable, you either have to (a) confess that you were snooping through his stuff or (b) keep it a secret, which also really sucks. I would prefer to just remain ignorant and not know.

While now I could probably converse with Simon cordially, I needed to clean him out momentarily so that I would not continue to be attached. I told Simon that, if he did not see this going anywhere at all, then we needed to not talk. At the time, I saw no point in trying to date other guys because I thought Simon WAS Prince Charming and did not see the point in developing relationships with anyone else. However, now that things were over, I needed to unattach myself so I could start meeting other people without feeling guilty. This was probably the best thing I did for myself because it allowed me to start processing our 'relationship' without adding on a bunch of other complications.

STEP THREE: GO THROUGH CATHARSIS
Since it had only been a few months since my first 'dreaded phone call', I still had my sad song playlist on my iPod. I revisited these familiar songs, and allowed myself to cry, cry, cry.

STEP FOUR: LEARN MINDFULNESS
Because I had already practiced so much mindfulness, I was quickly able to assess myself. Interestingly enough, I also had dreams about Simon, although these were not about beating up his mom like I had with Kent's mom. When Kent dumped me, I was easily able to figure out what happened because I had known him for so long; I knew he was in an identity crisis, I knew he used the phone call as a cowardly way out, I knew that he would get another girlfriend as soon as possible. But because I did not date Simon as long, it frustrated me that I could not figure him out as quickly. We never quite got to the point where we had full-fledged heart-to-heart conversations, partly because we had so much fun together, and partly because I was avoiding those kinds of deep conversations. So, I began dreaming about what those heart-to-heart conversations might have been like. I would say, "Simon, I know why things didn't work out. It was because you knew the next time we hung out, I would force you to go to yoga".

Of course, in my dreams, it was mostly me talking and spilling my skeletons, and I never gained much from his end. But, when I woke up the next morning, I felt a sense of relief. It's as if once the material is processed, the brain is satisfied and ready to move on. So, I went on with my day without even thinking about those things that previously bothered me.

STEP FIVE: ABOLISH THE ANGER

Since I did not date Simon for that long and we ended our relationship in a very mature, very nonchalant way, there were not as many things that I was angry about. One thing I did feel a tinge of anger about was that I sensed that he led me on. I felt a little embarrassed that I let myself get played and had no idea what was even happening. He sweet talked me, told me that he has not dated a girl worth mentioning in the last four years, and even flew me out to San Francisco and did not work for an entire weekend so he could spend time with me. But, when I went back through it, I realized that it was probably not him exactly leading me on, but rather myself projecting that onto him. And, once I took accountability for my own actions, I suddenly was not angry anymore.

Outside of anger, I also felt a little disappointed because I felt like he was letting a really great thing go: we were almost perfect for each other. Dating him would have been SO much fun; we had talked about me flying out to Phoenix to join him at a work convention, going hiking and camping together, traveling to Greece or Ireland. We had a phenomenal connection and I was disappointed that he was letting that go. However, what I had to remember was this was *his* choice, not necessarily mine, and I did not necessarily want to be in a relationship with someone that I constantly had to talk them into dating me: that is fake, unnatural, and a waste of my time.

STEP SIX: FINDING FORGIVENESS

In some ways because I went into the relationship with no expectations and because I put most of the blame back on myself, there was not much to forgive about Simon. I felt blind sighted, like I did with Kent because the phone call was so sudden and random, but I also had to appreciate Simon for being honest with me and not dragging on the relationship if he didn't feel it was going anywhere.

The area I had to forgive myself in involved the break up letter I sent Simon after our trip to Vail: at the end of the day, the letter was the catalyst for the break up. I am not sure if Simon got scared from the amount I shared with him, if bringing Kent into it offended him, or if there was some other kind of trigger, but the letter definitely changed his perspective on our relationship. I had a tendency to blame myself and to wonder if we would still be together had I not sent that letter, and kind of felt ashamed, like I had made a huge, huge mistake. However, what I had to remind myself was, at the end of the day, what happened had happened. I always want to plan out my life, and I always want things to work according to plan. Love and relationships are not scripted perfectly like a movie and are not exactly something that goes to plan. Much like with Kent, I wished there were things I would have said and things I would have done differently: I wish I would have not called him back after our initial conversation, I wish I had told him I thought he was acting out of fear, I wish I would have explained to him that I would never regret quitting a job for him if I made the decision myself. However, I had to accept that—that is what happened. I sent the love letter. It opened a can of worms. Had I not sent the letter and opened up the conversation, we probably would have been skimming this uncomfortable, un-natural line, and pretending that there was nothing to talk about. We would have been pretending until eventually something happened, whether it was a break up letter, a conversation, a text message. The letter just happened to be the catalyst for this conversation.

STEP SEVEN: UNDERSTAND WHY IT WOULDN'T WORK

Unlike Kent, the reasons Simon and I could not be together centered more on logistics. For one, we lived 1,300 miles away from each other. Since both of us are very busy and very career driven people, this would mean that someone would have to make a huge sacrifice in the near future if we wanted to see if it could turn into marriage, and I do not think either of us was really willing to take that leap of faith. After visiting his place of residence and seeing how proud he was of the work he did in his office, I knew that it would probably be me who would uproot and move out, since I was just beginning my career. Long distance relationships are fun, but they also move much slower because you do not see each other on a daily basis, so you have to wait longer intervals for those crucial checkpoints to occur.

Perhaps the biggest logistical issue, however, was just that we were in different parts of our lives. He was 32, I was 23. He was "looking for marriage", wanted to settle down, and start having kids ASAP before his time clock ran out. I, on the other hand, had a few other things on my bucket list to cross off before I came to this step. I needed to spend some more time exploring myself, solidifying that I wanted to marry someone just like Simon; he did not want to chance waiting that long, in the event it was not working out. So, while everything else lined up perfectly, the timing did not. And for that one, meager, but very important factor, it wouldn't work out.

STEP EIGHT: LIVING AND LEARNING

Simon served a few purposes for me. First of all, Simon taught me my worth. When we had that "dreaded phone call", it was actually a very mature conversation. No one yelled at each other. No one got upset and threw the phone. No one followed up with capitalized YOU MADE A HUGE MISTAKE text messages. My arguments with Kent were brutal; he would yell, I would end up in hysterical tears. These arguments with Kent were not healthy (I always think of him whenever I hear Taylor Swift's lyrics, "Screamin' and fightin'/cursin' in the rain/2 AM and I'm callin' your name...except, unlike Taylor Swift, I DON'T miss that one bit). Being dumped by Simon was actually quite refreshing.

I learned what it felt like to be in an adult relationship. I now have very high standards, but I think that every girl should. A conversation I had with my roommates about Kent made me very angry. In that conversation with my roommates, I learned that Kent made some pretty disrespectful, pretty derogatory statements about me that were not necessarily true. After learning this material, and being with Simon, I hit a few crises during this time. First of all, I realized that Kent saw me as his trophy girl, a pretty attachment that he could parade around his college campus. And, when he knew he would move and did not need that anymore, he dumped me. After dating Simon, and not seeing myself perpetuate the same dysfunctional tendencies as with Kent's relationship, I felt a relief: I was not destined to repeat the past and I would NOT end up with someone like Kent.

Second, Simon forced me to completely filter Kent out of my life. It would be inaccurate for me to say that I was 100% over Kent by the time I met Simon. Guys do not like to talk about other guys because they do not want to know about your shared experiences with someone else. Because I wanted to be respectful to Simon, and did not want him to think of himself as a 'rebound', I had to learn how to let go of whatever small attachments I still had to Kent. For weeks, I literally practiced what I would say to Simon when he asked me about my past relationships; "I dated a guy in college, we broke up last summer, and I am really glad we did because then I would not have met you". Rolling that officially off my tongue was awkward (good thing I had a nice glass of wine in me) but I did not want to bring Kent-baggage to Simon.

I also began going through my entire Facebook page (yes, we are in the digital age, unfortunately) and deleting every single remnant of Kent; every single picture, every single status, every single conversation. This took me sometime to get there because I still kind of wanted to hold onto those memories, I wanted the option to go back anytime I wanted and visually see Kent and my relationship (and also because in some of those pictures, my hair looks damn good). But, I surrendered: if I wanted to date another guy, I had to let go of those things because they were in the past. This time, deleting Kent from my Facebook history was not about cutting contact with him, but rather a signal that I was learning to navigate the world by myself, irrespective of his influence.

Because Kent and I dated during one of the most crucial parts of adult development, I also had to learn how to sift him out of the stories I told about my past. For the last six years, the stories I always told were through the lens of us as a couple, but now I needed to learn how to shift away from that perspective.

Simon would talk about putting a dead fish under a girl's pillow and I would want to tell the story about the time Kent's lacrosse friends arranged goldfish races and the loser had to eat the goldfish, living. Or, Simon would be concerned about me being cold and I would want to reassure him that I used to sit in six inches of snow at Kent's lacrosse games so I knew how to withstand the cold. This was very challenging, and I definitely was very awkward at first. I stammered, uttered incoherent sounds, stumbled through some very awkward pauses. But, I had to learn how to be me, and I had to recognize that those moments were me, of my doing, separate of Kent, and that Kent could have just been a minor character who witnessed the story.

So, I learned to re-tell the stories of my past from a perspective about me. The story about Kent's lacrosse team's keg race suddenly became a story about me being named "The Official Pumper and Beer Distributer" for my group of friends. Or, the story about the last summer at Cheyenne Frontier Days when Kent got so impatient when the taxi cab was late that a neighbor from across the street came out, gave him a beer, and told him to "chill" suddenly becomes a story about "I once saw this guy at Cheyenne Frontier Days...". Or, the time in high school he asked me to homecoming with a giant poster and I completely passed by it became a story about, "This one time I was asked to homecoming".

On the flipside, I began figuring out which stories were good to tell, and which stories I could probably leave out. This was difficult because most of the stories I could probably leave out were prideful stories that I would often share when we paraded around his college town as a couple. Like, I should probably leave out the story of when we got caught in the high school parking lot sleeping because we were too tired to drive home. Or, the story about how I cried the first time he scored his first college goal and how

I used to rub his feet after a lacrosse game. Or, the story about the time I cut out 72 hearts, wrote things I liked about him, and snuck into his apartment to tape them on the walls and then he tried to bar-be-cue for me but the steaks ended up half pink, half charcoal because the grill was so dirty. Or, the story about the time I thought he might propose because he took me to a nice restaurant and I freaked out. I can re-visit those moments myself—they happened and will never go away—but someone else probably does not need to know about these stories because they are really irrelevant. I took myself back to all my favorite moments we shared together, I re-positioned myself, and I discovered how to sift the Kent out. I now have a handful of really great, really funny stories about Britany to share with any new guy I may date.

In getting over Simon, it was not his physical address that I was avoiding (since he lived so far away), but rather a few songs that had special meaning to us. "Dayum Baby" by Florida Georgia Line was one I just could not listen to because it reminded me so much of Simon; I would skip it or change the station every time it came on. So, I made that my test towards healing. When I could finally listen to the entire song without becoming an emotional wreck, I knew I would be ok. And, a couple months later, I rolled up to the stoplight, jamming to "Damn Baby", and did not even think about the Simon-connotation.

Similarly to Kent, I wanted to take some time to try to figure out what went wrong in our relationship, so that I could either prevent that from happening again, or would be able to see those red flags a little sooner.

When Simon told me, "I have been trying to figure out how to get you to open up to me. You are kind of like a guy. I feel like I have to dig a mote and swim over and climb into the tallest room of the highest tower". I did not really think much of it at the time, but this could definitely have been a point of contention in our relationship, which is why he potentially could have lost interest; while I was busy trying to stay protected and telling jokes, he wanted to get to the deep rootedness of what made me tick. Upon reflecting on this statement, I realized that I am this way for a few reasons: as a dancer, I had to learn how to wipe whatever internal turmoil I was going through off, walk in front of a crowd of 80,000 people, and plaster on a smile. I have learned to perform happy, even when things are not happy.

Also being from a divorced family, I have had to learn how to support myself and be independent because there was not always someone around to help me. In retrospect, I definitely carry this trait into my adult life; I don't ask for help, I like to do things on my own. This can be extremely detrimental, especially when it comes to a relationship because it lends me to do all the work without any expectations of return.; healthy relationships should see an equal return of giving and taking. This is an extremely difficult construct to breakdown because it is so engrained into my being, but I also know that, if I want to have a successful marriage someday, I need to learn how to rely on other people. I wasn't letting Simon take care of me, rather, I smothered him because I felt like I could be the only one to take care of someone in our relationship. I often hold the fulfillment of taking care of other people sacred; for some irrational reason, I never understand why someone would want to take care of me. However, I realized that any guy I am going to work well with will probably get the same pleasure out of caring for me as I do them, and like Simon, if I stomp on those caring tendencies, I am forbidding the guy from his natural inclinations, and that in itself is not fair.

One of my most favorite parts of dating Simon, and of being a girlfriend in general, is to dote with random acts of kindness. Shopping for other people, writing "I'm thinking of you cards", and sending care packages brings me absolute joy. So if Simon was not going to be the recipient, I would find someone else who would still fulfill that role. In fact, I made a goal for myself to do one nice thing for someone else once a week. Research has proven that doing something for someone else not only makes the receiver's day better, but also makes you happier, and thus, on average, live longer. So, I compiled a list of random acts of kindness that I could do to not only make myself feel better, but to also brighten someone else's day.

1. **Support a friend by going to one of their functions**
   The thing about being out of high school/college is that we no longer have school sporting events that we are socially motivated to attend. However, we can still support the people around us by being their date to a work party, going to an award presentation they are receiving, watching the sports team they coach play a game, etc. I am a huge advocate for trying new things because I get to learn about someone else's lifestyle. I attended a Special Olympics basketball game a few weeks ago and that was one of the most humbling experiences, especially to see the parents and how they interact with their children. So, even if the event is anticipated to be boring, I still volunteer to show up because I get to see someone else's life in action. We all know that time is precious, so showing up to someone else's function will make them feel special. And, if nothing else, hopefully there is good food!

2. **Write someone a thank you/appreciation card**

As a teacher, I experience just how unspoken we are about our appreciation. We are always so in tune to our own lives that we forget other people have to make sacrifices for us. So, think about a person in your life that has made an impact, even if it was ten years ago that you never thanked. Or, someone in your life that you have been able to learn something from, such as a way that they raise their family that you appreciate. Or, someone in your life that you know is going through a difficult times and needs a reminder of how awesome and loved they are. In my opinion, I would MUCH rather get a nice, thoughtful card from someone rather than a gift because words and a message are things I can read over and over again and never lose.

3. **Volunteer your time to help someone else**

Whether this be offering to watch someone's kids, clean an elderly person's house or do yard work, walk a neighbor's dog, help someone move, offering to paint an office, etc., donating your time to someone else can be incredibly humbling. We all know that there is never enough time in the day to get everything you want done so donate a portion of your time to make someone else's to do list a little smaller.

4. **Invite someone to happy hour and offer to pick up the tab**

I believe spending time with someone is the best thing you can do because the conversations you make can never be erased. We grow through experiences and by learning from other people. Offer to take someone to happy hour, or lunch, or coffee, or whatever your preference. Put your technology away for an hour or so and divulge in conversation. It will distract you from your life and maybe even help the person you are in conversation with.

5. **Shop, not for yourself, but with someone else in mind**
The general tendency when you are at the mall is to look for stuff for yourself—I am completely guilty of this, especially since I have to live on a small teacher's salary. However, a few months ago, I began to change my perspective. Money is just money. Yes, I don't get paid much as a teacher, but I will always find a way to make ends meet. So, when I shop now, even if the purpose is for myself, I always take inventory of the store and see if there are little trinkets or items that someone in my life could benefit from, even if it is a scoop of peanut butter cups from Sprouts. My favorite thing to do when I dated Simon and had extra time was shop for things I could send in a box for him. The best feeling is when you give an unexpected gift to someone because you are letting them know you are thinking about that person and are hopefully making their day a little brighter.

6. **Offer to bring someone a treat**
If you are out at Starbucks or (my personal favorite) Sonic for lunch, offer to bring a co-worker back something. If you are on your way home and stop by Chick-Fil-A, bring your roommates a shake as well. I believe that what comes around, goes around, so if you are nice to someone now, then someone else will return the favor to you later on.

7. **Call someone you haven't spoken to in a while just to check in**
We all have that grandparent or that aunt or longtime friend that we know is isolated and can get quite lonely. So, give that person a quick call and let them know you

are thinking about them. The beauty of technology and Bluetooth is that you can multitask and do this while you are sitting in traffic.

8. **Strike up a conversation with someone you don't know**
Think about all of the people you encounter on a daily basis, sitting in the doctor's office, waiting on the light rail, standing in line at the store, etc. And, think about how many of these people you actually talk to. Probably none. But, I am always reminding myself that you never know what is going through someone's head, what obstacles they are tackling in their day. Maybe they just found out they had cancer. Maybe their spouse just lost their job. Maybe there is nothing going wrong in their life. You never know how striking up a conversation can change someone's day and you never know what you can learn from someone else.

9. **Hold the door open for a stranger**
Yes, we all complain about how un-chivalrous our society is becoming. How many times do you walk inside after someone else and they just slam the door in your face? Be thoughtful of those around you and don't be that person.

10. **Give someone a compliment**
I don't know why we don't compliment each other enough (of course, my answer to everything is that we all have insecurities that, by complimenting someone else, gives away something about ourselves that is uncomfortable). Find a way to give five compliments each day, whether it be commenting on what someone is wearing, a new hairstyle, a cute pair of shoes, or whether you comment on something you noticed them doing, something you heard them say that you liked, a positive change you have

noticed they have taken in their lives, etc. But, remember—these must be genuine compliments, otherwise the purpose is defeated.

In our lives, we get so busy and so trapped in ourselves: we are constantly thinking about what WE have to do, what WE have to buy, what WE are dealing with, that we forget about the needs of those around us. Think about that awesome feeling when the Starbucks drive-thru attendant says, "The person before you bought your order". Be that person that does that to someone else. Be altruistic.

While dating someone is so validating and is such a unique experience, we sometimes forget that we can get those same kinds of fulfillment in other ways. For my birthday, Simon was supposed to take me skiing. I was so excited for my newfound love for this sport that I spent every night watching videos, practicing my form, preparing for the next time I could hit the slopes. So when Simon obviously did not take me skiing, I called up a friend and went with her instead. I loved the deep, philosophical conversations that we would have on Wednesday-Night-Date-Night. So, when we broke up, I recruited a few of my friends to engage in intellectual conversations with me instead.

Most importantly, Simon taught me that my method of surviving a break up did in fact work and would probably continue to work, no matter what I went through. I felt a kind of triumphant feat in this way: that no matter what, I wouldn't be broken.

And that sense of agency, realization of choice is powerful.

Yes, relationships require some shifting. At the beginning, you have to learn a lot about each other. You have to adjust your life, make room in your schedule. break ups take even more work. Right now, everything with Simon was so intense that I am not necessarily interested in starting another relationship. I need to take some time away for a while. But, knowing that I have the potential to start and end one without my life being over is incredibly liberating. I am giving myself agency: I have the CHOICE to date whenever I want, and if that relationship fails, I already developed the tools to survive. Right now, however, I am busy writing a book.

Part III:

Prepping for "Prince Charming":
Marriage, Relationships, and Being Single

The Modern Meaning of Marriage

Since dating Simon, I spent some time exploring what it really means to date in the modern world and how I see myself fitting into some of those categories. If the outcome of dating is marriage, I had to work backwards to figure out what I wanted. First, I needed to figure out what marriage meant to me. Next, I needed to look at how I could position my relationships to reach that outcome of marriage. Then, I needed to figure out my dating style, and how choosing who I wanted to date would lead to the kind of relationship that would end in the marriage I wanted. And, in order to do all of that, I needed to figure out who I was as a "single-ite" in society.

It used to be that you met someone, spent a few months dating, realized they did not have some kind of weird disease, and decided to get married. Then, you moved in with each other and the real part of being in a relationship began. In books like, *Gone With the Wind,* Scarlett O'Hara meets her beau somewhere (for Charles, it is at Ashley and Melanie's engagement party, for

Frank, it is at his general store, for Rhett, it is also at Ashley and Melanie's engagement party). Scarlett and each one of her suitor's probably feel 'butterflies' about the relationship, court around for a couple months, throw a marriage celebration, and spend an engagement period, touring the county. It is during this time that Scarlett picks up on Rhett's bad habits: his drinking, his aggressive tendencies, his bad moods and gambling addictions.

Of course, the modern meaning of marriage no longer looks like this Southern-belle style. I discussed this meaning of marriage with a Saudi Arabian immigrant in my graduate class one evening. She came to the U.S. on scholarship with her husband to study English as a second language teaching and we spent some time discussing the differences between American and Saudi Arabian culture. Amongst these topics was marriage. As an ignorant American, I asked how she met her husband; in America, we have these elaborate stories: "Oh he is my best friend's brother", "Oh we met in high school and recently reconnected via Facebook", "I was a waitress and he was a customer", "He accidentally backed into me in the Wal-Mart parking lot and had to pay me restitution and we fell in love and it's been happily ever after". But, of course, that is our romanticized culture. The Saudi Arabian woman replied, "Well, our culture is not like your culture. It doesn't work the same way. In our culture, your mom and your sister find someone they think you might like and they arrange a meeting. If you feel something for him, then you might talk on the phone for a little while and then announce your engagement. It's really important that you marry someone who is a virgin. I don't think I could date in your culture because everyone is so promiscuous and has so many partners. I don't think I could handle my husband being with other people." I thought this was a very accurate perspective on American dating culture.

But, she is exactly correct: the modern meaning of marriage in American culture has indeed changed since Scarlett O'Hara's time. Instead, we meet someone, date them for a really, really long time, move in together to test the waters, and once we decide there are no extreme deal-breaking tendencies (such as, "does he get up too many times in the middle of the night to go to the bathroom that I will never sleep?", or, "does she pick at her teeth after dinner in an annoying way?", or, "will I be able to live with the fact that he has a funny smell coming from his big toe?"), we decide we can sign the piece of paper and marry our significant other. So, when the marriage transaction actually occurs, the learning about each other stage already happened and you just go on life as usual. For many people, it becomes a requirement that you live together before you get married. In 1865, co-habitation would have been unheard of. However, it is almost against societal conventions these days to NOT live together before you get married.

I think this shift can be attributed to a few factors. First of all, with the economic recession in 2007, it became an economic necessity for some people to move in together; why spend $3,000 renting separate apartments, paying for separate cable and internet packages, when you watch the same T.V. and use the same internet all the time anyways? (In a study conducted by Harvard, 36% of college graduates in 2009 moved home with their parents—I am assuming these were mostly the "single-ites" who did not necessarily have a significant other to split the bills with, so the parents had to suffice).

But perhaps more prominent than just an economic necessity, cohabitation allows us to see every single side of a person before making a commitment. Being products of divorced families, we have seen our parents struggle that we want to ensure we will never put our families or ourselves in those painful situations of loneliness and suffering. I think the Millennials are being very picky and taking their time selecting mates to avoid future strife and suffering. We want to know everything about a person before we make that marriage commitment: we want to know who your previous relationships were, so we can figure out if there is a chance of you passing HPV onto us; we want to know how you react when you lose a job or go into your own economic depression; we want to know how you adapt to change and how you interact with children. We saw what our parents went through, we know what we had to go through, and we want to take every precaution possible to make sure we do not go through a divorce ourselves. So, we do the learning about the person prior to the marriage.

In addition to co-habitation, the function of a marriage itself has also shifted in recent decades. It used to be that marriage was seen as two separate spheres coming together to complement each other. This philosophy began in the Victorian era; men were seen as the breadwinners, the protectors, the knowledge to the outside world, and women were seen as the moral and emotional epi-centers, the child providers, the knowledge of the house. The man worked while the woman cooked, cleaned, and took care of the children. The man went out to pubs and coffeehouses to discuss politics, economics, and legal affairs, the woman invited other women to her house to discuss music, church, and social affairs. The idea was that the man and the woman occupied separate spaces, and together, they would complete a whole.

However, with more women earning college degrees and entering the workforce, this old-fashioned marriage structure no longer works. Instead, marriage has become about two people coming together who can do things together. We coined this term, "I want to marry my best friend". Well, a best friend is someone you enjoy being around because you share common interests; it is someone that you can travel with, you can talk about the same kinds of books, you can enjoy viewing the same movies. Today, we expect whoever our significant other is to accompany us on our leisure activities; we want to have a companion. In Victorian society, this type of relationship would never fly. In fact, during the latter half of the era, men started traveling to exotic countries all by themselves in order to get away from these marital constraints and the women were expected to continue remaining idle and stay at home (I honestly can't blame the men though. The idealized "Angel in the House" wife sounds so boring).

It is important to recognize the shift in the function of marriage. I grew up in a predominantly conservative area and do feel pressure to fit this traditional man-breadwinner, woman-housewife kind of role. For some 20-Somethings, this is exactly what they want, and to that, I would say, don't give up on your dreams because these types of traditional marriages often breed the morality and stability that we are missing in our society. But for other 20-Somethings like myself, I know that I would be miserable in this kind of set up. I spent four grueling years (and $80,000) earning a college degree. I fought for my first job and worked very hard to maintain it. For me to dump all of that to be "An Angel in the House" would make me, and many other 20-Somethings, very miserable because our society has opened up so many opportunities for us. More or less, I am not looking for someone to support me, but rather someone who will support me, supporting myself, which looks like a very different potential husband, and completely changes who and how I choose to date.

Recognizing this shift is important because if the ultimate goal of dating is to get married, then it alters the way in which we date. For example, with the greater than 50% divorce rate and rising looming over my head, I know that, as a female in society, I need to ensure independence and stability to protect myself in case something really tragic and unpredictable happens. I personally know so many brilliant women who dropped out of school or quit their jobs all together to be an idle "Angel in the House", and either their husbands lost his jobs, lost his life, or lost their marriages, and the women end up in some really devastating positions, where they are scrambling to make a mortgage payment and put food on the table. An old family friend, for example, met her husband when she was 20 and dropped out of college. They divorced, and she has spent the last four years working part time, selling merchandise part time, and going to school part time to support her three children. They live in a townhouse with three other people and accept food stamps while she finishes her degree. This was never in her plan and had she anticipated a divorce, she probably would have (a) not married him in the first place and (b) probably would have finished her degree and started a career. Knowing that this could definitely be a possibility I know that I need to date someone who allows me to have my independence and my own rainy day fund (My grandma's best advice to me: what's yours is mine and what's mine is mine. She still puts money into her divorce fund, just in case my grandpa, who is 87, dying of Parkinson's disease, and can barely walk, decides to leave her someday).

Or because I take my privilege to vote very seriously, before I decide on a stance, I always make sure I do my research. In the Victorian era, it would have been the man who was the holder of this research. And since women were not allowed to vote, the

"Angel in the House" did not necessarily need this information anyways. But because I can vote, I know that I need to date someone with whom I can share my research with, bounce ideas off of, and who perhaps can help me see the opposing side to an argument. So, while the Victorian woman might be looking for someone who can handle those affairs on his own, and vote for her, the modern woman is looking for someone with whom she can share those conversations with and help her make her own decisions.

I was always under the impression that the way it works is you find someone you love, that you are most compatible with. And, then you love each other so much that you can't live without and you get married. I always thought it was the way you felt about each other that drove everything else. That is it. End of story. Nothing else matters but the fact that you love each other and have the most electric chemistry.

But, the more I think about it, the more I think this fairy tale romance idea is very, very wrong (as depressing as that is). Perhaps just loving someone is not enough after all.

I recently read the part in *Gone With the Wind* where Ashley Wilkes finally declares his love for Scarlett, they make out secretly in the ditch, and then he explains to her how they can never be together because he is a coward and she is valiant and those two characteristics don't go well together. Up until this point, Scarlett has had a very difficult time with Ashley's marriage to Melanie because Scarlett **knows** that Ashley loves her and does not understand why that love is not enough. Ashley, on the other hand, knows that he is a wimp and is not willing to live up to being the man that Scarlett deserves and has to let her go, as painful and heart wrenching as that may be. No, in this case, loving and caring about each other is just not enough.

This scene made me wonder how many real life people cannot be together, despite their passion, their electric chemistry, their strong connection because of some kind of circumstance—whether it be a personality flaw, a job re-location, some kind of past baggage. I feel like so many 20-Somethings are breaking up right now because, "they just aren't in the same places in their lives". They could be completely perfect for each other—check off every single box on their list of what a potential mate must have—and timing, or a job, or an event draws them apart and they cannot be together, no matter how much they care for each other.

This happened to me in some degree. I never quite understood Emily Bronte's quote "Whatever souls are made of, his and mine are the same" from *Wuthering Heights* until recently. Simon, I believe is the male version of myself; nerdy, contemplative, "wanderlustful". He wrote the same way I did, talked about the same concepts I did, enjoyed the same activities I did. And, despite all of those things being perfect and completely compatible, circumstances forlorn us from being together. In this case, love is not enough because other things weigh more heavily.

And, what if what we think we are looking for, what we would be most compatible with, is completely wrong for us? I personally am very attracted to guys who are of the John Grady type—pensive, independent, wise, flighty, reckless. But, this could actually not be very good for me because (a) it probably means I get a guy who is instable and (b) he doesn't really know how to handle his feelings. Another one of my friends was head over heels for this guy—he was smart, ambitious, mature. And then, she realized that his obsession with gluten free, dairy free, carbohydrate free, sugar free, etc. diet would never fit into her eating schedule and probably cause her to die of starvation. Of course, some other things lead to their break up, but my point is that perhaps who we *think* we are compatible with, who we feel this electric chemistry and passion for, may not necessarily be the best option for us. Maybe we need someone a little more mellow, a little less exciting, a little more predictable—because that is what is going to work in the end. As it turns out, who I want to date, and who is good for marriage, can be completely different people. I may really be into a rocker, who gets up and leaves to go travel the world on a moment's notice, and when it comes time for children, he does the same thing, and that won't work.

I am not sure I like this new revelation because it makes me question everything I have been told about 'love' growing up; maybe it is not what I expect it to be and maybe I won't find absolute happiness and romance like they promised and that I will have to compromise a little less chemistry for something a little more stable. It is kind of like when you are in kindergarten you are told that you can be anything you put your mind to. And then you get to college, and realize that you really are not smart enough to get into law school and you should actually probably just be a fry cook at the local diner instead. It's actually kind of depressing to think about how life does in fact have limitations and that there are certain factors that will impede who "Prince Charming" actually ends up being.

I am a firm believer that marriage (and college, for that matter) is not for everyone. There are certain people who are meant to be single for the rest of their lives, which is perfectly acceptable. As a single person, there are so many great benefits. You can do whatever you want, whenever you want. You can save your money for things you want to do, rather than spending on your child's extracurricular activities. You can decide to take any day you want off work to sit around in your underwear and eat Captain Crunch while watching sappy Lifetime movies. So if this is you, excellent. Do not change your 'selfish' ways. We need you kind of people in our society.

However, if you are like me, you really hope to get married in the somewhat near future. I cannot wait for the day I can come home from a long day of teaching and coaching and put my smelly foot in my husband's face and beg him to massage them. I cannot wait for the time I discover I ran out of feminine products and force him to go to the grocery store to pick some more up. I cannot wait to have someone adorn me with compliments and jump at the opportunity to cook me dinner (although, I think I can wait to pick up someone else's sick-ridden used tissues and fold someone else's laundry).

The best-selling book *The Secret* talks about how, if you put something out in the universe, it will likely happen for you; if you want something, you have to act like you have it. If you want to be married, you have to act like you are married; the book suggests altering your sleeping arrangement so you are not starfished in the middle of the bed, but rather sleep off to one side; when you park in your garage, park to the side, as if another car imaginarily fits alongside (in my garage, I am really, really hoping this imaginary car turns out to be something cool, like a Corvette or Porsche), or wearing a pretend wedding ring on your ring finger.

I am not really sure if I believe in going to this extreme. Like, if I wear a pretend wedding ring on my finger, then I am giving a false impression that I am in fact married, and then (a) it scares all the potential eligible bachelor's off, or (b) I have to awkwardly explain to someone why I am wearing a pretend wedding ring on my finger, and then I just sound loony.

But, what I do value in this theory is that if you want to get married at some point in your life, you must keep yourself in the practice of relationship-type skills so that when the time comes, you are able to let someone else in. I have seen too, too many times people who spent the last ten years of their lives, running around, "being selfish", that when they are confronted with a real and serious relationship, they freak and end up derailing it all together because they have not stayed in the practice. Like anything in life, you must practice towards your goals; things do not just happen out of the blue. For example, I knew that I someday wanted to write a book, so I started a blog so I could stay in the practice of writing; if I decided one day to just sit down and write, I probably would have stopped at the first page. But, the more I practice, the more I write, the easier it gets. The same thing is true with athletics. If I wanted to be a faster hurdler, I could not just daydream about it and suddenly become a better hurdler; I had to practice my technique. The same thing is true of marriage: if you want to be married at some point, while you should spend this time "being selfish", you should also open yourself up and continue practicing aspects of a relationship that you might lose being a "single-ite".

In researching what marriage meant to me, I gathered my evidence from a variety of places: old married couples, newly married couples, people I have known my entire life, people I have just met. I have seen some people at the very beginning of their marriages, and witnessed some at the very end. Everyone loves to share their relationship advice with you, so it is never difficult to pull stories out of people.

From my observations and questioning, I learned that marriage looks so different for each couple. Some married couples work for the same companies, carpool to work together, eat lunch together, and go home together. Others work in completely different spheres, leave at different times, work different hours, have different business strengths. Some married couples met at 17 and knew right away they were each other's soul mates. Others go through one or two relationships (sometimes even marriages) before they find each other. Some married couples grew up with the same exact faith. Other married couples grew up Catholic and Jewish and learned to mediate in between. It makes sense that marriage would look so different on each couple because there are so many different kinds of people in the world. What works for some would not work for others (Like, I really need a husband who works a lot and is gone often, but I know other very happily married couples who spend a significant amount of time together).

So, instead of attempting to define what marriage *IS*, I have spent some time thinking about what marriage *IS NOT*.

Marriage is NOT the wedding: Especially in our society, we get so caught up in putting on a big showcase. We traditionally set aside a year, between engagement and wedding, just so that we can ensure enough time to tour the best venue, book the best DJ, choose the best cake. We must have the most unique photographs. Then, we need to have these elaborate bachelorette parties, bridal showers, rehearsal dinners. Our hair and make up must be spectacular, our nails must be perfect, our skin tan and glowing. We spend obscene amounts of money, and stress, throwing a five-hour party. Sometimes, I think we spend so much time planning the wedding that we forget what we are celebrating: the actual marriage. When all the guests go home, the decorations torn down, what we have left are two people, who made a commitment to stick together and tackle the world together for the rest of their lives, no matter what. I think we sometimes get so blinded by the flashiness of weddings and strutting around, impressing everyone with our money and skills and so caught up in the day that we forget what the celebration is actually about.

Like everyone else, being a 20-Something is the season for attending your friends' weddings. Working at the golf course for the last seven summers, I have been afforded the privilege to witness hundreds of weddings; some good, some bad (like the groom who had to be retrieved from Colorado Springs because he refused to attend his own wedding after a debacle the previous night), some a drunken mess (like the one wedding we found the groomsmen in the closet, trying on Rotary vests?), some fun, some awkward (like the one 40 person wedding with an hour private orchestra session, at which the bride and groom were the only ones who enjoyed themselves).

Last summer, I worked a very casual wedding, And, of course, everyone's response to the bride and groom was, "Congratulations on your marriage". Generally, we use this term when someone has worked really hard to achieve something, whether it be a job promotion, some kind of award, or achieved some kind of goal.

So, I started thinking (which is what I do best): When we use this term about a marriage, what are we actually congratulating?...

Are we saying, "Congratulations. You survived the wedding process and didn't die from the stress/drama"?

Are we saying, "Congratulations. Now you can finally take a tax deduction and put more money back in your savings account to pay off those student loans?"

Are we saying, "Congratulations. Your have finally found someone who can latch onto your insecurities and validate your existence. You no longer have to feel like a nobody"?

Are we saying, "Congratulations. You finally found someone who you think is attractive enough to produce children and who will put up with your bad habits"?

Are we saying, "Congratulations. You found someone who can support you so you can quit your job and finally live your dreams of being a stay-at-home husband/wife"?

Are we saying, "Congratulations. You are finally mature enough to stop thinking about yourself and commit to one person" (which, in our society, how often is that really true?)?

Are we saying, "Congratulations. Now you get to enter the really fun part of marriage where you fight all the time, have to compromise your sleeping positions, and adjust to someone else's schedule"?

Are we saying, "Congratulations. You finally decided to join the status quo, do what everyone else is doing, and put on a wedding"?

Now, I don't want you to think that I am anti-marriage because I am not and I love being in a relationship. I completely understand that relationships take hard work, dedication, and sacrifice. Some of my best friends are very happily married and I too hope to gain that experience someday. However, what I think is corrupt is the emphasis society puts on the institution of marriage. By creating a big hoopla out of weddings and saying all this, "Congratulations" crap, as a society, we are kind of making "marriage" the ultimate goal, as if there is ONE thing we are striving for (and in this case, the event being the wedding itself), and that is finding someone who can validate our existence. And, if we don't have a marriage, then our lives don't really count because marriage is the one and only 'goal' that really matters.

Now, I also believe that every girl has her own special "thing". Some of us are going to be the greatest wives and moms in the world ever, and that is what we were put on this earth to do: to teach others to be the greatest wives and mothers; our brains are wired to do best wife and mom things. Some of us are going to be the greatest career women ever. Some of us are going to be the greatest servers, the greatest coaches, the greatest athletes, the greatest horseback riders, etc. Each of us fulfills a specific purpose, but not one of us can fulfill them all.

Society telling us that 'marriage' is the end all-be all goal is kind of rude because what if some of us have other 'things' going on outside of 'finding someone worthy enough to spend our time on'? What if some of us have goals to teach in a foreign country, to construct an energy efficient house, to visit all the restaurants featured in *Diners, Drive In's, and Dives*? Why does it have to be that finding your significant other and getting married is the 'pinnacle' of your life? I would say I personally have put a lot of thought and a lot of work into finding myself and determining what kind of significant other complements me best, so if I ever get married, it will be, "Congratulations, Britany. You overanalyzed everything there is to think about in the world that you finally found someone who you can officially determine is a decent human being". But, not everyone is me—some people just fall into it, no analysis needed.

The next time you are at a wedding, think about what you are saying to the couple when you congratulate them on their marriage. Is your congratulations genuine—is there some kind of significant milestone you believe the couple has reached—or, is your congratulations just perpetuating an unfair social expectation? Perhaps the more appropriate term is, "I am so happy to see you so happy".

Marriage is NOT a guaranteed *happily ever after*: We have this Hollywood-inflicted notion built into our schemas that once you meet your "Prince Charming", nothing bad will ever happen; your marriage will never hit turbulence, you will never disagree on how to discipline your children, you will never look at someone with lustful eyes ever again. Like, suddenly you sign this piece of paper and all of your animal instincts go away because "you are married". Unfortunately, the romance peaks and valleys. You will sleep on the couch some nights because you get into some big, blow up argument about whose turn it is to take out the trash and come to work the next day with bags under your eyes. You feel very bad when you wake up one morning and think to yourself, "I made a big, huge mistake. What was I ever thinking?" because our Hollywood-inflicted ideas tell us *happily ever after* means we should never doubt our marriages. However, marriage is a huge endeavor and we are human. Life is messy, we make mistakes, we are fragile, wounded creatures and are constantly suffering, making selfish choices. We are thrown unforeseen obstacles. Everyone, at some point, questions his or her decision. But, it is those who question those decisions, and then make a commitment to stay together with their spouse, to work through issues, no matter what that stay together and choose to make it as close to a happily ever after as possible.

Marriage is NOT easy: Yes, marriage should not necessarily be hard, but it does require work. During marriage classes, the Catholic Church spends a majority of the time focusing on forgiveness. In a marriage, forgiveness is key. And, if you have ever had to personally forgive someone, you will know that it can be exhausting, it requires introspection, admitting your own faults, your own participation in the act, and letting go of something someone did to hurt you (like Kent's mom). It is very difficult, but absolutely necessary in a marriage. If you plan on spending the rest of your life together, eventually one of you will do something hurtful, and if you want to make it as close to that *happily ever after,* you have to sacrifice something about yourself in order to move forward.

Marriage is NOT two people coming together: I used to think that the way it would work is: there is me, there is him, and then we live together. But, it is actually much more complicated than that. It is more: *this is my side of the bed, this is your side of the bed, this is where we intersect. This is where I sit to do work, oh, and you want to sit here too, so I either have to move or you sit on top of me. This is our favorite meal, but you pick out the mushrooms and I guess I should eat them so we don't waste money. I want to go to Las Vegas next weekend, but you have a softball game, so let's find a fun brewery tour instead.* It is much more about two people learning to mold into one. It is dark blue sometimes, magenta others, and maybe purple when they blend nicely together.

Marriage is NOT finite: One of my favorite places to observe is at the golf course. Interestingly enough, some of the happiest, most in-love couples I see are those on their second marriages, I think because they learned so much from the mistakes made in the first one. As humans, we are always changing, progressing, evolving, both individually and as a couple. What you marry when you are 23 is not what you will die with when you are 103. But, hopefully, you make a commitment to each other to support each other, and your relationship, no matter what changes occur.

Moral of the story is: Marriage is not quite what we think it will be. It is a struggle, it costs us our selfish desires, forces us to question our own strength. But, so I have heard, the reward is so, so worth it.

Now that I knew what marriage was NOT, I began thinking forward thinking to my future and what I want in a marriage and how I want my family to look. If the ultimate goal of dating IS marriage, then I needed to figure out what I wanted that to look like. Dating Kent, these kinds of thoughts had never crossed my mind; I would try really, really hard to envision what our wedding would look like and I could never quite get to even walking down the aisle (and, I tried to avoid thinking about having his children because he was a big guy and I am little girl and that just sounds painful).

It was true that I was not going to marry my high school sweetheart, so I wanted to hear other people's stories. I love hearing people's love stories because it somehow gives me hope for my own.

One of my saving graces was all the old people in my life. Seriously, if you are struggling with a break up, find some old people to talk to. What you will find is they once upon a time went through the same exact obstacles that you are currently going through. Realizing that these emotions and these struggles are innate to human nature is actually very relieving because you start realizing that if they survived and are still relatively kicking, you can too.

I asked these old people the same two simple questions: When did you meet your spouse? How did you know your spouse was 'the one'? I wanted to know, out of all these very successful couples, what the magical component was. I got all kinds of different stories:

The couple at the golf course: He was from Detroit, she was from San Francisco. They were both in Chicago for a fitness and health industry conference. He walked into a bar with his friends.

She was standing with her gay boss, doing their favorite thing: checking out guys together. They were checking out one of his friends. The friend caught their eye, went over to talk to them. He and she started talking, spent the rest of the night hanging out. They both ditched training the rest of the weekend to hang out. Eleven days later (which happened to be Thanksgiving), he borrowed $160 from a friend to buy a plane ticket to visit her in New Jersey. For Christmas, he cancelled his trip home to Minnesota to go out to San Francisco to spend it with her. They dated on and off for six years, switching off months to see each other. They never had any intentions to get married, until she got pregnant, and realized he would not be allowed in the delivery room. So, they marched down to the county courthouse, raised their right hands, and it was happily ever after.

When I visited my friend in Detroit, I spent some time observing her parents. They are perhaps one of the cutest, still most in-love couples I have ever met. They met when they were both students at Michigan State University. Around graduation, the husband pulled his now-wife into her sorority's front room and proposed to her. The couple moved to Florida, she stopped working to take care of the two children, and went back to work later. Now, a thriving business woman, she travels, goes to conferences, works on projects while the husband, retired, stays home and is "the Haus Frau". What I think is so romantic about this couple is the husband says, "My wife scarified her career to raise the kids so I could focus on mine, so now I have to support her as she climbs the corporate ladder".

One of my co-workers's dated a guy for a couple years before they realized religion was too much of a impediment for them to get married. So, she went on her way for a few years. When she was 27, she decided she was going to teach abroad and right after she signed her contract, she met her now-husband. They got engaged four months later, she went to South America to teach, he planned the wedding, and now they have been very happily married for 30 years.

Another one of my friend's met her husband when she was a bartender in Chicago. At the time, she was dating this "way hotter" DJ, and when she realized what a scum he was, dumped him and a few months later, started talking to her husband.

Some dated twenty other people before running into their significant other in a bar (while he was dancing with another girl). Some met their significant others at 23, lost touch, and reconnected at 26. Some met their significant others on a study abroad trip, others through a friend, and more increasingly, some through online dating services. Some experienced that romantic "love at first sight" shindig and others had friendships that grew into relationships.

So, based on my research, here is the one defining conclusion I can give you: **It happens differently for everyone.**

Being a single 20-Something during this time (aka wedding season) can be very intimidating. It's really depressing to see all of your friends who are so happy to get married, and think to yourself, "Ok, so even if I met "Prince Charming" today, I probably want to date him for a year, then we will want to be engaged for another year, so it looks like I will be at least 27 when I get married, and then I will want to wait two years to have kids, which puts me at 29, and I don't want to be an old mom, and I have always wanted six kids, so looks like I will just have to plan on being pregnant between the ages of 29-35, since doctors suggest you stop at 35 anyways". All this thinking and planning and watching the time tick away kind of puts us single 20-Somethings into a panic. Um, hello Prince Charming, show up NOW before I get more gray hairs and become a cat lady and then no one wants me at all!

From what I gather, when it happens, you just know. Something I struggled with when Kent dumped me was the time it would take me time to get to know someone else before I knew I wanted to marry him; at 23, I didn't necessarily have six years again to decide it's not going to work. Kent and I really grew up together; we experienced our high school graduation together, our first drinks as 21 year olds, we endured the stress of college finals together, let go of broken friendships, saw our friends get married (and dumped, and put in detox, and cop cars too). So, when I started dating Simon and wasn't necessarily privy to all this information, I kind of freaked. I didn't know what his college friends were like, what kind of obstacles he had overcome, how he handled stressful situations. And logically, I needed to know those things before I decided if he was a potential husband and getting these crucial elements out of him might take a long time. Then, I realized that I was attracted to the person he was *today*, and that whatever experiences he had previously *crafted* him into that person, positive or negative, so I could be patient in waiting for some of those crucial elements to surface.

For those of us who start dating young, I think we have to spend a longer length of time together to ensure a successful marriage because we do so much changing, shifting, and growing in those post-high school years; we have to make sure the person we are with is changing, shifting, and growing in the same ways that we are. Kent and I obviously did not grow together. But, as research suggests, the older we become, the more rigid our personalities and beliefs become. Yes, marriage is a life altering decision and yes, you should be conscientious and rational about your decisions. So, while it is important to know each other well, perhaps we do not need that six-year dating period as we get older because we already have established a strong enough identity. When it happens, it happens, and it will go quickly. After all, once you get married, you are committed to spending the rest of your life together and getting to know each other.

The conclusion I have arrived to is: **DON'T PANIC**. It happens differently for everyone. We are all at different places in our lives, different stages of development. Just because your three best friends are getting married this summer does not reflect anything about you.

And, when you are in a relationship, those developmental milestones happen differently for everyone as well. You experience your first fight, drop the L bomb, meet each other's families at all different times, even at different times within your own relationships.

Plus, there is some excitement in the unknown. Actually realizing that I may not know right now who I would end up marrying was also relieving because it meant I did not need to focus so much energy on finding a mate. When it was supposed to happen, I would know, and I should just live my life until then.

I began by creating a list of all the things I wanted to accomplish between now and when I die. Writing a book, of course, was at the top. I also included applying to graduate school, teaching in a foreign country, learning to play guitar, reading all of the literary classics, mastering the halfpipe at Copper, visiting all yoga locations. Suddenly, marriage was not so urgent.

Last, I began reflecting on how my own tendencies might show up in a dysfunctional way in marriage. We come from the generation of "50% of marriages end in divorce and rising", which means that many of us come from very broken homes where we did not necessarily grow up watching good examples.

My childhood was extremely dysfunctional and I knew that, if I wanted to have a shot at a successful marriage, I needed to recognize my own dysfunctional tendencies and figure out how I was going to change them.

For example, money was a very touchy subject in my household. We, as the kids kids, felt like business transactions for my parents; they were constantly going to court to get the child support and alimony payments changed. And, none of us kids really ever saw any of that money, so we all got jobs as soon as possible so we could afford daily living expenses. Because of all that tension and stress that surrounded money when I was growing up, I don't even want to deal with it in my adult life; my form of budgeting is to spend less than I make, which will not necessarily work when I have a family. So, I did some research, tried to cut free from my Dutch-spending habits by purchasing some more expensive jeans, got a credit card, and dumped some money into a savings account.

Or, some dysfunctional habits: ultimatums and jabs. My family grew giving ultimatums to each other: "If you call your friend to pick you up, I will break your cell phone"; "If you walk out of this house, I will call the cops and have you arrested"; "If you don't pick me up tomorrow, I am not paying for your field trip". While I knew these were dysfunctional forms of manipulation, I did not realize more minute places they came up in my own life: in my teaching, at home, with my friends. I used to do this with Kent all the time. One time, I got mad at him for not spending enough time talking to me and booked a trip to California to visit a friend and told him once I landed in the airport. Or, if he cancelled plans on me, I would say, "I am glad lacrosse is more important than me" and stop talking to him. No wonder we fought all the time.

Or, perhaps the hardest thing that I have struggled to break because of my parents' divorce and all of the chaos that came of it, my siblings and I learned to raise ourselves, which means that I am very good at taking care of myself, being independent, and not needing anyone's help. While this is great for a single person, it could potentially be hazardous to a relationship because in a relationship, you must learn to mold together and compliment each other; you do this part, I do that. And, not only that, but it could attract me towards guys who take advantage of my independence. Even with Kent, I did everything and accepted no help from him; I did the driving to hang out, I did his homework for him, I did the foot massaging and hand rubbing, and never did I ask for anything in return--because that was my nature, and that was what I was used to. So, I began finding other ways in my daily life that I could learn to give up some of that dependence and rely on other people. I delegated tasks to my assistant coach, asked my friends to pick me up from the airport, let my sister do my laundry (well, actually, she just got tired of seeing it strewn in the hallway). But, recognizing these tendencies, and beginning to break them helped me to prep for my next relationship.

Like unhappily married families, divorced families come with their own set of struggles. I am still not perfect at fixing these things; I still jab, give ultimatums, have anxiety about my money, struggle to let other people help me. But, the important part is that I can recognize those dysfunctional tendencies and make an effort to correct them. I wanted to ensure that, whoever "Prince Charming" ends up to be, I was not carrying unhealthy baggage into our relationship because I do not believe others should suffer from other people's poor choices and behaviors.

Relationships

In order to get to the marriage step, I must also determine what a good relationship looks like to me. I love being in a relationship, I love having a boyfriend. So, what could I offer someone else? If we are talking about being on a time crunch to meet "Prince Charming", then I needed to come prepared with my own ideas of what a successful relationship might look like. If he fits my mold, perfect. If not, then there would be no hard feelings and we would both just move on. Of course, like marriage, relationships come with their own misconceptions:

We are searching for "Mr./Mrs. PERFECT": I am sorry to break it to you, but humans are flawed. There is no such thing as a perfect person. We all have our backgrounds, our judgments, our misconceptions. If you are looking for a "Mr./Mrs. Perfect", you are probably never going to find him/her because he/she/it does not exist. The trick is finding someone with whom you are willing to compromise things about yourself and your own expectations to make it work.

But, the important thing is to have your non-negotiables: No, I will not be with someone who brushes their teeth once a week. No, I will not be with someone who spends more time playing video games than he does talking to me. No, I will not be with someone who wears Birkenstocks and socks.

Relationships shouldn't require any work: Notice that I didn't say "relationships shouldn't be hard". I think there is a difference between a relationship being HARD, one which leaves you physically and emotionally exhausted at the end of every day, where you are constantly arguing or vying for each other's attention, and a relationship that requires work. When you get two humans together, inevitably there is going to be some conflict. You will question each other. You are going to experience some bumps in the road. You will disagree on things, you will fight, scream at each other, and threaten to sleep on the couch. You will experience awkward silences, you will run out of things to say to each other, and you will say things you didn't mean or act in ways that are unconventional to your personality that you will regret. But, what we have to remember is relationships are about learning how to live in tandem with another person. And that takes a little bit of work, mediation, and compromise from both ends.

All relationships should follow a similar set of steps at a similar set of time: I think the worst thing you could do for yourself is compare your relationship to another, whether it be a friend's, a family member's, or a previous relationship you have had. Again, we are all humans and have so many different factors

going on that will determine the speed and strength of a relationship. Just because you aren't in the same place as your best
friend does not mean there is anything wrong with you. Since I
went to high school with Kent, we knew all of the same people
growing up, we knew all of the popular hangouts, the gossip, the
history of each other, etc. Then, I dated Simon, who was completely out of left field and had no connection to my roots whatsoever. So, of course, Kent took less time to get to know because I
was already familiar with his life. With Simon, it took more time
to get to know because I had to explain situations, landmarks,
personalities of my friends, my own background, etc. And, I
would say each situation had benefits and drawbacks; with Kent,
I could share more common experiences with, but with Simon,
who came out of left field because we didn't know many of the
same people, it saved me from lots of gossiping and allowed me
to share other ideas, like big life philosophies. I have even tried
to ask people approximately when your first fight/major argument occurs (because the way that goes is a huge indicator of your
relationship). Some told me three months, others said six. Some
said I love you within the first week, some said it six months in. I
think this is a testament to how each relationship must follow its
own natural pattern. And, for someone like myself who loves order and answers, this is really hard to accept, but also necessary.

We have to reserve ourselves for our "one true only".

No, I don't mean that you should enjoy a bunch of promiscuous behavior. But, I do believe that we are destined and able to
love many different people throughout our lifetimes. One of the
scariest parts about relationships is that we must open ourselves
up to be vulnerable, not just to someone else, but also to ourselves. Being in relationships helps us to learn about ourselves

and can sometimes reveal some uncomfortable notions we have. For example, say you are dating someone who is a Backgammon pro--lives his life to play Backgammon. And you suck at it. Well, this might drudge up some insecurities and anxieties you have about your Backgammon abilities and yourself, which might cause you to be in uncomfortable territory. And, instead of overcoming that discomfort, you just decide to ditch the Backgammon pro and find someone who plays at the same ability level as you. Or, say you are in a relationship with someone who is completely devoted and selfless—someone who is always putting you before themselves, always sending you thoughtful messages, someone who never expects anything in return but appreciation. So, this person starts giving and spending time on you, and you start realizing that you are not willing to give up as much time and effort on them, or that you are psychologically unable to, so you start feeling selfish and begin realizing insecurities and conflicts within yourself that are really uncomfortable to experience. So, instead of re-evaluating yourself, you just decide there is something wrong with the other person because that is easier and less harmful to your sense of self.

After synthesizing these misconceptions, I am aiming to look at relationships in a different way. For one, I am trying to look at how every significant relationship I encounter in my life can teach me something about myself—not just romantic relationships, but also friendships, student-relationships, acquaintances, etc. It is kind of like going through a wringer: when you begin a relationship, you start in one way and by the end, you come out completely different, hopefully as a stronger, wiser, more confident, less selfish, better person. Opting to start a relationship is a scary decision to make, but I think, if you can look at it in this way, whatever the outcome is, it will have been worth your time. This task requires reflection, which is also scary territory because you might have to go back to awkward, uncomfortable, embarrassing things that you did or things that you say (or that love letter you sent that did NOT go the way you had planned). But, if life is about making mistakes and learning and growing, why not allow yourself these very daunting, but also very rewarding, experiences?

And, there are many ways I can prep for my Prince Charming in order to keep myself in relationship practice. I read an article recently that discussed the casualness of 20-Something dating culture, both the jargon and the behavior involved. The article basically said that because we are afraid to put ourselves out there and get hurt, instead of asking someone on a date, we ask them to "hang out". That way, if it goes poorly, we do not have to deal with necessarily being rejected because we can just chalk it up to us "being friends". Girls pay, guys pay, sometimes we split the bill. There is no such thing as courting anymore.

Furthermore, the article also looked at the casualness of hooking up and how hooking up leaves both people unsatisfied. We might selfishly say, "I need this libidinal desire taken care of", so we just randomly hook up with someone for the sake of hooking up, disregarding all emotional attachment because that could be too painful to deal with. Just randomly 'hooking up' with someone leads to this idea of 20-Something selfishness: I want my sexual urges taken care of so I am going to go on some random, meaningless sex spree because it is what I want and what will make me feel better. But, engaging in these activities is supposed to have that emotional attachment, and we are too afraid, leaves us unsatisfied. Sadly enough, we even have songs about this; 'Stay With Me' by Sam Smith has been the top of the charts. If you listen to the lyrics, he basically says, "I know we are not meant to be together, but I am lonely, so stay with me to fill this void". It's not a song about romance and falling in love, but rather being unsatisfied and trying to just selfishly fill that abyss.

In our society, we use this world "selfish" to describe the period of being a "single-ite". We might say, "Since I am footloose and fancy free, this is my time to be selfish". But, I think we have to be careful that we do not abuse that term "selfish". "Selfish" often has a negative connotation and really means lacking consideration for others; only thinking about one's own personal profit or pleasure.

What we need to be careful of, however, is that we are not taking this "I am doing ME" thing too literally. Yes, as a single 20-Something, I am going to focus on myself. I am going to enroll in graduate school because I have the ability to take a night class that no one needs me home in the evenings to cook dinner. Yes, I have the ability to go to yoga every Saturday morning because no one needs me to split chores. Yes, I can stay out late on a Friday night without needing to warn anyone because I am not accountable to anyone else. Those are all things that I am doing for myself that is not necessary detrimental to anyone else's existence. Being completely "selfish" would be running to the front of a buffet line at a wedding because I am ravished and want to get to that perfectly grilled steak before anyone else. Being completely "selfish" would be sprawling out on the couch because you are tired and not leaving any sitting space for your housemates. Being completely "selfish" would mean forcing all of your friends to go to an opera for your birthday because you want to go, even though everyone is bound to fall asleep. We need to be careful that we are not taking advantage of people, but rather just spending this time, developing ourselves with the betterment of an eventual someone else in mind.

For example, I know that someday, I will be expected to cook for my family (unless, of course, my dreams come true and I marry a personal chef). I, like many other 20-Somethings, am a notoriously terrible cook. I once tried to cook breakfast for some of my friends after a sleepover. I left a burner on, the stove erupted, and all the smoke detectors in the house screamed. When I was in college, I never had to worry about feeding anyone else but myself. My dinners would usually consist of a bag of carrots or honey mustard pretzels. I recently tried to cook Spanish rice, and I SWEAR the back of the box said to add milk instead of water. Knowing that cooking is a skill I obviously need to practice for my someday family, I made a goal to cook one new thing a week. Some weeks, this new thing might be heating up store bought orange chicken (a realistic meal when I have kids), other weeks it consists of making risotto from scratch. While statistics suggest I will not get married for four more years, I am practicing the skills I will need *now* so that they are already pristine for later (and by pristine, I mean that I can cook macaroni and cheese without burning the noodles).

Another part of being in a relationship that can easily be lost when we are running around, "being selfish" is accommodating to someone else. Because we are selfish by nature, it is really, really easy to get caught up in yourself. One of my friend's recently asked if she could come visit me for the weekend. On the surface, I pretended to be ecstatic. However, underneath, I was slightly cringing because all I could think about was how she was going to undermine my selfish bedtime rituals of writing on my blog and reading my book. Of course, you need to ensure that how you are serving others is genuine and not "just to get a boyfriend" at some point. I am very fortunate to coach an outstanding group of young women that allow me to practice this skill. When I make my practice schedule, I have to always take into consideration their schedules as well. Like, we probably should not practice at

10 p.m. at night; even though that might be what is best for me, that may not be what is best for them, and I must find a way to compromise. While you may not have a team, there are many other ways you can practice this skill: perhaps it is negotiating a cleaning schedule with your roommates, offering to pick up a shift for a co-worker, managing to meet a friend around his or her busy schedule. As "single-ites", we get so used to accommodating around ourselves, that we forget how to compromise with someone else (a necessary skill in marriage).

Regarding a more serious topic, arguments are an inevitable part of a relationship. The way you approach an argument can really make or break the relationship. I once dated an "older gentlemen" and it ended, in part because he did not know how to deal with confrontation. He spent the last few years of his life just worrying about himself, so he did not need to practice confrontation and argumentation. Instead of approaching me as, "Hey, I think we have a problem and I would like to figure out a solution", he more or less said, "Yeah, um, this isn't working". Looking back on it, I do not think he want it to end this way, but because he approached me in that way, I checked out and did not even bother trying to work things out. While you certainly should not force a bunch of arguments "just to practice arguing", there are ways you can stay in the practice. Whenever my friends tell me about their relationship-arguments, while offering a listening ear and advice, I often put myself in their position and consider, "WWBD" (What would Britany do?). Whenever my roommates argue, which is usually about trivial things, such as pot pies and the sizes of chicken eggs, I think about how I would react. I build schemas and role play situations to test how I might react in order to prep for whomever my "Prince Charming" ends up to be.

Defining My Dating Style

Ok, so if I had a sense of what good relationships require, I needed to turn to dating in order to find that relationship in the first place. I was not ever getting married if I did not at least date someone first. My grandparents, who grew up in small town farming communities, met their sweethearts in high school, got married at 20, and started having children right away (which is why my family's clan has approximately 200 descendants at family reunions). Sorry to say, but the world is much larger, much more connected, and love does not necessarily work this way anymore. The way this modern form of dating usually works is, one night, you go to the bar with one of your friends. That friend will either bring a new friend or you meet someone at the bar, decide you like each other, and exchange phone numbers. You text for a little while, maybe hang out a couple more times with your friends, and then decide you like each other enough to go on a first date. Then, a week or two later, you go on a second date. By the third date, you decide you like each other enough to 'commit' to each other (but, since we are not in high school, you do not change your Facebook relationship status *just* yet). You exclusively date each other for a few months, until one day, someone does something that the other person does not think fondly of, or you just decide you are in different parts of your lives, and you end it. Then, you go through the break up process before you are ready to meet someone else. All in all, the time between meeting each other, determining you like each other, dating each other, breaking up, and healing, this could take anywhere between nine months to two years. And, you might go through this process a couple times before you finally find someone it will work with.

At 23 years old, I was still young enough to have hope of finding love, but not really young enough to waste my time. The way I saw it, even if I met someone *tomorrow,* that would mean we probably would not go on a date until, oh let's say December, when I am pushing 24. Then, we would need to date each other exclusively for a bit; he would need to meet my family, I would need to meet his (and that definitely does not happen until at least date three), probably get a dog together so I can ensure he will be a competent father. We would need to go through some stuff together, talk about marriage, so I would probably be 25. He would need to propose, we would spend at least a year being engaged before we got married, which makes me at least 27. I would want to wait at least two years before we had kids, which brings me to 29. And, like my grandparents, I wanted to raise a family of six and research suggests women should stop having kids at 35, which would mean I needed to pop one out every year until I turned 35? And, of course, if the guy I met tomorrow did not work out, I would need to push my timeline forward a little bit. And, what if I actually did not meet someone for another year? Then I am getting married at 30, starting to have children at 32, and could definitely not pop out six children by age 35, so I would either have to give up my dreams of raising six children, or hope Prince Charming came ASAP.

And, since I had NO idea what my new version of "Prince Charming" was, I knew I would need to test the waters, see what kind of fish were out there, before I started exclusively dating (but still not F.B.O) someone. As it turns out, I am not really good at dating two guys at once. At one point, I was 'texting' (not even really dating) three guys and that was too much for me. I found myself texting while I was driving one time and almost hit a deer grazing on the side of the road and decided three was too much texting for me.

From what I have gathered, many single 20-Somethings feel the same exact anxiety; they feel like the time clock is a-ticking and if they do not find someone to settle down with soon, they will be cat ladies for the rest of their lives. So, I started researching ways that I could get my "Prince Charming" to come rescue me from the tallest, tallest tower.

First, I needed to figure out what love meant to me and what it looks like in the modern world. The first place I began searching was popular culture. And why not? It is interesting because we often use popular culture as a means to instruct how we should live our own lives. Just the other day, I conversed with a gentleman at the golf course. He mentioned that his wife's favorite show is *Real Housewives* and that he noticed a significant change in her after she started watching it; suddenly, she became more materialistic, would talk back to him, expected him to buy her more stuff. Whether we are aware of it or not, popular culture influences our perceptions of the world.

Of course, what better way to deconstruct popular culture than what we are taught in school. I read *Romeo and Juliet* with my freshmen every year, which is my absolute favorite unit to teach to them. I love teaching this unit because when I mention we are reading it they all moan and groan about how terrible it is and "can we just watch the movie instead?" And by the end of the unit, most of them will be saying, "this was my favorite book I have ever read" (Ok, so we read the whole thing in class and could very well be the ONLY book some of them have ever read). I love seeing how immature and squirrely they get when they read, "I have my naked weapon out", and "Thrust the women against the walls", and "I want to take their maidenheads" (this part, of course, requires them to look over at the translation, which means "virginity"—I know when they have read the translation because their faces get red and embarrassed). And, of course, all of the boys rush to read the girl parts so they can speak in high voices and all the girls rush to be Juliet so, like in *A Walk to Remember* or *Boy Meets World*, a boy magically falls in love with their reading of lines.

If you think *Romeo and Juliet* is "the greatest love story of all time", then your English teacher taught you incorrectly. In my class, we spend the entire time making fun of how desperate and impulsive the two "lovers" really are. Like, in the infamous balcony scene, Romeo starts by creeping in the bushes and talking to himself while Juliet seductively strokes her boobs?

One day in class, we were talking about this concept of "Romeo" that we have in our society. We see this everywhere in pop culture: Taylor Swift sings, "Romeo save me, I've been waiting for so long", Jason Aldean says, "You can be my tan-legged Juliet, I'll be your redneck Romeo". When we are growing up, we have these conceptions that we are all searching for our Romeo and if we find him, then we will live happily ever after and have a beautiful wedding, with happy, cheering people, delicious cake, a pretty white dress, never get divorced or have any major problems. We don't really realize all the stress, the sacrifices and compromises we have to make, the disagreeable in-laws and annoying siblings.

Ok, so let's think about Romeo and who he really is. First of all, at the beginning of the play, he is hopelessly in love with another girl (Rosaline) and basically wants to marry her so that he can have sex with her. Rosaline does not want to marry him—her excuse is that she wants to remain a virgin the rest of her life and Romeo spends the first few pages of the play, complaining about how beautiful she is and how her treasures will never be utilized. Red flag #1: Romeo is only in it for the good looks.

So then Romeo spends the entire first act moping around. He walks around in the early morning, crying, not talking to anyone, being a loner, and then sits in his room, by himself, still not talking to anyone all because Rosaline doesn't like him back. He complains that he is not himself and dramatically tells everyone to just leave him alone. His friend, Benvolio, tries to give him advice and say that there are plenty of other fish in the sea and Romeo shoots him down and says there will never be anyone better than Rosaline. Red flag #2: Romeo is extremely sensitive, dramatic, and desperate.

So then, at the end of Act I, Romeo sees Rosaline, she rejects him for a last time, and so instead, he sees Juliet and falls madly in love with her. Red flag #3: Romeo is clingy and is one of those people who must always have a girlfriend.

Um, Romeo does not exactly sound like a guy I would particularly want to date. We can't even call him a "ladies' man" because he only got one girl and the only reason he got her was because her other option, Paris, is ugly and pompous. He seems extremely high maintenance and I wouldn't even know where to start with cleaning his tights.

In our culture, our girls are raised to have this ideal image of Romeo. Or, of "Prince Charming": a man with strong muscles, blonde, flowing locks who will save us from a mean monster and sweep us off our feet. Or, of a Ken, who has stunningly good looks, tans at the beach every day, drives a really nice car, and always has the best gadgets.

So girls, if this is what you are looking for, I think you are going to be sorrowfully disappointed because these guys don't exist. And if they do, I am not sure they are the type you exactly want to be raising your children because they are probably more concerned with their dashing good looks than making sure your child isn't drowning itself in the bath tub....

In our society, we are taught that girls are supposed to be the homemakers—the cookers, cleaners, kid-raisers—and the men are supposed to be the money makers and the disciplinarians. We are taught that our man should always be taller than us, know how to fix a leaky faucet, and buy us red roses on Valentine's Day, our birthday, Christmas, Mother's Day, Father's Day, our first date, FB official, and wedding anniversary, and any time he made us mad to make up for it.

We need to remind ourselves that our Prince Charming's are going to look different for each person because each of us have different goals, experiences, perspectives, motivations. One of my friends loves that her boyfriend has a strong work ethic, even if it means he has to make some sacrifices. On the other hand, I have another friend who wants to spend as much time as possible with her significant other.

If we search for the societal definition of "Prince Charming" or "Romeo", I think we are going to be thoroughly disappointed. The only girl I can think of who would work well with that kind of guy is someone who is meek, quiet, insecure, and immature (which I know none of you really fit that profile anyways).

I, for one, would probably meet Romeo and give him a fake e-mail address if he were to ask for my phone number because I have enough of my own emotions to handle...

Next, I turned to what I thought we would traditionally define as "the greatest love stories": aka Nicholas Sparks' movies. First of all, *The Notebook* is a really cute story and it is really cute that the two old people die 'hand in hand' together. However, I think it is kind of pathetic that Noah buys a house, lives by himself, and desperately waits for Allie to break her engagement and come back to him. I am really happy it worked out for them, but what was his backup plan if it didn't? (And, I couldn't even really get past the first ten minutes of *The Last Song* or *Safe Haven*).

While popular culture did not necessarily teach me what I **wanted,** it did teach me what I did not want. I did not want to be the traditional wimpy, helpless, pathetic damsel in distress character, the kind of girl who can't even lift a stack of menus without help. I need not want to be the needy, clingy, high maintenance type who wanted her boyfriend to go shopping together and get their nails done and go out to dinner every night. Because movies are written and reality television could be manipulated, I began looking at the relationships I knew in my own life.

Research suggests that the brain is not fully developed until 25, so now is the time to explore. In regards to dating, this means pinning variables against each other and looking for the perfect combination. I am very confident that my "Prince Charming" will eventually show up, and so will the other variants of "Prince Charming" for all of my friends, whether he end up being the gym rat or the intellectual lawyer, the Old Navy sales manager or the biker/hiker/mountain biker type. We have to remind ourselves that it will happen when it is supposed to. Some of us already met our "Prince Charming" and just need to meet some more people to solidify that decision. Others of us need to spend more time figuring ourselves out before we can even share that with a significant other. For me, I am in no hurry—I know it probably won't happen for a while (or at least until Christmas time because that is what my psychic said) because I am still searching, meeting, dichotomizing.

I always joke with my friends because on my search, I am not just looking for myself, but also for them as well. While we are all looking for a gentleman, someone who is successful and has acquired strong morals, we are all slightly looking for a different version: one of my friends is looking for someone with chocolate brown eyes, another is looking for someone with a nice body, one more is looking for a lumberjack (My ideal guy was once a Boy Scout). We are single women, flocking together, and looking out for each other.

I thoroughly have enjoyed this process because, although I do not think I have found him yet, exploring other people allows me the opportunity to learn about myself and the world at large. I am taking the approach that every person I meet, good or bad, can teach me something and will lead me closer to knowing what I want in a "Prince Charming" (for example, I learned that I need someone who knows how to spell because I had to un-install an ap for saying, "R U sure U want 2 quit?"...the English teacher in me cringed). You may meet someone who goes to church and youth group and volunteers at the church once a week, and realize that religion is very important to you, or that religion is not important to you. If you are like me, you might have awesome family members who do your laundry and cook dinner for you, so you might realize that you need someone who can accommodate your busy schedule. Or, you might not have a busy schedule like I do, and realize that you want someone who can hang out with you all weekend. Any interaction has potential to be a positive interaction if I make that choice. As much as I rag on social media, I think it is a great tool for us to look into other people's lives and make connections with ourselves. I stalked someone the other day whom I noticed made the same exact goofy, not normal smiling facial expressions as I do in my pictures and decided that I would probably really get along with this person. I asked my roommate if I could go hunting with him sometime, since it is an expedition I have never been on before. Then he said, "Britany, you know you can't talk right?..." and I learned that I probably am not cut out to be a hunter.

From my investigations, I think it can go one of two ways: either spend the whole time looking for a particular kind of person and find someone who fits those exact qualities or you spend the whole time looking for a particular kind of person and end up with someone completely different. One of my mentors said she never expected to end up with a redheaded, 5'10" businessman, but they have been married for twenty years. On the other hand, my sister was looking for someone who grew up in the country, had a strong work ethic, and could be a fix-it man. She found exactly that.

For those of you single ladies, I encourage you to meet as many people as possible. Meeting people is fascinating because you get the opportunity to inquire and learn about someone else's life, even if you experience a clash of opinions or lifestyles; it makes you more confident in your own decisions. I met a guy a couple months ago who made me feel like the most important person in the world (ok, the most important person at the bar...)

and then I met one this weekend who was incredibly vulgar, impolite, and self-absorbed. Both of these experiences allowed me to learn something about myself: the first guy restored my confidence a little that I do deserve the best and the second made me realize just how many douchey guys there are in this world. So, while it would be ideal to find the love of my life every time I go out, both of these experiences are important to my development.

Next, I began thinking about what kind of suitor would fit me and what kind of things I could gain from a relationship. If I knew what marriage meant to me, and I knew what I thought a successful relationship looked like, then I needed to start thinking about what kind of boy fit that. Dating Kent, and then dating Simon gave me very enlightening, and different, experiences to compare. I have been spending some time re-evaluating my past relationships. In an effort to learn from these, I recently have been spending some time pondering the question, "was it HIM I liked, or was it the IDEA of him that I liked?"

As people, I think we really like to have relationships; in particular because relationships validate our existence. We kind of realize this when we go to college: if I don't show up for class one day, virtually no one would know and no one could care. It's fear driven really: I could be laying on my dorm floor somewhere, convulsing, choking on my saliva, and no one would ever think to search for me. We frantically scurry to find relationships so that, just in case we don't wake up one morning, someone notices our absence.

And, we always feel some kind of need to be making some kind of relationship progress, whether it is the step of just getting to know someone, being knee deep in the actual relationship, or getting over a break up; we are always suspended somewhere in between those stages.

In reflecting upon a relationship, something that I think is especially important to determine is whether it was THE PERSON that you were attracted to, or rather the IDEA of having the person that you were attracted to. I have been in both situations.

Now that I reflect back upon it, dating Kent was totally due to the IDEA of being in a relationship. While he was nice and we had some decent moments together, I was more so attracted to the things he offered me. For one, being 18 years old, I was really attracted to the status he offered me. We were the All-American couple; I was the dancer/cheerleader, he was the lacrosse player, and we would parade around places like that together. I LOVED wearing his jersey on game day because it gave me some kind of status as well; people would ask me about him, and I, the proud girlfriend who knew "everything about him" would be able to talk up his game. It was really cute—for 18 year olds. People would joke about us being husband and wife and I would laugh, swat their tri-cep, and say, "Oh stop it".

For two, he was really, really big, which meant that I could run around my dorm in my half-top dance outfit and no one would think to touch me. When I went out on the weekends, no one tried to get fresh with me because they knew him (or at least saw pictures of him) and did not want to get beat up. I never had a problem feeling claustrophobic at concerts because no one wanted to be around him since they couldn't see. To me, he offered a sense of protection.

And, he also allowed me a little bit of stability. It turns out that I am NOT the dating around type. I don't really like having lots of boyfriends. So, while everyone else was going around, dating up a bunch of people, he allowed me to focus on other things: graduating college, getting a job, starting a dance team, etc. We all know that dating requires a ton of work and I would not have been able to accomplish as much as I did had I been required to date up a bunch of people in college.

But, when it really came down to it, there was really not much about HIM that I was really attracted to; it was more the IDEA of him and what he offered me (which is a really terrible thing to say). As it turns out, I haven't been violated, I haven't needed anyone else's protection, and I have made my own name--I don't necessarily need him. I didn't really like the fact that chewed with his mouth open. I didn't really like the fact that he never wore his seatbelt while driving and I never really liked the fact that he only brushed his teeth once a day (I am a four-a-dayer at minimum).

Upon this journey of "understanding why it wouldn't work" and "learning from the past", I have realized that I have no idea what even attracted me to him in the first place—which is an excellent realization to come to because now I know what kind of guys to check off my list. Unfortunately, we usually cannot discern whether we really like a person or the idea of the person until we have already left the relationship; it's not like we date around saying, "I really don't like YOU, but I like that you offer me status, protection, and stability".

I can usually answer this perplexing question based on how difficult it is for me to get over the break up. Yes, breaking up sucks, but it also sheds light on some things that we are often blind to when we are in the relationship. If it is something I just pass off and don't really think too much about, then it was most likely the IDEA of the relationship that I was attracted to, not the actual person. If I don't really miss him and can live my life even better without him, then I probably did not like HIM that much.

However, if I am kind-of screwed up for a while afterwards, then that probably is a good indication that I was attracted to the PERSON, and not just the idea of being in a relationship. Being sad and lonely kind of sucks, but a lot can come out of it, too. I can think of two instances in my life when this actually probably occurred. And, interestingly enough, both of these cases included a very similar kind of guy: a pensive, reckless soul who has a good heart. The first one was when I was in high school and my diaries are so dramatic I can't even handle reading them anymore to extract meaning. In the most recent case, Simon, I realized after we stopped talking that I actually missed talking to HIM. I didn't just miss talking to someone in general like the last one, but there were things I thought he was the only person in the world I could discuss certain things with. I wanted to share my travel adventures, I wanted to share with him my new philosophies in teaching, and even months later, I wanted to share my ultra nerdy revelations from my Victorian Lit class. So because I felt like he was the only one in the world I wanted to share these things with, it was revealed to me that I liked HIM. There was something inherent about him as a person, and not just the idea of him, which is an extremely important revelation for me to come to and really great information for me to now know.

I think deconstructing the idea of a person to the actual person is especially important if there is a possibility of you "getting back together in the future", which one of my friends is currently debating: if she decides she liked HIM originally, then it would be worth her time to try things again; if she decides she only liked the IDEA of him, then she should probably try someone else out and not waste her time.

As 20-Somethings, we tend to have a very pessimistic view of dating these days. We think that because one relationship doesn't work out, it puts us "back at square one". I do not necessarily see it this way. I think that any relationship, no matter how significant or insignificant, gets us one step closer to knowing what we want. I now have these two categories built for myself: boy for boy's sake and boy for idea's sake. I think that, if I can find a boy that offers both together, I will be set.

...but don't worry, my 24 year old self is not currently interested in those ideas of status or protection anymore—it's more a question of who can pay off my student loans or not, who can take me on the nicest plane rides, who can afford to buy me a Greek servant who fans me with olive branches and feeds me grapes all day long...

As it turns out, since I did not really like Kent, but I really did like Simon, I began using that information to inform my search for Prince Charming. Oh where, oh where could I find him?

In *Snow White and the Seven Dwarfs*, Snow White eats an apple, faints, and her "Prince Charming" comes to rescue her with a spell-expelling kiss. The problem with that attempt is I didn't know any witch doctors that could mix up a magical potion.

In *Cinderella* (my favorite), Cinderella loses a glass slipper, "Prince Charming" scours the countryside to find her, fits the slipper perfectly to her foot, and rescues Cinderella from her evil stepmother. The problem with this scenario is I weigh too much to even wear a glass slipper and I see no ball coming up in my near future.

And in *Shrek*, "Prince Charming" actually never arrives at all because it turns out he is a coward. No thank you.

Unfortunately for me, none of these were viable options and I definitely could not risk getting poisoned for "Prince Charming". But, what I did do was devise other ways I could prepare myself for my "Prince Charming" while I was waiting for him to show up. You do not necessarily need to strictly *date* other people to get practice. There are plenty of other ways you can learn.

I first began with learning about myself. The most common advice I get on how to have a successful marriage is to be confident and independent with yourself before you can attach to and share your life with someone else. The break up threw off so many notions I thought I had about myself that turned out to be completely incorrect; I *thought* I enjoyed spending my Saturdays, sleeping in until noon because I was out socializing and partaking in eventful, social activities the night before, but it turns out, I would rather go to bed early so I can make my yoga class and do fun afternoon social activities. I *was not* sure if I ever wanted to have kids, but it turns out, I actually do. I *thought* I wanted a labradoodle puppy, but it turns out they are extremely expensive, I am Dutch, and a rescue from the pound would be just good enough.

I learned about myself through observing the world around me, and tracking my reactions (that is mindfulness at play, folks!). If something happened that made my heart swoon or make me smile, I would put it into my list of "things I like", and if I got really heated, really angry, really disgusted, I knew it was something that did not work for me.

For example, when I went to see a sports' broadcaster speak at a conference, I learned that I actually do not like high society. The broadcaster talked about how, after she graduated college, she worked as intern at a local radio station, submitted a tape to a producer on a whim, and now is best friends with all of these really famous athletes and goes to their houses for dinner all the time. I found myself thinking, "Wow, that is really great for you. But I don't really like people who brag about all the 'celebrities' they know and how cool they are. I would rather talk to someone, like myself, who works with the people in the trenches, who sees the obscurities of the world, who gets invited to normal people's dinner parties (and clad in jeans and a t-shirt is perfectly acceptable) because I sure as hell do not like to dress up that often".

I learned about myself through reading. I read *The Happiness Project,* which is basically about this lady, who decides one day she is not really happy, and spends a year researching ways to be happier, and writes about it. While her ideas about happiness are not necessarily jaw dropping or drastic, she focuses on changes such as cleaning the clutter out of the house, trying to stop nagging her husband, spending more time doing crafts and art projects. I really enjoyed the book, but the entire time I was reading about her apartment and riding the subway and the masses of people, all I could think about is, "Ug I would hate to live in New York. My pores would clog so bad in that pollution."

Or, I went to a festival and my whole day was ruined when someone lit up a cigarette and blew smoke all over the unprepared crowd. All I could rant about all day was how inconsiderate it was for that person to smoke in front of everyone, and how they should have noticed the rest of us were not smoking for a reason. Lesson learned: don't date a smoker.

I took my very first trip to the strip club. It was an incredibly enlightening experience, one that I am glad I now have a firsthand account of, and one that I hope to never have again. Here was my experience: I walked in, saw a mechanical, ride-able penis in the front, laughed so hard I almost peed my pants (due to immaturity) and spent the remainder of our time there sitting very uncomfortably, with my shoulders hunched over, signaling through my body language, "I DARE YOU TO TOUCH ME AND SEE WHAT HAPPENS". From this crouched position, I observed the rest of the customers. It was actually very sad to see the desperation—the strippers, of course, are after money, and they know exactly who to target—the most unfortunate souls who probably don't get any action from anyone else. And, while the play-acting and insincerity of the strippers was apparent to me, it was very sad to me that some of these customers fed so ignorantly on this attention. The whole experience is just kind of a momentary illusion that will not extend past those walls, but it is the stripper's job to make the customer feel some kind of value. So, I probably could not date someone who would require regular trips to the strip club.

Of course, I paid attention to some positive emotions as well. I really liked it when guys held the door open for me, even random strangers. Although I am perfectly capable of opening the door myself, it made me feel respected. I remembered my favorite literary character, John Grady from *All the Pretty Horses* by Cormac McCarthy, and realized that I am attracted to pensive, thoughtful, private, wandering guys. I moved out to the 'countryside' and realized how much I love just sitting on my porch swing, listening to the calming sounds of nature.

I began creating my dichotomist key. Strangely, I found myself doing this process when watching *The Bachelorette* the other night; as the guys stepped out of the car, I immediately starting putting them into "husband" or "not husband" categories (and of course, they all kind of sucked so the "husband" category was *not* very big at all).

We need to date a variety of people in order to (a) figure out what works and what does not work for us and to (b) figure out what works for us. A plethora of second-married couples are so happy because they figured out what did not work in the first marriage, and vowed to prevent that in the second. Dating serves similar purposes.

Of course, we all know that the primary goal of dating is to find a significant other. You go around, meeting a bunch of people, and hope that someday, one encounter blossoms into something a little more. However, I think it is just a little more than *just* stumbling into the right person on a crowded street; through meeting different kinds of people, you start constructing an outline, or a schema, of what you want.

It is actually a very interesting phenomenon. And, the more you date, the more you hone in on what your "Prince Charming" should be. Through each person you meet, you start picking and choosing characteristics that you like, and making note of the ones you don't like. You decide, "Oh, I really like boys who are motivated and passionate in their career, and I really don't like boys who are still in frat-party mode", "Oh, I really like boys who have done some traveling and have cool stories to tell, and I don't really like boys who chew gum like a cow", "Oh, I really like boys who have read a couple of books in their lives, and I don't really like boys who send provocative SnapChats".

You start creating a list of non-negotiables (not interested if he talks about his money all the time, can't go through the rest of my life reading mis-spelled text messages, won't work with a mama's boy). You devise a list of look-for's (Does he drive a truck? Would he be content living away from the city? Is he active and outdoorsy?)—of course, these kinds of things can be adjusted and are not necessarily deal breakers, but if a guy hits on most of these categories, he automatically becomes "potential bait". You know what kind of professions fit your personality well (firefighters, engineers, construction, military, pilots), and those that probably will not (sales-man, insurance agents, "entertainers"). And, you test different traits with your own (Is it better for me to be with someone who is just as Type A as I am, or do I need someone a little more mellow? Am I able to date more than one person at a time, or am I a one-guy kind of girl? Do I need someone who is the same age or someone who is older?). You formulate a list of questions (What is your past relationship experience? How important is religion to you? Do you want to have a family someday? What is your credit score?)

All in all, your job is to construct a "type" for yourself. It's not to say that you end up *exactly* with that type, but ultimately, you do all of this work and this entire meeting people to find out what complements you the best. At this stage in our lives, you get kicked into two categories: (A) husband material or (B) not husband material. If you get kicked into the 'not husband' category, it doesn't necessarily mean you are out of the picture, but my approach with you is probably going to be a little different.

It is quite an existential thought and is like using a dichotomous key in science class. You start with one question: Do I like blondes or brunettes? (Sorry, redhead lovers, since there are generally only two options, your significant other will have to find you another way). This question leads you to another choice: Do I prefer boys who dress well or boys that don't care if their clothes get dirty? And, each person you interact with and each experience you have helps you to refine your "type". I personally have been stuck contemplating characteristics (Do I want a big weight lifter, or someone who does more cardio?) and I will meet someone or have an experience that helps me to make my choice. Or, just recently, I met a guy. He asked me what I did on my weekend, I said I had to take care of my grandma because she got her toe cut off. I thought my comment was funny, he didn't, so I decided I am not going to waste my time on someone who doesn't appreciate my sense of humor. Some of us only have a few questions to answer; others may have hundreds (which, would be me because I am so analytical).

The way I look at it: nothing is a complete waste of time. You might have a really awkward, long drawn out conversation with someone, but then that will just help you to put more traits into your "not husband material" category. You may go on an amazing date with someone that doesn't go anywhere, but then you can put more characteristics into your "husband material" category.

And, at the end of this long, selective process, you hope that there is a knight in shining armor, waiting for you on his stead-fast horse to pull you out of the tower.

The way in which I now date looks a little different. I personally get really tired of the monotonous, "Hi, I am Britany. I am 24 years old, grew up in Colorado, and teach high school English and coach a dance team. What do you do?"

It's so lame and gets so redundant. If I am speed dating a bunch of people, asking the same questions and giving my same answers, dating kind of starts losing the fun and excitement. So, I came up with a list of unique questions to ask people. Of course, I have the advantage because I devised the questions, so I have already thought about how I would answer them. Their responses tell me a few things: first of all, can they handle my sense of humor? If you can't already tell, I am very sarcastic, very cynical, so if they are not able to keep up with me, it most likely is not going to work out.

If you were a kind of cereal, what would you be and why? (I would be Frosted Mini Wheats because I am sweet, wholesome, and crunchy).

If you were to write a book, what would the topic be about? (Surviving a break up, duh! But, I would also like to write a book about my childhood stories, a book about teaching, and a book about coaching young women).

What is the most magical moment of your life? (Mine would definitely be singing and dancing in the V.I.P section of the Disney Princess Parade, but winning a state championship and receiving a standing ovation was pretty awesome as well).

If you had one superpower, what would it be and why? (I would have the ability to go back in time so I can relive some moments in my life).

What is the best place you have ever traveled to? (The Black Forest in Bavaria, Germany by far).

What is the best present you ever gave someone? (The best present I ever gave someone was a car phone charger with a picture of my face plastered to it so the recipient would not have an excuse to forget to call me).

In addition to asking quirky and unexpected questions (that often lend themselves into interesting conversations), I also began paying attention to the kinds of stories someone tells about themselves. As an English teacher, I am a connoisseur of stories, both well-written stories by famous authors and perhaps not-so-well-written stories by students. I love reading and hearing stories for a variety of reasons. Upon meeting a new friend, instead of asking her, "What is your favorite color?" and "Who is your role model?", I try to share a story about myself and ask for her to share a story in return. If you pay very close attention, the stories people tell about themselves can be a much more accurate indicator of who they are as people than any of these typical interview questions will ever be. Depending on the stories, you can determine (a) how they feel about themselves, (b) how they feel about other people, (c) what kind of reactions they have in certain situations, (d) what kind of beliefs they have, (e) what insecurities might be looming—basically, how they view and get along in the world.

For example, you might ask someone to tell you a story about the most magical moment in his/her life. They might respond with something about walking outside with a loved one while the snow gently blanketed their jackets while they heard the melodious sounds of the drunks at the bar across the street. They might respond with something about scoring a game-winning touchdown in the last ten seconds. Or, if they are like me, they might respond with that story about being 20 years old and being asked to sit in the V.I.P. section of the Disney Princess Parade while Cinderella and her fairy godmother sprinkled glitter all over....

We are all warehouses of stories: things we have done, seen, tried, failed, regretted, learned from. The experiences we have make us the people we are today, whether those experiences are positive, negative, neutral. So, next time you are conversing with people, pay attention to the stories they tell about their lives; it will be more telling about who they are as people than any lame interview question you could ever ask.

My new dating checklist looks a little different, a little more solid than before. Instead of focusing on menial characteristics, I am focusing on character; I would much rather be with someone who perhaps makes some bad decisions but is overall a good person. In thinking about Kent, Simon, and all the other lovely gentlemen I met along the way, I created a new dating checklist for myself.

1. **Must be respectful of women:** Call me old-fashioned, but I believe that women should be respected. We sacrifice our last names, sacrifice our bodies to have children, sacrifice our jobs for our husband's. I love it when a guy calls me 'ma'am', knows how to swing dance or waltz. Although I can certainly do it on my own, I love it when a guy holds the door open for me, carries my bags, pulls out my chair. I need my boundaries respected, my needs met, my intellect challenged. In a previous life, I was probably a Scarlett O'Hara. And, if you show me that respect, I

will in turn take care of you and show you the same level of respect that a woman should show a man.

2. Must be willing to solve problems: Learning how to argue and solve problems together is crucial in a relationship. Whenever I got into an argument with Kent, it would always end in us screaming at each other, me hysterically crying, him blaming me for everything that happened. Feelings were hurt and we never got anywhere. I can say I did and said somethings that were completely out of my character and I am ashamed of to this day. I am not really into that kind of "passionate" relationship anymore; it is too much work, too frustrating, too energy draining. Life is messy, unexpected things come up. You are bound to disagree with your significant other and make each other mad. HOW you solve those problems, however, is more important than the actual disagreement itself. I am a problem solver and need someone who is willing to problem solve with me. If his first instinct at a crossroads is to turn around and run, then I am not really interested.

3. Must have a sister:...or close girl cousin, or mom who was a teacher...I have found that the most respectful gentleman had some kind of significant female presence in his life. My poor brother grew up with four women in the house (he is the youngest). We used to paint his fingernails, make him walk around the house in dresses and heels. His favorite color until he went to kindergarten (for the second time) was pink. But, now that he has a girlfriend, he treats her very well. He understands that women have mood swings, they can be irrational and emotional. He understands that it is his role to fix things, lift heavy things, light the barbecue grill. So, I need someone who understand women because we all know woman is a complicated and charged "term".

4. Must be goal oriented: As mentioned previously, I am highly motivated by goals. They keep us from becoming stagnant and plateauing in our lives. I think that, as 20-Somethings who are out of college, we tend to stop setting goals for ourselves because we don't see an immediate need any longer. We may not need to build our resumes to get a job, take challenging classes to get into grad school, save our money to pay rent, etc. I am constantly setting goals for myself because I never want to stop learning, growing, and progressing., even if those goals are small, such as cook one new thing a week (this week, it was making frozen orange juice?) or create a new outfit to wear to work (mainly just to motivate me to wake up in the morning). To keep up with my crazy, busy, awesome life, I need someone who shares a similar drive.

5. Must have some life experience: I know that I have certainly been through some life experiences and, although I suffered during, I know that each one of those obstacles led me to the person I am today—and I am very grateful for that. Some of the strongest relationships I have seen stem from people who have overcome something in their lives, whether it be a divorce, an injury, disease/cancer, a substance abuse issue, etc. I now know that life will never stop spurting out problems and obstacles, so I want to be sure I am with someone who is going to tackle those things head on with me and come out on top. The best indicator of future behavior IS past behavior and I want someone who has proven his strength, courage, and resiliency.

I have been interviewing other 20-Somethings and asking them about what qualities their perfect significant other should have. The responses are typically something like, "tall dark and handsome", "successful", "doesn't have a lot of baggage".

Yes, as a 20-Something, I do not necessarily want to be with someone who has credit card debt, who struggles to manage his money, who can't do his own laundry or clean his own house. But, what about the other kind of baggage?

As young women, we often find ourselves judging people who have been through hard times. We don't want to be with someone who has already had a divorce, who has a child, who had a life changing injury or some kind of family drama, has already gone through some kind of rehab. To us, this signals that this person could perhaps be "broken" and "unstable" and we might have to compromise something about ourselves for this person (because, after all, 20-Somethings are very self involved).

But, what about those who have had some kind of significant event in their lives that we might deem as "baggage", but have taken the necessary steps to heal, overcome, and triumph above it? To me, this would be an indicator towards the quality of their character. And, the best predictor of future behavior is past behavior. The older I get, the more I realize life sucks. As I said previously, when I graduated college, I thought I had finally gotten through "the hard stuff". Now, as I get older, I am learning that the world really is an unfair and problematic place. Sometimes, I feel like I am hit with problem after problem; my projector breaks, the copy machine breaks, my sister's truck breaks, my car breaks (ok, that could have been my fault...). I am realizing that these kind of things will never cease; there will always be something to deal with; life is never going to be peachy keen, no matter how hard you try to control that. So, someone who might have overcome some of this "baggage" proves that they would be able to get over these life obstacles with composure and optimism. It also suggests that they have a strong character, are willing to learn from their mistakes, and have some kind of depth; I mean, who wants to talk about the weather with your significant other for the rest of your life?

Yes, it is all a matter of perspective and yes, some of us haven't had the opportunity to be in situations where we would carry this "baggage". I would say my life has confronted me with a plethora of obstacles; between my parents' divorce, my dysfunctional family, living with roommates, job searching, paying bills, Kent, etc.—I have definitely had my fair share that some may consider "baggage". And, each one tests a different part of my character and through each obstacle, I learn to become a stronger person and to not be so stressed/anxious in the future. Although it may not have been ideal to go through some of these experiences, each one has shaped me to be the person I am today and has taught me a great deal about resiliency.

So perhaps as young 20-Somethings, we need to be careful about what we consider "baggage". Yes, we should be cautious about our relationships, Yes, there certainly are many red flags we should be looking for. But perhaps we need to re-consider this term "baggage"; we all have something we are not necessarily publicly announcing; because perhaps it could signal the beginning of a healthy and appreciative relationship.

Combating Anxieties 20-Something's Face

$\mathcal{I}$n addition to compiling a list of non-negotiables, I also started compiling a list of all the anxieties 20-Somethings feel when dating, and I began de-bunking them, to my own taste.

ANXIETY: "ALL THAT I ATTRACT ARE DOUCHEBAGS"

I would argue that attracting douchebags serves a sort of function. We all have to date some not-so-good choices so that we learn to appreciate a good choice when it comes. I personally never attract douchebags because as soon as I tell them I am an English teacher, they realize they never paid attention during grammar instruction probably because they were doing douchey things to the teacher, they can't spell, are unwilling to take the time to use spell check, so they don't even bother continuing the relationship.

If you are worried that all you attract are douchebags, then maybe you need to indulge in some introspection as to why you are attracting those douchebags in the first place. Is it because you are so caught up in finding a super attractive mate that you only go for the GQ model who is cocky? Is it because you only search for potential mates at bar, where everyone is drunk, out of control, and just looking for a hook up? Is it because you wear super skimpy clothes that sends the message, "I am easy", and attracts those kinds of individuals?

I always tell my dancers and students: dress like the kinds of people you intend to attract: If your intentions are to attract a horn dog, then certainly wear a tight skirt, low cut top, and stiletto heels. I am not saying you can't dress like a slut because sometimes we need to do that to caress our egos and exert our feminine powers, but just be aware of the kind of message you are sending—and the kind of person you are most likely attracting. I personally do not expect to meet my future husband at the bar anymore. When I go out, it is usually to people watch, spend time with my girlfriends, and put on my dancing shoes. I have been known to tie a jacket around my waist or wear my Birkenstocks or do the chicken wing dance to deter potentially creepy guys because, at the end of the day, it is about ME having fun—not about me having to ward off pervs.

Or, perhaps there are some deeper underlying issues that cause you to attract douchebags. Perhaps you date the douche-bag who walks all over you and treats you poorly because you, yourself, do not have much self worth. Maybe you do not feel you deserve any better. Maybe your parents never said, "I love you", maybe your dad left your family when you were a child, maybe you never knew your dad. But, if you are attracting a

HAPPILY NEVER AFTER: A 20-SOMETHING'S ...

douchebag for any of these reasons, there is something more going on, and if you want to eventually have a successful marriage to a non-douchebag, it might be important to recognize that now. Because no one deserves to be in a douche relationship. The good news is, at this point in our lives, we hopefully have good enough health insurance that can take us to counseling so we can take charge of those dysfunctional tendencies; we have the power to alter our paths.

Most likely, if something keeps happening over and over again, it is probably you. So, if you fear that you will end up with a douchebag because no one else seems to be attracted to you, perhaps it is time to change something about yourself. Remember that YOU have the choice to date whoever, whenever, whatever you want. No one said you had to date the douchebag.

ANXIETY: "I MUST ALWAYS BE DATING"

Anytime we as "single-ites" go anywhere, people are always trying to hook us up, as if there is something wrong with us if we do not have a significant other.

If dating is practice for the big kahuna later on (aka marriage), I sometimes feel that, if I am not constantly dating, then I am not getting in that practice, and there is a good probability I will end up alone, that crazy cat lady. After Kent dumped me, I was really eager to get myself back into the dating circuit. I identified all of the problems in our relationship, I came up with a list of potential solutions if those happen again, and I was ready to try my hypotheses. Boom. I needed to find my future husband ASAP.

I sometimes also feel that, if I am not running through and testing a bunch of guys out, then I will never find my "Prince

Charming". It is about quantity: the more I date, the more types I can assess, the more likely I am to find "Prince Charming".

But, the real world does not work like *The Bachelor*. I do not have 20 guys at my disposal and I do not eliminate one each week until I am left with "The One".

What I remind myself is that, at the end of the day, I am just looking for ONE "Prince Charming". I really just need ONE. I could date fifty guys, or I could date one and still probably end up with the same outcome. While I think it is important to put yourself out there, I do not necessarily think it is absolutely required to be constantly dating someone. I see so many girls who just run through guy after guy after guy because they feel this perpetual need to get married and for some reason, they think that if they do not constantly have a boyfriend, they are not on track to get married. For most people, it is when you are not even looking (and not being desperate) that you find "Prince Charming". I realized that, if I dated a bunch of guys, had a bunch of really strong connections and inside jokes and "specifically us" moments together, I would probably desensitize myself to the great things relationships brings; suddenly, one would run into the other, and being in a relationship would not be as exciting anymore. I wanted ensure that, whoever my future husband ends up being, I am saving those special, intense moments for him.

And, as it turns out, I actually really hate dating. It is the demise of my soul. It makes me feel guilty, it's often a waste of my time. It forces me to reject people, break hearts, say and do things that are out of my character. The good news is, "Prince Charming" probably hates dating for all the exact same reasons as I do. No need to serial date to find him because he is most likely fishing right now anyways.

ANXIETY: "I CAN'T MEET ANYONE"

The thing about dating is, you have to put yourself out there. If you are hermitting in your house during the week and hanging out with the same friends on the weekends, you are likely not meeting anyone new, and if any of those people were potential bait, you would have dated them now already. And then yes, your options will be a little limited.

Many of my friends in this case turn to dating websites and aps to help them meet someone new. For some situations, I believe that online dating is a great way to connect people who would not normally cross paths. However, I am not sure about some of those dating aps because they often seem to function as a hook-up finders. Many of my friends use these aps because "they can't meet anyone else" and then they wonder why their dates always end up being creepy, pervy, and chauvinistic. It goes back to the attracting a douchebag argument: know your platform. If you want to attract these kinds of men who are only looking for a good time, then of course date off aps. One of my friends dated one of those "older gentlemen" for a few months that she met off a dating ap He supposedly worked for the government, busting up the Mexican cartel and told her she was not allowed to go downtown because it was too dangerous. Then, he "used his FBI" privileges to hack into her Facebook account and started messaging threats to all the guys on her friend's list. Yes, a real winner. But, if you are looking for someone who is committed, kind-hearted, and prude, then church is probably a much better venue to do that in.

After Kent dumped me, I really felt this anxiety. I spent the last six years of my life intentionally NOT meeting any new potential suitors. And I knew sitting at my house was not going to introduce me to anyone new. So, I had to figure out how to build my base back up again.

Making lists always seems to be a way to cure my anxiety, so I began making a list of all the places I could meet a potential "Prince Charming".

The next time it snows, I could slowly drift my car into a ditch and say I "hit a patch of ice". That way, I can meet anyone who stops by to offer to help. And, if they look really old and creepy, I can just run inside my car and lock the doors.

There is a small airport up the street, so my sister and I were thinking that we could accidentally trip over one of the landing strips and hope the planes see us before taking off. Pilots are great suitors, correct?

We could also accidentally light the fireplace on fire and call the fire department to come put it out. We have renter's insurance, right?

Or, some day when the neighbors are outside, we were thinking that my sister could drop me off and I could pretend I am on a long run (but really, I would just run a couple of feet) and stop in front of the house to "stretch" provocatively, and then have my sister pick me up at the bottom of the street (we live on five acres, so the houses are kind of far apart—it would be too much running to just do it by myself).

We could drive around with the dogs in the car and then let them out in front of someone's house and go running after them because we have "been looking for our dogs for hours now!" Or, we could do what my older sister and I did when we were younger—make a sign that says, "WE NEED FRIENDS" and post it on the mailbox.

In reality, however, there are so many places I go to and so many places I gained social membership that allots plenty of opportunities to meet new people: teacher trainings, concerts, weddings, yoga classes, church, the ever-so-romantic grocery store or parking lot run in/over. Or, just hanging out with different groups of friends allows me the potential to meet someone new.

Engaging in new activities is also a great way to meet new people. One of my co-workers met her husband while playing ultimate Frisbee and they have been together for over twenty years. I joined an adult softball league this last spring. I never turn down an opportunity to meet new people because you just never know. Did I meet my future husband playing softball? No. My team was a bunch of mismatched players between the ages of 20 and 65. But, I did have a great time and made some new friends. And who knows, those new friends could have a brother, a cousin, another male friend. People love setting other people up on blind dates (I think because it is really entertaining for the outsider to watch the awkwardness ensue), so as long as I put myself out there, I should not be afraid that my "Prince Charming" will never show up.

Once I realized how many potential places I could meet "Prince Charming", I started not worrying about it. It seems a little counterintuitive, especially for someone so Type A like myself; once I realized I would not be able to predict when and where I would meet "Prince Charming", I stopped worrying about it because I knew it would take all the fun and excitement and magic out of it when it actually happened. So for now, I just have to believe that it will actually happen, that it will happen when it is supposed to, and I am supposed to just be focusing on something else right now. As George Michael reminds me, I "just gotta have faith".

ANXIETY: "I DON'T WANT TO GO THROUGH MEETING ANYONE ELSE"

When we have been in these long-term relationships, we have a tendency to get comfortable. We recognize the work and the time it takes to break up, date around, and find someone else to start a new relationship with. Being in my mid-twenties, sometimes I feel like the time clock is ticking and sometimes I do seem to panic. A couple of my friends are currently in long term relationships; they met in college, started dating, and are now thinking about marriage because "that is the natural thing to do". I was totally in this position with Kent; I already knew how to make him mad, he already knew where all my ticklish spots were; we had this routine of hanging out every weekend, and would always just eat at Qdoba. It was easy, convenient. I would say, "I mean, I love him and we work well together. I don't really like his addiction to reality television, but I think I can live with it because I really don't want to have to find someone else".

My response: We are now 24, which means that we are looking at hopefully spending the next 86 years with someone else. Why make a decision that fulfills your desires in the short term when you have the long term to suffer? My question to my friends is always: What do you want your quality of life to look like?

For me, my quality of life is the most important thing, hands down. I want to be doing what I want, having fun, learning, connecting, and making the most meaning out of life all the time. I recently visited one of my friend's at her office building. It was a flat plane of little partitioned cubicles. All I could hear was the silent "type-type-type" of people "working". Some people were listening to music, some had their feet on the desk, others were staring at blank spreadsheets and catching up on the latest episode of *Orange is the New Black*. If someone had a question, they would try, as inconspicuously as possible, to roll over to someone else's "office space" and whisper the question. Of course, since the only other noise was the "type-type-type" of the keyboards, everyone could hear the question anyways. All I could think about the entire time was how miserable I would be in this environment. No thanks, I will stick to my meager teacher salary and continue talking as loud as I want.

As Americans, we love working and we love making money. The more we work, the more money we make, the more nice things we can afford. We get our paychecks, we get excited about how much money we made, and we work even more to make even more money. It's a vicious cycle.

I am completely guilty of this. Despite the fact I teach high school English and coach a dance team, I still work at the same golf course I began at when I graduated high school. As anyone in the service industry knows, Fridays, Saturdays, and Sundays are the best shifts. I am motivated by money, so I would work all day, every day on Fridays, Saturdays, and Sundays. Most weekends, I would probably pool between $500-$600, which, as a poor college student, and now a poor teacher, is very attractive. My family would take trips to Iowa, my friends would want to go to concerts, and I would always turn down those opportunities because I had to make money. Taking off a Saturday night could mean the difference between me buying 100 thread count or 400 thread count sheets for my dorm bed. Or, the difference between me eating at Whole Foods, or Sprouts. And, as I graduated and started my first job, I had this same exact mentality. Despite the fact that I work a salaried job, I could not give up those incredibly lucrative weekend shifts because money "makes our lives easier". I sometimes taught all week, worked at the golf course all weekend, and started my Mondays completely exhausted, unprepared, with no good weekend stories to share. I constantly ate on the run because I didn't have time to go to the grocery store, my dad offered to do my laundry to save me from wearing dirty, wrinkled clothes because I didn't have time to do that either. I often lesson planned during my bev cart shifts and forget ever sleeping! I worked all day, all night, and was never able to enjoy the proceeds because my life was just work; my bank account surely grew, but my quality of life did not. This is the American way of life.

I think this is partially why Americans are so addicted to substances: coffee, alcohol, fast food, etc. We live in such a fast paced society and we feel the need to constantly be on the go, constantly be working, constantly one-upping everyone else, that we don't take time to enjoy our lives and we have to rely on other substances to get us through our days.

The Italians, on the other hand, live a much slower life-style. The Italians value their quality of life. I remember visiting Italy on my European excursion and feeling very perturbed that I could not do my tourist-y stuff during the afternoon. No business or learning occurs approximately 11-1 because every-one goes home to have lunch with their families and take a siesta before returning to everyday activities. As an American, this didn't make sense to me; why close when you could be making money? But, then I noticed all the men sitting in cafes, laughing and telling stories—enjoying each other's company and acting as though there is not a care in the world. Sure, their economy might be tanking and businesses might be suffering, but there is something to be said about this slower-paced lifestyle.

Since my existential crisis, I re-evaluated my life and my priorities. It is very easy to get caught up in wanting to make as much money as possible. But, what is your quality of life if you are working fourteen hour days, constantly exhausted and having to run on twelve cups of coffee a day because you get up early and get home late, and spend your one day off catching up on things, such as bills, grocery shopping, and laundry? What happens when you work so much that you can't even enjoy the money you are making? Or, what happens when you spend the rest of your life, 'devoted' to living with a dead-beat significant other? It just sits and collects dust.

Just like money, because so much of what we do is centered around relationships, relationships play an enormous part in our quality of life. I certainly would much rather spend a little more time waiting for "Prince Charming" to come around to ensure happiness in the long term rather than just be with some-one because "it is comfortable". I can suffer for the next four years of my life (statistics say I should be married by 27)

NAVIGATING AS A SINGLE-ITE

For some unknown reason, an urge arouse to re-read *Gone With the Wind* before writing this book. In the beginning, Scarlett O'Hara is 16 years old—prime-marrying age. She attends a party in which she is the center of attention and attracts a plethora of potential suitors (My favorite part is when Charles Hamilton confesses his love to her and her response is, "Ummmm....."). Everything she does is targeted towards enticing someone to marry her—in the way she dresses, the girls she chooses to engage in conversation, the way she eats (or, doesn't eat in that matter—her nanny forces her to eat before they go to the party so she doesn't over indulge herself and ward off potential husbands).

In my senior class this past year, we also talked about this same 'marriage' issue in accordance to *Fahrenheit 451*. In one of the sections we read, Montag (the main character) asks his wife, Mildred, where and when they met—neither of them can remember. In one conversation, Mildred and her friends talk about having children. One lady says, "I have had two children by C-section. No use going through all that agony for a baby. The world must reproduce, the race must go on. Besides, they sometimes look just like you, and that's nice". Another friend talks about how she re-married right after her husband died, just for the purpose of being married.

Both of these diverging literary works have caused me to think about this idea of singleness and the "need for marriage". For one, in Scarlett O'Hara's world, if you are not married by a certain age, it means that there is something unattractive and unavoidably wrong with you; maybe you have a huge, hairy mole on your face or you did something to earn a poor reputation (like Rhett Butler). Maybe your family earned a disgraced name or you were involved in an unfortunate accident. Basically age seventeen, if you are not slotted to be married, it means that you failed at attracting men, and that is a bad, bad thing. Even Melanie, the pale, sickly, cadaverous, meek girl got married...

In *Fahrenheit 451*, marriage really means nothing; they do it because society tells them they must have a significant other and they must reproduce children, but, as signified by Montag and his wife, there isn't any real attraction, real emotion, real reason TO get married. Mildred's friend, in fact, gets married right after her husband dies so she doesn't have to deal with the pain and agony of his absence; she just moves on, like an assembly line, to the next. What is exceedingly eerie about Bradbury's "dystopian society" is the presence of these relationships in our own society. How many people do you know who are on their second, third, fourth marriage? The first one didn't work out, so we might as well just throw it out and move onto a new one, hoping it will be different.

I know quite a few 20-Somethings whose sole purpose right now is to **GET MARRIED** (some of us are even in some widespread panic to "find the right one, right now"). Everything they do, everywhere they go, every conversation they have revolves around marriage. I cannot judge because I certainly occupy this space myself. After Kent and I broke up, the men could probably track the desperate-for-a-mate smell that reaped through my pores (which is probably why none of the approached me). But, I think we sometimes get so caught up in the here and now that we forget about what marriage is supposed to be about—we forgot that we are supposed to be devoted to that person for the rest of our lives, and making a rash, ignorant decision at 21 or 22 could jeopardize very important aspects of our futures.

Now, I don't want to make it seem like I am anti-marrying-young because I do believe that meeting our soul mates comes at a different time for each of us. However, I don't think that being single should necessarily be given the negative social stigma that it often does. How many times have you gone to a relative's house and the first question they ask you is, "So, are you seeing anyone?" And, you respond with, "NO", and they respond with a somber, "oooohhhhh", and you feel like you have let them down? I think society has taught us that, if you don't have a significant other, it means that you have failed at something in life and there is something really wrong with you. Yes, maybe in Scarlett O'Hara's time period, this could be true because the life span was so much shorter, but thanks to modern medicine, our lives now span at least 83 years (my grandpa just recently obtained a prescription for nightmares—I didn't even know that existed!)

I remember when Kent dumped me, I was in a very tumultuous state of being; "If I am not going to marry Kent, then what if I get stuck with someone that I don't love, that I am not attracted to, that I don't get along with?" And, then I realized that I have a **CHOICE** in whom I want to date and whom I eventually want to marry; this is the 21st century and no one was going to force me to do anything I did not want to do. Realizing that I have a choice was the most liberating and empowering epiphany I had (especially since I am a little oppositional-defiant).

Right now, I am *choosing* to be single because it means that I am not settling. I encourage all of you "single-ites" out there to embrace your singleness because it no longer means there is something wrong with you—it just means that you are choosing to be picky and true to yourself.

I think, during this season of my life, I am meant to navigate the world by myself. I am meant to attend my friend's weddings as a "single-ite", I am meant to eat bags of carrots for dinner because I am busy doing other things, I am meant to go to my yoga class whenever I want to. I think I had to learn how to be myself before I could share that with someone else, and I have complete faith that, whenever that time comes, it will be well worth the wait. There are quite a few benefits to being single:

1. I don't have to check in with anyone: When I am at work, I don't have to constantly check in with someone. I don't get fifty text messages from someone, wondering why I am not responding and then consequently getting mad and blowing up my phone. In fact, I often just leave my phone in my car. I have absolutely no obligation to call anyone back, respond to any messages I don't want to, be home at certain times. I can leave my house when I want, go on an extended trip when I like, and not talk to anyone at all when I need my alone time. Today, for example, I started my day at school. Then, I decided I wanted to go shopping and after, I met a friend for happy hour. No one cared where I was, what time I would be done, how much money I spent shopping. Someone texts me on my way home and wants to meet for ice cream? Sure, I will be there in a jiffy! I can do what I want, when I want.

2. I can travel all by myself: When traveling with a significant other, it doubles the cost. You have to purchase two plane tickets, two dinners, two prescriptions of Xanax. You have to chit-chat about what restaurant you want to eat at, discuss what part of the restaurant you want to sit at (inside or out? upstairs or downstairs? bar or dining room?), figure out whose turn it is to pay the bill, blah, blah blah—all of those decisions that suck out so much time and energy because you are trying to compromise with the other person. If I want to take a trip to Egypt, I buy myself a ticket, drive myself to the airport, eat what I want, sit where I want (on Southwest, there are way more seating options when you travel alone). I can plug in my music, take a nap, grade papers, or strike up a conversation with my neighbor—whatever I want. No one else cares.

3. No one cares who I talk to: Since becoming a "single-ite", I have attended two really great weddings. I arrive to the wedding, by myself, and leave the wedding, by myself. I can talk to whomever I want, dance with whomever I want, sit next to whomever I want. I don't feel responsible to introduce my dead-weight-significant-other to anyone and force awkward conversation. I don't feel bad when I want to tear up the dance floor and my dead-weight-significant-other is being self-conscious and refusing to dance. I don't have to worry about my dead-weight-significant other pouting and wanting to leave early because oh, wait, I can leave whenever I want. Oh, and, I only have to buy a gift from me, aka one person, not two.

4. I don't have to worry about getting in arguments with someone: I feel very privileged that so many of my friends share their arguments with me, or feel comfortable enough to actually argue with their significant others in front of me. That makes me feel like a very special person in your life, since you trust me enough to share your inner most insecurities. I am so happy to be your confidant. And seeing these arguments reminds me just how much inner turmoil, distress, and work they take. Of course, I completely recognize that disagreements are inevitable and necessary in every relationship; that is how you strengthen your bond and get to know each other better. I just think about all the really taxing arguments Kent and I had and I am so glad I don't have to sacrifice myself, my sleep, or my time "trying to work things out" right now. Instead, I can role play through other people's arguments, and still go to bed, with no one upset with me.

5. I don't have to go to functions I don't want to go to: There is nothing more upsetting than having to miss out on a really fun party because your significant other's brother is in town and there is a tradition that the family "gets together and bakes cookies together". Or, you have to get up before the rooster crows to travel all the way to BFE to sit in six inches of snow to watch a lacrosse game because you "are a supportive girlfriend", even though you know they are going to lose. Or, you have to go out to purchase an appropriate dress for the company Christmas party, which is full of fake conversation, fake laughter, and fake hugs with people who add absolutely no meaning to your life, you don't care their child goes to a Montessori school, and you will most likely never see again because they are probably quitting right after the company party. No thank you. I would rather spend my time on something substantial.

6. I get my bed to myself: How many of you actually get a good night's sleep when you share your bed? No one because the majority of people either kick, sprawl out like a starfish, talk in their sleep, steal the covers, wake up way earlier than you do, etc. etc. I can sleep with a blanket and no one will make fun of me. Every night, I go to bed whenever I want, however I want. I can watch T.V. if I want, surf the net, read my book. And, I wake up (relatively) whenever I want.

7. I don't have to worry about buying birthday/Christmas/ anniversary/Valentine's Day/Earth Day/Columbus Day, etc. presents: Gifts are always very tricky in relationships because getting someone a gift signifies just how serious the relationship is. Say you give someone a book, but they give you a diamond necklace. Oops. Or, someone makes you a really nice scrapbook and you do—nothing. Or, someone pours out their soul to you in a love letter and you, forget to read it? I definitely have been dumped multiple times on my birthday, in part, I think because the guys start thinking about how serious the relationship actually is and start freaking out (you know because boys and their feelings...). I personally do not have a ton of time to be shopping, especially since we seem to have a gift-giving occasion about every two weeks, so it is really nice to save my time and my money.

8. I am in better shape: When you date someone, you eat out. A lot. Everyone establishes these really cute "Friday night date night" traditions, where you go to dinner and a movie, eat some popcorn, candy, an Icee every week. It's great to spend that time together and be in that routine, but the calories really add up when you are (a) eating so much rich food and (b) sit inside a movie theater for three hours. I am in waaaayyyy better shape since becoming a "single-ite". My abs look bomb (can we also add, as a side note, I don't have to watch really terrible, violent action movies as well?)

9. No one expects me to do house-wifey things: Let's be honest, the whole cooking/cleaning/baking shebang is not quite my cup of tea right now. But, no one really expects me to ever cook. My bathroom and my room can be as messy as I please. I can do my laundry once a month and no one notices. I probably don't even really need to brush my teeth (but don't worry, I am too much of a hygiene-freak to let it get *that* far).

10. People feel bad for me being the third wheel all the time: Not to brag or anything, but being the third wheel is definitely one of my best traits. I had a campfire at my house a few weeks ago and noticed that there were three couples, and me. It's great. I get lots of attention. People feel bad for me (although they really shouldn't), so they are constantly trying to set me up with their friends, introduce me to new people. They invite me to gatherings, let me tag along on date nights, listen to my "crises". I love it and would definitely consider myself a professional at being the third wheel.

Being single is awesome, and don't let anyone talk you out of it. Most likely, those people (aka your mom and grandma) are empty nesters and are looking for a grandchild to add purpose to their lives again. In that case, tell them to rescue a dog from the local shelter.

The Conclusion

As I stood in front of my class this last spring, teaching 'No Exit' and modernism, it suddenly dawned on me that I had been in my very own existential crisis. An existential crisis begins with some kind of traumatic event, which sends an individual questioning his/her own existence and the meaning of life. This traumatic event could be reaching a certain age, a life-threatening episode, the death of a loved one, a change in relationship status. Hamlet experiences this when his father dies and he spends the rest of the play contemplating his own values and existence. More commonly known as a 'mid-life' crisis, one of my mentor's occurred when she was 43 and the result was a biker tattoo of a cross and a rose, one thorn for each of her children.

My boyfriend of almost six years dumping me one night on the phone triggered my own existential crisis. I didn't think much of it at the time, but as I reflect back on it, it was a big deal. I normally do not like to attribute significant life changes to boys because I like to be independent and I like to think there is much more to life and don't like them to have that much power, but in this case, it was the best thing that could have ever happened to me; it rocked every single perception I had about myself, about my future, and my reality of the world.

Within the wreckage of what I thought was my life, I found beauty.

I would say it probably took me about two weeks to realize how miserable I would have been had I married Kent. I remember distinctly sitting on the bike at LifeTime Fitness with my sister and having this wave of feeling rush over me, this pit in my stomach, that he was NOT the one for me. I always told myself, "I will wait for Kent to graduate and get a job before I decide how I want my future to look". I always waited on him to make decisions for me because I was too scared of making them for myself. So, I went to my grandma's, the counselor, the next day, sobbed in her very comfy chair for about three hours, and decided to devote all the break up energy towards re-defining myself. This last year, I embarked upon a huge journey of self-exploration. I would not say my existential journey centered on the loss of Kent in my life, but he became the trigger; I needed to go on this journey anyways. At the beginning, it was very tumultuous. I could literally feel the turbulence of my soul, sloshing inside of me, anxious, uneasy, and unsure, like an open boat in the midst of a perfect storm.

The first thing that I did was book a plane ticket to visit my best college friend in Detroit. This lead to more spurts of trips. I explored San Francisco, Orlando, Las Vegas, Chicago, Los Angeles. I went to concerts: Joe Diffie, Dave Matthews, and Imagine Dragons. I started avidly writing on my blog and I tried new activities: skiing, BMXing, cooking. I got a new cell phone, moved houses, and started grad school. I met some really excellent people—and some really not excellent people. I got closer to my family, my co-workers, and my friends. I strengthened my spiritual relationship. I made new goals and started looking at the world through a different lens. And, within these things, I learned a tremendous amount about myself.

I started solidifying my own personal beliefs. I embraced my inner nerdiness. I realized I am a bomb-ass girlfriend. I dove into my yoga practice and re-connected with some long lost friends. I made some good decisions, and some bad ones. I felt complete adoration from one guy, and violation from another. I dedicated myself to the motto "less work, more play". I laughed, cried, felt lonely, and realized that this spectrum of emotions is what we call "life".

When I look at who I was prior to that "dreaded phone call" and where I am now, I could not be a more different person. I spent about nine months in crisis purgatory and absolutely loved every minute of it. I look back fondly on all of the experiences I had, people I met, the lessons I learned, and I believe my existential crisis is starting to round down with the publishing of this book. Although I still have much to learn about myself and the world around me, I feel like this uneasiness is starting to greatly subside and I am emerging a better, more true version of myself. I no longer need to actively seek guidance from other people because I am confident in myself, and I can now share my wisdom with you.

For anyone who is on their own existential journey, I encourage you to embrace it. It is beautiful. I think about all the moments that helped me figure out something new about myself and am so fortunate for the turbulence the crisis created. From pain, we find growth. From guilt, we create morals. From dysfunction, we learn how to cope. For anyone who has never been on an existential journey, I am so excited for you. I think it is important to trudge through turbulent times because otherwise, we stay stationary and our lives become monotonous, mundane, mediocre.

I tie my existential crisis not only to Kent, but to also a new formation and resurgence of my own identity. The thing is, especially in our early adolescent years, we will go through so many identity crises. I went through one when I entered college. My next began when I stopped dancing for my college dance team, and the break up stemmed my third. And, I am sure I will continue to go through many more identity crises: when I get married, when I change careers, when my children go off to college. But, what I have proven to myself is that I can not only survive, but also thrive.

What ultimately healed me was this skill of *metacognition*, which is thinking about your thinking. I encourage you to track your thoughts, too. It is not only useful in grief and loss, but also just as a life skill and getting to know yourself better. It works like this: you think of a thought. And then keep thinking about that thought, asking yourself why it could potentially be bothering you. You devise a list of possibilities until suddenly you become fixated on one. And what I have found, amazingly, once you hone in on that conclusion, the thought does not seem as bothersome anymore. It is as though putting language to your anxiety causes it to completely dissipate.

For example, I have an irrational fear of fish. Once, my roommates went fishing, put the frozen fish on the pizza rolls in the freezer, and I could not even open the door. A couple weeks ago, they came home with a crayfish in a Ziploc bag and chased me around the house with it. Then, the restaurant I work at served little lobsters for dinner. I had a physiological reaction to seeing them on the plate—my palms got sweaty, my heart palpitated. So, the thought I have in my head is, "Where did my irrational fear of fish come from?" I keep thinking about it and listing some possibilities: "Perhaps it came from watching Planet Earth in the IMax at the museum?" "Perhaps it came from a fish brushing up against my leg while jet skiing?". "Or, perhaps it came from seeing my older sister's fish jump out of the tank and flop around her floor when I was eight". Yes, that last one is definitely right. Now that I have debunked my irrational fear of fish, I can properly tackle my fear.

The same is true in relationships. Of course, the older we get, the more hardened, coarse we become. We get put through the wringer of life experiences and we come out a little starchier. The more we date, the more experiences we have, the more baggage and fears we could potentially carry. For me, my greatest fear is that I will end up in the same dysfunctional relationship that I had with Kent. For others, there is fear about perpetuating a cycle of abuse, fear of *marrying your mother*, fear of being with a cheater again. But, I believe that if you can take these proper cognitive steps to re-evaluate and learn from your past and to recognize your fears, you are already setting yourself up for success.

I believe that the brain is an extremely malleable and capacious space. If we let pain slip between the recesses, it does not go away; it festers, until one day, it explodes uncontrollably. I did not want to carry my maladaptive behaviors and emotional baggage into a new relationship; I didn't think that would be fair to whoever my "Prince Charming" ends up to be.

About a year ago, that "dreaded phone call" reached my ears and now currently, when I think about Kent, I am not sad, I don't feel a sense of loss, I don't long for something I once had. I think about all the gifts he gave me (which is really just two). First of all, he protected me during that time that so many girls are running around, "finding themselves" and finding plenty of other things too; he allowed stability so I could focus on myself, my education, my relationship with my family.

And, I just forgot the second gift, so perhaps there was just one.

Just kidding. Kent and I spent a very critical time growing up together. When I think back on him today, he served as the best friend that I needed at the time; he saw me through college, stood by me when I graduated, attempted to comfort me when my family went awry. We learned so much together. Because we were both college athletes, we spent a plethora of time learning about efficient workout techniques, I learned a lot about lacrosse player diets, and how to stretch out any sore muscle you could think of. And, mostly importantly, we could be each other's backboards, playing fields, for how a relationship should—and should not—function. We eventually just outgrew each other. Sometimes that happens, and I am so glad it happened before there was a marriage, and a family, and a mortgage in the picture.

Whenever a black Ford Escape pulls up to the stoplight next to me, I always check to see if Kent is sitting in the driver's seat. I will probably always do this because I did it for six years of my life, but I know that if one day, it does happen to be him, I will be able to give a friendly smile and energetic wave. I recognize that I am not the same person I was a year ago—I spent the year growing, reflecting, identifying, finding myself—and know that because of this change, we may not even be friends amongst the crowd anymore.

To this day, I have not spoken to him since he came to pick up his stuff at my house. I resist the urge to stalk his social media profiles. My friends tell me he appears to have a new girlfriend and I genuinely wish him well in his life (although I hope to never make any appearances in it ever again). I am a completely different person than when he left me all those months ago, staring blankly at my wall while sitting on the blue floral patterned sofa, but I am so grateful for the experiences he gifted me, both During-Kent and Post-Kent. As for Simon, I told him not to talk to me, and being the gentleman that he is, stuck to that request.

And now, it is just me, navigating the world as a very happy, very content, very enlightened "single-ite". As I drive to work in the morning, my new theme song plays: Michael Buble's, "I Just Haven't Met You Yet", which gives me hope that, although I am currently very, very single now, it just means that I have not met the right person. But, "Prince Charming" is coming. And, I know he will be so worth the wait.

Made in the USA
Middletown, DE
26 September 2017